Countering Terrorist Finance

In Memory of Tim Arnold
1961–2002

Countering Terrorist Finance

A Training Handbook for Financial Services

TIM PARKMAN and GILL PEELING

Routledge
Taylor & Francis Group
LONDON AND NEW YORK

First published 2007 by Gower Publishing

Published 2016 by Routledge
2 Park Square, Milton Park, Abingdon, Oxon OX14 4RN
605 Third Avenue, New York, NY 10017

Routledge is an imprint of the Taylor & Francis Group, an informa business

British Library Cataloguing in Publication Data
Parkman, Tim
Countering terrorist finance : a training handbook for financial services
1. Terrorism – Finance – Prevention 2. Money laundering – Prevention
I. Title II. Peeling, Gill
363.3'2516

Library of Congress Cataloging-in-Publication Data
Parkman, Tim
Countering terrorist finance : a training handbook for financial services / by Tim Parkman and Gill Peeling.
p. cm.
Includes index.
ISBN 978-0-566-08725-7
1. Terrorism--Finance. 2. Money laundering--Prevention. I. Peeling, Gill. II. Title.
HV6431.P364 2007
363.325'16--dc22

2006032960

ISBN 13: 978-0-566-08725-7 (hbk)

Contents

List of Figures

Supplementary Resources Disclaimer

Additional resources were previously made available for this title on CD. However, as CD has become a less accessible format, all resources have been moved to a more convenient online download option.

You can find these resources available here: www.routledge.com/9780566087257

Please note: Where this title mentions the associated disc, please use the downloadable resources instead.

List of Abbreviations

AML	anti-money laundering
APG	Asia/Pacific Group on Money Laundering
ARA	Asset Recovery Agency
ARS	alternative remittance systems
BCBS	Basel Committee for Banking Supervision
BIF	Benevolence International Foundation (Illinois)
BSA	Bank Secrecy Act (US)
CDD	customer due diligence
CFATF	Caribbean Financial Action Task Force
CFR	Council of Foreign Relations
CMIR	Report of International Transportation of Currency or Monetary Instruments
CTC	Counter-Terrorism Committee
CTF	counter-terrorist financing
CTR	currency transaction report (US)
DTROP	Drug Trafficking (Recovery of Proceeds) Ordinance 1989 (HK)
EAG	East Asia Group
ESAAMLG	Eastern and Southern Africa Anti-Money Laundering Group
FACT	Federation of Associations of Canadian Tamils
FARC	Fuerzas Armadas Revolucionarias De Colombia

FATF	Financial Action Task Force
FBI	Federal Bureau of Investigation (US)
FinCEN	Financial Crimes Enforcement Network (US)
FIU	Financial Intelligence Unit
FSA	Financial Services Authority (UK)
FSAP	Financial Sector Assessment Programme
FSRB	FATF-style regional body
FSU	Financial Sanctions Unit (Bank of England)
GAFISud	Grupo de Accion Financiera Sud America
GRF	Global Relief Foundation (Illinois)
HICFA	High Intensity Money Laundering and Related Financial Crime Areas
IAIS	International Association of Insurance Supervisors
IDD	integrity due diligence
IMF	International Monetary Fund
IOSCO	International Organization of Securities Commissions
IRA	Irish Republican Army
JFIU	Joint Financial Intelligence Unit (HK)
JI	Jemaah Islamiyah
JMLSG	Joint Money Laundering Steering Group (UK)
KYC	know your customer
LAPD	Los Angeles Police Department
LTTE	Liberation Tigers of Tamil Eelam
MLCA	Money Laundering Control Act (US)
MLRO	money laundering reporting officer
NCCT	Non-Cooperative Countries and Territories
NCIS	National Criminal Intelligence Service (UK)

NCTAUS	National Commission on Terrorist Attacks Upon the United States
NPO	non-profit organizations
OFAC	Office of Foreign Assets Control (US)
OSCO	Organized and Serious Crimes (Amendment) Ordinance 2000 (HK)
PEP	politically exposed person
PFLP-GC	Popular Front for the Liberation of Palestine – General Command
PIRA	Provisional Irish Republican Army
PLO	Palestine Liberation Organization
POCA	Proceeds of Crime Act 2002 (UK)
RUF	Revolutionary United Front (Sierra Leone)
SAR	suspicious activity report
SDN	specially designated national
STR	suspicious transaction report
TFOS	Terrorist Financing Operations Section (FBI)
UNATMO	United Nations (Anti-Terrorism Measures) Ordinance 2002, as amended (HK)
UNSC	United Nations Security Council
UNSCR	United Nations Security Council Resolution
USA PATRIOT Act	Uniting and Strethening America through the Provision of Appropriate Tools to Restrict, Intercept and Obstruct Terrorism Act (US)
UTO	United Tamil Organization (UK)
VHCT	very high cash turnover

Acknowledgements

The authors wish to thank Faith Glasgow for her hard work in the preparation of this book, particularly in relation to Chapters 2, 3, 5 and 6 of Part One.

We also with to thank those MLROs and Compliance Officers who gave their time so generously in speaking to us about CTF and AML issues generally and in suggesting ideas for inclusion in the book.

Finally, we wish to thank the editing team at Gower for their support and guidance in converting the initial drafts into this finished product.

Many thanks to all.

Tim Parkman and Gill Peeling

PART ONE

Countering Terrorist Finance

CHAPTER 1

Training in Countering Terrorist Financing

ANTI-MONEY LAUNDERING AND COUNTER-TERRORIST FINANCING TRAINING PROGRAMMES: AN IMBALANCE?

Banks, insurance companies, fund managers and other mainstream types of financial institution around the world are doing a great deal of training on anti-money laundering (AML), but they are tending to do much less on counter-terrorist financing (CTF).

That statement is a generalization, and like all generalizations there are no doubt many to whom it doesn't apply. It is not an official statement from any relevant body and it certainly isn't based on the results of any empirical survey. It is, however, the view we have formed, based on our own experience as trainers and training developers in this field. Since January 2001, our company Lessons Learned Ltd has spent thousands of hours running or participating in practical AML training programmes for clients and their staff in multiple jurisdictions around the world. We have worked with clients on programmes in Britain and in America, in the Arabic countries of the Middle East, in the Asia Pacific Region, in Africa, in Eastern and Central Europe and in all the countries of the former Soviet Union in Central Asia. Yet, almost always, the subject of terrorist financing ends up getting much less airtime than money laundering. In some cases, at least outside of the United States, it seems to us that it holds the position almost of an add-on, if time allows, to the main topic of the day, money laundering.

Why? After hours, perhaps even a day or so, of a Money Laundering Reporting Officer (MLRO) engaging staff in training activities on the minutiae of identification procedures, on 'know your customer' (KYC) and 'customer due diligence' (CDD) exercises, and different case studies on what is, and what is not, suspicious in a money laundering sense, why is it that the training treatment of the issue of terrorist financing for some financial institutions still seems to consist basically of the following three points made at either the beginning or the end of the session?

- *Point 1* Terrorist financing is like money laundering, except it is the other way around; that is, it is usually legally obtained money being used for an illegal purpose.

- *Point 2* The amounts, revealed by 9/11, are much smaller than with money laundering, so they are much more difficult to spot – almost impossible, in fact.
- *Point 3* Accordingly, there's much less we can do about it; other than refuse to do business with anyone on the UN terrorist suspect list, and make sure we keep good, accessible records in case the authorities come asking.'

We found ourselves wondering: is this all there is to know about terrorist financing? And if there is more, then is the above actually all that staff really *need* to know about it and, therefore, all that we should be teaching them? Surely banks, insurance and investment companies couldn't be any *less* concerned about becoming a conduit for a terrorist group than for, say, a drug cartel or an organized crime syndicate? We could not reconcile in our own heads, on the one hand the enormous legal, political and media effort expended on terrorism and terrorist financing since 11 September 2001 and, on the other, the relatively subsidiary treatment of the subject in the training programmes of many financial institutions.

Relevant research materials *do* exist. The Financial Action Task Force (FATF) and associated regional groups, various industry associations such as the Wolfsberg Group, the International Association of Insurance Supervisors (IAIS), the International Organization of Securities Commissions (IOSCO) and others, and numerous other high quality AML and CTF consulting firms who advise and consult in this area, have conducted studies, run workshops and published guidelines and typologies. But our sense was that, valuable as these resources are (as we ourselves have found in the writing of this book), they were not actually getting through to the front line as effectively as they might. Terrorist financing, it seemed to us, was an issue that most people felt that they *should* be training staff on, but far fewer actually were.

WHAT ARE THE DIFFICULTIES WITH CTF TRAINING?

In reflecting on this, we were drawn to the conclusion that there were a number of apparent reasons for this mismatch between the importance of the subject and the amount of training time it was getting. In no particular order, we identified these as:

Absence of 'suspicion features' as a basis for sound, practical training

As one MLRO put it to us, quoting a well-known post-9/11 saying:

> *Searching for terrorist funds within a financial institution isn't just like looking for a needle in a haystack; it is like looking for a needle in a stack of needles. There is nothing which we can usefully do to improve our organizational capacity to detect unremarkable, sub-$10000 payments, whether through systems, training or anything else.*

Another put it equally succinctly, stressing that in his view, neither training nor transaction analysis were at the heart of the matter:

Transaction analysis just doesn't work for terrorist financing, and neither, really, does training. It is only name screening that is going to be effective and that is where the focus will be...

In other words, given the relatively minuscule amounts required to prepare for and execute terrorist attacks (for example, see Chapter 3 for detailed accounts of the financing of the 11 September and Bali bombing atrocities), and given the otherwise completely non-distinctive nature of these customers' activities, effective suspicion recognition training was all but impossible. And since, as we all know from our AML training, suspicion recognition training lies at the heart of any training programme, that was why there was much less focus on terrorist financing as a suitable topic for staff training.

Relative recency of terrorist financing as a topic of concern

Even though financial institutions are used to adjusting their behaviour immediately in the face of sudden legal developments such as sanctions and injunctions, their long-term, embedded training programmes always take longer to adapt. Although governments and relevant international bodies had started to instigate measures against terrorist financing well before 11 September 2001 (see Chapter 4 for a summary of the legal, treaty and regulatory history of the subject), as a topic of concern within the financial services industry, the authors believe that terrorist financing only really achieved prominence in the aftermath of the al-Qaeda attacks of that date. As this book goes to press, therefore, little more than five years have passed, during which time financial institutions around the world have had to focus heavily on ensuring that they do not provide services to individuals and organizations named on UN suspect terrorist lists – primarily an operations and technology issue, not a learning and development issue.

Financial firms, at least in FATF countries, have had a lot longer – ten years or more – in which to develop effective AML training programmes, a period during which the various legal and best-practice requirements have remained far from static, and have required a regular updating of compliance programmes. Who could blame them for keeping the training focus primarily on AML, especially when CTF training objectives may appear less than clear in the world of the bomber, whose final (and often only) mission can be funded well within the limits of an anonymous average salary? And, as for those financial institutions situated in the emerging economies of the world, who have only very recently become subject to AML and CTF laws at all, the solid wall of new regulatory requirements – particularly reporting requirements – has left many whose primary challenge is to file the necessary number of mandatory transaction reports within time, with little time and resource left to devote to training – and particularly to CTF training.

Status of terrorist financing as a political issue

Training staff in CTF is likely to involve financial institutions – particularly international financial institutions operating globally – in at least some level of political discussion with some staff, some of the time. Terrorist financing has a political edge which money laundering does not. After all, regardless of our political or religious beliefs, all of us can agree that drug dealers, kidnappers, protection racketeers and child pornographers are bad people with selfish, worthless objectives which the financial services industry should be playing its part in combating. Not everyone thinks that the objectives of terrorists are worthless, however, even if most abhor their methods. Indeed, as we discuss in Chapter 2, the issue of what a 'terrorist' actually is remains one of the most intractable problems in the whole CTF debate.

Take, as an example, the following exchange witnessed by one of the authors at an AML/CTF conference he attended in one of the states of the Arabian Gulf some years ago.

> *Speaker: ...and so the use of the global financial system to finance terrorism is just as unacceptable to the world community as the use of the financial system to help criminals profit from their crimes...*
>
> *Delegate: (interrupting) Who is a terrorist?*
>
> *Speaker: Excuse me?*
>
> *Delegate: I'm asking you, Who is a terrorist? How do you decide who is a terrorist?*
>
> *Speaker: Well, there are many definitions, but basically the term as I understand it refers to those who deliberately maim and kill innocent civilians – women, children, non-combatants – in order to draw attention to their cause and advance their political aims...*
>
> *Delegate: Are Western leaders not then terrorists? Do they not send their aeroplanes to bomb villages and towns to kill women and children to advance their political aims?*
>
> *Speaker: Madam, the issue is vexed. I'm not sure I can address this and say everything else which I have prepared. Maybe afterwards...*
>
> *Delegate: But it is critical, a terrorist or not a terrorist, who is to say?*
>
> *Speaker: Well, since you seem to be insisting ... the pilot who drops the bomb is not deliberately trying to kill the child, it is an accident. He does not celebrate it afterwards and neither does his family. But the terrorist suicide bomber is actually aiming to kill innocents...*
>
> *Delegate: But both are following orders from their superiors, this pilot and this suicide bomber! And in both cases those who give the orders know that the death of innocents is bound to follow, so which one is the terrorist?*
>
> *Speaker: But it is completely different! The pilot's superior tells him to avoid civilian casualties, the terrorist's tells him to aim for them...*

This exchange continued in similar vein for a few more minutes before the facilitator intervened, and the two were seen in animated discussion during the next break.

We do not mean to suggest for one minute that financial institutions have shrunk, in a governance sense, from training on CTF because they fear a conversation on politics. But at the point of delivery, the subject can be more challenging than the more straightforward issue of money laundering.

As one MLRO we talked to said:

> *We had all just about worked out the approach to take with money laundering. And then along comes terrorist financing which is far less clear-cut. I mean, what on earth can you train people on, when it comes to terrorist financing, and how do you deal with the fact that some people actually probably sympathize with the grievances, even if they do not support the method?*

HOW CAN FINANCIAL INSTITUTIONS OVERCOME CTF TRAINING DIFFICULTIES?

If we are right; if these difficulties and others are generating a more restricted approach to staff training in CTF than is the case for, say, anti-money laundering, then we need to question whether that is the right response. Is detailed staff training in the CTF elements of the whole AML/CTF compliance programme really less worthwhile than the more well established AML elements? Is it really the case that, as another MLRO put it, '90 per cent of what you need to do for counter-terrorist financing, you're already doing for anti-money laundering anyway, so it is just a question of filling in the gaps.'

The stakes could not be higher. Reputationally, the risks for a financial institution being implicated in a terrorist financing plot are of a completely different order of magnitude when compared with those surrounding money laundering – and everybody thought they were bad enough. There is no 'materiality test' with terrorist financing. The final act of the terrorist – killing people – is so heinous that those implicated through negligence, or bad practice, can expect swift retribution. And this retribution goes beyond the reputational hits and regulatory censures which routinely attend money laundering defalcations by financial firms. They extend to account closures, potential lawsuits at the hands of victims and victims' families, and total exclusion from the global financial system.

Ultimately, financial firms will make up their own minds on this, but we believe that the industry can usefully do more on CTF training, and that in doing so it will greatly enhance its overall contribution to the wider fight against terrorism. We outline below some observations on the three difficulties with such training which we identified earlier. In doing so, we hope to set out some ideas for a positive approach to the design of effective CTF training.

The absence of suspicion features

In one very important and specific way, it *is* true that the kind of account profiling and training exercises which are meaningful in an AML context, are not effective in a CTF context. If a bank customer, say, is motivated to commit or otherwise involve themself in acts of terrorism, then as long as reasonable care is exercised, they need have little fear that their account will reveal any financial information indicative of the attack. The 7 July 2005 bombings on the London Underground and bus system are estimated to have cost under £1 000 to plan and execute – less than the UK average monthly salary. So there is no point in sitting bankers down and searching for 'unusual or unexplained patterns of transactions' as one would in an anti-money laundering scenario.

But there are still a number of areas where specifically focused training *would* be beneficial, such as:

Suspicion recognition – Type 1 terrorist financing

We write later in this book about distinctions between 'Type 1' and 'Type 2' terrorist financing. The scenario involving the bank customer above is Type 2. It refers to the funding of an individual attack or series of attacks, often within a relatively short space of time and using amounts of money which are relatively small, both in their totality and in the individual amount of each payment or withdrawal. Type 1 terrorist financing, on the other hand, refers to the longer-term funding of a particular terrorist movement or group of movements from a variety of different sources and, typically, in much larger amounts. There are features of Type 1 terrorist financing which *should* be detectable by knowledgeable staff who have been attuned to the issues, and we discuss these in greater detail in Chapter 5. As with suspicion-recognition training in AML programmes, its purpose is as a red flag identifier – look out for these things and report them, they may be indicative of terrorist financing.

We are talking here of issues such as:

- the detection of potential front companies, shell companies and shell banks;
- opaque ownership structures with no clearly apparent commercial purpose;
- accounts or groups of accounts with unusual or unexplained signing arrangements;
- activities by charity and NPO customers with higher risk profiles;

and the host of other 'large money' suspicion indicators which are familiar material for those used to training in AML, but which are also applicable to Type 1 terrorist financing.

Many will point out that it is, of course, possible to conduct training in such issues almost exclusively with reference to potential money laundering networks, and merely to mention at the end (or at the beginning) that they may also apply to terrorist financing networks. But if you do that, as we aim to show in Chapter 5, the focus *on the risk* is lost. We believe that, to be most effective, training on CTF should take place in the context of a discussion about terrorist financing, not one on money laundering. Despite sharing many of the same characteristics, they are fundamentally different activities, undertaken by different types of people, with very different motives. The training should reflect this.

Terrorist financing typologies

Training in typologies is an excellent way of raising staff awareness of all the potential ways in which the organization could become involved in a terrorist finance chain. It complements Type 1 suspicion recognition training by describing a wide range of methods used by terrorist financiers, which may or may not, however, produce suspicion indicators. Typologies are descriptions of actual reported cases issued by bodies such as FATF. A good knowledge of typologies helps staff to build awareness and to generate internal reference frameworks against which to judge and measure situations and information that they encounter during their daily work.

Enhanced importance of identification and know-your-customer principles

It is one thing to collect KYC information as a routine part of your company's AML policy, or to comply with the regulations, or in order to ensure that your department passes its next internal audit inspection. It is quite another to do so in the knowledge that the treatment of this information, if obtained diligently, stored safely and updated regularly, actually constitutes one of the single most valuable contributions which financial firms can make in the battle against terrorist financing. Studying examples of the kinds of instances where diligent collection of identity and KYC information actually makes a difference when it comes to investigating and disrupting funding for terrorists, helps to motivate staff to undertake KYC work to a high standard.

Forged documentation and fraud

Staff who are involved in the identification of customers are not required to be amateur sleuths, but an awareness of some of the key differences between genuine documents and forged ones may be useful when dealing with false ID documents of lower quality – for example where they have been prepared by ideologically inspired but poorly equipped and organized individuals in an attempt to hide their identity. Relevant staff who have been trained, say, in which aspects of the typically used identification documents in their country are the most difficult to forge, will be better placed to detect potential forgeries than those who have not. Likewise, given that low level under-the-radar fraudulent activity such as credit card and cheque fraud is frequently used by terrorists to fund operations, focusing on building a greater awareness by relevant staff of the various scams and techniques used (whether by terrorists or by plain, ordinary fraudsters) ought, by default, to improve the organization's capacity to combat terrorist financing.

International background and conflicts knowledge

In our experience, employees of financial institutions around the world tend to be bright and educated, drawn from amongst the most talented people available to any sector of the economy in their country. But not everyone is always well informed about the various political, religious and nationalist disputes which exist in the world at any given time; disputes which currently involve terrorist activity and which will therefore involve terrorist financing at some level – maybe internationally. Staff who have been trained in these areas will be able to exercise more informed judgements about the actions they are taking and the reports they are filing.

Recency of terrorist financing

There is an understandable and completely rational desire in almost all organizations to amend existing training strategies and programmes to reflect current developments, rather than to develop new ones. This applies across the whole range of the organization's learning and development platform, not just to AML and CTF.

This approach works perfectly well, as long as the amendment process is regular and thorough enough to detect all the changes which need to be made. Practically, in many organizations, that is not the case. Lack of resources, the pressures of dealing with an ever-expanding list of more pressing operational issues, or simply the sheer speed of change, make it all but impossible to do much beyond the addition of piecemeal amendments over time: a change of wording here, a couple of extra slides there. This is the way things tend to happen in organizations. But there are problems with this approach. Whilst it may technically tick the boxes of programme updating, over time the programme becomes ill-fitting, too long, less sharp and not really geared to the organization's needs. We have seen a number of examples where this has happened with an organization's AML and CTF training: the CTF element has been added in, post-9/11. It is not really full enough and does not contain enough detail – particularly since the AML elements have themselves been expanding to meet an ever-changing environment there as well.

The solution is the conduct from time to time of a training audit. A training audit allows you to step back and look at the bigger picture. It allows you to ask a mixture of generic and detailed questions, the answers to which will help you decide what should be in your training programmes for a designated period ahead. A training audit does not have to be a huge, lengthy and bureaucratic exercise, but it should:

- cover all the relevant parts of your organization;
- cover certain key areas, which we outline below;
- link in with any broader AML and CTF risk assessment exercise which your organization has undertaken.

Framework of a Training Audit

Establishing current provision levels

- What training has been done before?
- To which business units?
- To which people within those units?
- What did it cover?
- What format was it in (for example classroom, e-learning)?
- How long ago?
- What was the feedback on its effectiveness (for example test results, written comments)?
- Without intervention* what training is likely to take place this year and next?
- Which units?
- To whom?
- Content?

* that is, without any intervention as a result of the training audit.

Establishing the organization's needs

What risk levels[†] apply to particular business units?

Customers

- business locations with large customer base with ethnicity connected to conflict zone involving terrorism;
- charity/NPO customers with objects directed to conflict zones involving terrorism;
- customers with business operations in conflict zones involving terrorism.
  - geographic area of operations (for example physically located in or books business from conflict zone involving terrorism);
  - product profile (for example products with a proven usage value in low-level fraud, money distribution and/or origin and ownership disguise).

Products

- credit cards
- off-street cash conversion and forex purchase
- wire transfers
- trust and nominee accounts
- tax and offshore advisory services
- hedge funds
- single premium policies.

Corporate

- recent acquisition (new business purchased from another company);
- new leadership (for example a new business head and management team);
- massive staff change (for example the outsourcing of an entire department);
- other major operational change (for example restructuring, new reporting lines and so on).

† The above are given by way of example. Financial institutions will presumably have developed their own risk assessment frameworks with which to link their training audit work.

Legal and Policy

- What minimum standards of training are required by local law and local regulators? Here it may be necessary to look beyond the strict confines of CTF and AML, and into wider areas such as training and competence generally.
- What minimum standards of training are recommended by bodies of which the organization is a member (for example local bank, insurance or investment manager associations; international bodies such as Wolfsberg Group, IAIS, IOSCO and so on)?
- 'Clear and present danger' – are there any parts of the organization which need immediate attention (for example business units which have had regulatory fines, poor audit gradings or near misses)?
- What does the organization's existing policy say about training? That is, what standards does it commit the organization to achieving with regard to, for example:
  - Who gets what?
  - Frequency?
  - Level of detail?
  - Effectiveness/quality checks (for example testing and/or feedback mechanisms)?

Depending on your (honest) assessment of how credible the organization's current policy is, the above question may in turn give rise to a further line of relevant enquiry centred on policy development and, specifically, who needs what kind of training. Organizations will have different ideas about how to segment the various potential content combinations, but an example structure might be:

- Foundation
  - legal and policy framework and requirements;
  - background – 'CTF – why we do it';
  - basic examples of terrorist financing;
  - suspicions and the duty to report to the MLRO.
- Additional – *Foundation*, plus
  - conflicts knowledge – deeper awareness;
  - detailed examples of terrorist financing; typologies and structures; use of products;
  - 'red flags' training; symptoms that 'something may be wrong'; Type 1 terrorist financing.
- Specialist – *Foundation*, plus relevant combinations of *Additional*, plus relevant combinations of
  - KYC/CDD examples – how thorough data-gathering and records maintenance helps investigators;
  - identification issues – documentation; identity theft; forgery;
  - fraud – credit card fraud, cheque fraud;
  - terrorist lists – operational issues (client acceptance checks; procedures on incorporation of new names; 'false positives' and so on).

'The Near Horizon' – what impact will any forthcoming changes we are aware of (business, regulatory, political) have on the above?

Identifying the gaps and creating a training plan

Having obtained data on what level of training provision currently exists within the organization and determined what its actual needs are according to risk, law and policy/values, the final piece of the training audit is to map the needs against the existing provision, identify those areas where there is either a gap or a weakness, and create a training plan.

Mapping can be either matrix or questionnaire based, or both. We have seen some very effective matrix-based tools which list training needs on the vertical axis, with the adequacy of current provision for different business units in each country assessed in cells along the horizontal axis. Some have used variations on a colour coding theme; green for 'OK' or 'Not applicable', amber for 'Weaknesses in current provision' and red for 'Serious weaknesses/total gap'.

The depth of detail may vary: if you are a lone MLRO operating with little or no assistance, you are unlikely to have the time to get involved with colour-coded matrices. The important thing is that there should be a process, and that from it you should learn about how much or how little your organization is doing about CTF training within its overall AML training programme, and about what it would make sense for you to do next. The process and your findings should be recorded.

Prioritization is key when it comes to planning the training programme or programmes required to fill the gaps and remedy the weaknesses. Priorities should emerge naturally during the mapping process, but if they do not then they must be created and agreed with very senior management. No organization, however rich in resources, is likely to be able to do everything which needs doing, immediately. Some compromise is always necessary. Your task as an MLRO is to ensure that the compromises occur in what are deemed to be the least critical areas, and that the decision-making processes involved are logical and capable of withstanding scrutiny. This applies just as much to the development, hiring or purchase of training resources (personnel and materials) to help meet the identified needs as it does to which staff are going to be trained in what.

Finally, the training plan you produce needs to be very clear about:

- objectives
- resources
- costs
- timing (what, by when)
- value/effectiveness

with some kind of mechanism for measuring, or at least gaining feedback on the latter.

This latter point is important because it is as a result of its regular AML and CTF risk assessment processes that your organization will have identified those parts of its business which pose the most substantial risks of money laundering and terrorist financing.

Political issues

Who is a terrorist? Why does the US get to decide who the terrorists are, with everybody else just falling in behind? Why can't governments be terrorists too? Why are we only freezing the accounts of those who attack Western interests? Why do we not freeze the accounts of the Lockheed Corporation, McDonnell Douglas and the Israeli Government, *as well as* those of al-Qaeda and Jemaah Islamiyah?

We have conducted, participated in or attended enough face-to-face sessions and events touching upon terrorist financing to know that at any point in time they are only ever one question away from metamorphosing into a discussion – inevitably fierce – about anything from the politics of listing and de-listing, to ethnic profiling, the war on terror, freedom of speech or what constitutes an acceptable set of values for a civilized society. We shouldn't be surprised at it. For many people, all over the world, the wider issues constitute the biggest subject of our time. Many – and not just Muslims, in Muslim countries – have strong views, and they wish to express them. The scene is set for you, as the trainer, to find yourself as the facilitator of a political discussion, which was probably not what you intended at the beginning.

From a purely practical perspective, if you wish to achieve the technical training objectives which you have set, then there is no real way in which you can let such discussions take over. Your task is, after all, to explain certain vital requirements which are of huge importance to the organization, not put the world to rights. If the United Nations has been unable to agree a definition of terrorism after ten years, three volumes and 1866 pages (see Chapter 2), then you are unlikely to be able to achieve it in the course of an afternoon. And yet for a question as fundamental as 'How fair can these laws be, in a world which I see as unfair?' (which is the underlying thrust of all these arguments), for corporate employees simply to be told, in effect, 'I don't want to answer that and in any event, we don't have the time.' or 'I'm just doing my job' is in some way to impugn the integrity of your position and, therefore, of your message. What else can be said? Does anything else need to be said?

FINANCIAL INSTITUTIONS AND THE LAW

Stepping back for one moment from the issue of terrorist financing and 'who is a terrorist?', the truth is that if you're the kind of person who worries a lot about being required to observe laws which you do not agree with because they may turn out to have consequences that you consider to be unjust, then on a statistical basis alone, financial institutions are probably not the best places for you to work in. Financial institutions are creatures of licence. They exist only insofar as they observe the laws of the countries in which they operate, and because they are so critical to the economies of their countries and to their trade with the wider world, there tends to be a large number of laws and regulations which apply to them. We have all seen examples where financial institutions have been either dissolved or expelled when they have failed to observe the conditions of the licence. When you work in a financial institution – particularly a global one – pretty soon you get to learn the most fundamental rule, which is 'Obey the law of the country you're in', and the reality is that you don't really have the luxury of exercising day-to-day judgements about which laws you're going to comply with and which ones you're not.

One of the authors well remembers the anger felt by Indian and Pakistani employees in a bank they were working at during 1999, when both countries were subjected to UN economic sanctions following their reciprocal nuclear explosions of that year. Many felt that their respective countries had the right to defend themselves through production of the weapons and they resented having to assist in enforcing a sanctions regime which they viewed as basically hypocritical. Indeed, common opposition to the sanctions laws proved to be a source of unity between the two nationalities within the bank, with many a friendly discussion ending in hearty and cheerful agreement about each country's right to wipe each other off the map. The bank, however, had no choice: it had to apply the sanctions (except of course in India and Pakistan, where it was arguably illegal to do so, but that is another story). Other instances we have come across involved cases as diverse as:

- the application of employment quotas within the financial sector, in favour of a certain ethnic group, viewed strongly by another ethnic group as deeply racist and discriminatory, but by the protected group as being vital to their continued participation in the local economy;
- the unilateral freezing in one country of the assets of all nationals of another country following the outbreak of hostilities, and the very severe hardship caused to those who had their assets frozen.

FINANCIAL INSTITUTIONS AND SOCIAL RESPONSIBILITY

Beyond the law, many financial institutions have a moral sense to them as well. Many are now eschewing the old outlook, which was basically to book any business as long as it turned a profit and wasn't illegal, and taking a more modern approach under the broad banner of social responsibility. These range from so-called ethical banks and investment companies which will only lend to or invest in businesses which, for example, do not pollute the environment/employ child labour/experiment on animals, through to Islamic banks which will provide products and services only according to established Islamic principles, through to those multinational financial institutions which will no longer provide services to, for example, armaments companies, tobacco companies or political parties expounding extremist racist or religious views.

Victims of terrorism occupy a place beyond that of helpless innocents, loved ones mercilessly killed in the cross-fire of an unrelenting conflict between implacable enemies. They are murder victims, killed because of the message their deaths would send. Deliberately killing civilians in order to convey political, religious or ideological messages is not socially responsible, and most people's abhorrence towards it is clearly reflected in the fact that the CTF regime put in place since 9/11 is well supported in international terms. More than 130 countries have signed up to it (see Chapter 4 for details). Whilst a contributing consideration for some countries will undoubtedly have been a determination not to suffer the negative essentially US/EU-led economic and political consequences which refusal to ratify would have entailed, it is also the case that there is an innate recognition that *any* country, *any* people, might one day be the subject of a terrorist attack. No doubt there are many criticisms which can be levelled at 'western policy', as a potential contributor to injustice, some with a wider currency than others but criticizing the international CTF legal framework on the grounds that it discriminates against those who deliberately target and kill civilians is effectively to remove oneself from mainstream thought on the issue within the financial services community.

OBJECTIVES OF THIS BOOK?

What we have tried to achieve with our book is as follows.

Firstly, we have attempted to gather together within Chapters 2–6 researched summaries of key terrorist financing information, along with various views and commentaries expressed within the source documents. In the production of these chapters, and mindful of the title of the book, our guiding principle has always been 'Will this information be potentially useful to an MLRO who is trying to construct a training programme for their staff?' In addition, however, we also hope that the chapters will provide MLROs with a useful resource, in one place, from which to improve their knowledge and thereby increase their confidence levels for the task of training staff.

Secondly, in Part 2 and on the accompanying CD-ROM, we have taken what we believe to be the most important topics, and produced ready-to-use training resources which MLROs can, if they wish, deploy within their own organizations for training purposes. These are primarily presentation and case study based, with slides, diagrams, handouts and presenter's notes, but there are also some examples of a few of the other tools and techniques which we use frequently in training courses and programmes run by our company.

In various places we have made use of FATF or other typology reports. We have taken some license with these. We have sought to make them more accessible by in some cases assigning real locations to them, converting them to the present tense and giving names to the parties. These alterations are arbitrary, though also we think, realistic. Not being privy to the information on which country or countries the typologies related to (this information is never revealed by FATF in its typology reports) in particular our re-workings of these case studies should not be taken as guesses about which countries were actually involved, nor as allegations that those particular activities have actually occurred in the countries mentioned.

CHAPTER 2

Terrorism and Terrorist Financing in Perspective

TERRORISM – DEFINITIONS AND HISTORY

What is a terrorist?

Most people probably have a pretty clear idea in their minds of what constitutes a terrorist act. Yet no clear, universally accepted definition of terrorism has been pinned down. Different international organizations, different governments and even different agencies within the US Government each have their own working outline, although there's plenty of common ground.

The general focus, in the words of the Terrorism Research Center in the US, is on

> *... terrorism as the systematic use of physical violence – actual or threatened – against non-combatants, but with an audience broader than the immediate victims in mind, to create a general climate of fear in a target population, in order to effect some kind of political and/or social change. (1)*

But given the emotive nature of terrorism and the political, economic or religious grievances underpinning terrorist organizations, terrorism is inherently extremely difficult to define conclusively. The perspectives of the victims injured in an attack, the people living in the vicinity who must continue their lives in a climate of fear, and the government agencies whose job it is to hunt down the terrorists and keep social order are far removed from those of the terrorist organization and its supporters. Even within a discussion group or training session, individual views may differ about the legitimacy of particular causes or targets.

The problems in reaching a consensus on definition are grounded in part in the oft-quoted cliché that 'one man's terrorist is another man's freedom fighter'. Thus, American commentators used to exclude the mujahideen in Afghanistan and the Irish Republican Army (IRA) when they compiled lists of terrorist groups, while including the Palestine Liberation Organization (PLO), the Vietcong and similar groups that had an impact on US citizens – and the US is not the only country where such selective categorization has taken place. Many Middle East commentators have great difficulty with the notion of 'Islamic fundamentalism' as being a source of terrorism; for them, its very use suggests that Westerners are being antagonistic towards their religion. Egyptian commentators have been keen to distinguish between the PLO, which they see as a legitimate group, and the Popular Front for the Liberation of Palestine-General Command (PFLP-GC) or the group around Abu Nidal, which they see as illegitimate. (2)

Nowhere is this stumbling block more clearly illustrated than in the Palestinian–Israeli conflict, where the suicide attacks carried out by Arabs against Israeli civilians are viewed by their supporters as the only means of resistance against a brutal and unfair occupation, and by the Israelis and many in the West as barbarous assaults on essentially defenceless civilians, by fanatics who have no interest in even talking about a just political settlement of their grievances.

There are other questions also working against a clear, unambiguous definition. Given the focus on violence against civilian populations, do attacks against, say, an oil pipeline owned by a multinational oil company constitute terrorism? What about attacks against military personnel? Brian Whitaker, writing in the *Guardian* newspaper in May 2001, pointed out that the suicide attack on the *USS Cole* in Aden harbour in 2000, which killed 17 American sailors and injured a further 39, was classified by the US state department as terrorism, because the US was not engaged in hostilities there. (3) Then there's the vexed question of whether or not a government and its military forces can carry out terrorist acts such as the shelling or bombing of areas where civilian deaths are likely or perhaps even unavoidable.

Unsurprisingly, a universally accepted definition of terrorism is widely considered to be an important step in the fight against it. It lays the ground for international cooperation, and for the kind of mutual support called for under various UN counter-terrorist resolutions and conventions. Conversely, without a common definition of terrorism, countries are free to decide for themselves who are terrorists and who are freedom fighters.

The UN and other international bodies have been trying since 1996 to reach a consensus; even before the 9/11 attacks on the United States, articles on these have referred to attempts by the UN and other international bodies to define terrorism '[which] run to three volumes and 1866 pages without reaching any firm conclusions'. (4)

Early 2005 saw apparent progress in that respect, with proposals for a UN terrorism convention, including a 'direct and simple definition', hammered out at the Madrid Terrorism Conference in March 2005. But a consensus on wording could not be reached at the 60th General Assembly in September 2005: the US and supporting governments insisting on a definition of terrorism that would include all attacks on civilians and non-combatants – a proposal opposed by some developing nations sympathetic to the Palestinian cause.

Nonetheless, agreement on a definition is still at the heart of the UN's efforts; the definition has gone back to the drawing board and work continues. An October 2005 meeting of the Legal Committee, stressed once again that nations need to reach consensus on what constitutes terrorism in order to be able to unite against it. The reason for terrorist action did not matter, since there was no such thing as 'justifiable terrorism', commented the Iceland representative Hjalmar Hannesson. Any just cause for which terrorists might claim to be fighting was only harmed by the hideousness of the means they chose. But at the same time, others have sought to insist that the Legal Committee needs to find a definition of terrorism that also 'recognizes legitimate struggle and the right to self-determination'. (5) As the hunt for a universally acceptable version continues, a brief round-up of working definitions and summaries gives some idea of the range of nuances and views. Let us start with no doubt the least authoritative, but also probably one of the most modern sources.

Wikipedia

According to Wikipedia, the online encyclopedia:

> *The term 'terrorism' is largely synonymous with political violence, and refers to a strategy of using coordinated attacks which typically fall outside of the time, place, and laws of war ... or the manner of conduct commonly understood as within the bounds of conventional warfare.*
>
> *By most definitions, terrorist attacks are characterised as indiscriminate, involving the targeting of civilians, or are executed with disregard for human life – hence they are widely considered to be a violation of contemporary traditions for the conduct of conventional warfare.*
>
> *According to definitions typically held by states, terrorists are actors not belonging to or adhering to the rules and traditions of any established national armed forces, and thus are considered to be rogue actors – lacking any centralized coordination for their attacks, political goals, or unitary consensus to act.*
>
> *Hence the term 'terrorism' is often used in its relative sense to assert that the political violence of an enemy is immoral, wanton, and unjustified, when compared to the violence of state actors.*
>
> *Those accused of being terrorists rarely identify themselves as immoral or unlawful and often instead use terms which reference their overall struggle – such as separatist, freedom fighter, liberator, militant, activist, insurgent, paramilitary, guerrilla, rebel, jihadi, mujahideen (both meaning 'struggler'), or fedayeen (meaning 'prepared for martyrdom').*

Proposed UN definition:

> *Any action intended to cause death or serious bodily harm to civilians or non-combatants, when the purpose of such an act, by its nature or context, is to intimidate a population or to compel a government or an international organization to carry out or to abstain from any act cannot be justified on any grounds and constitutes an act of terrorism.*

It emphasizes that:

> *The targeting and deliberate killing of civilians and non-combatants cannot be justified or legitimized by any cause or grievance. (6)*

USA PATRIOT (Uniting and Strengthening America by Providing Appropriate Tools Required to Intercept and Obstruct Terrorism) Act 2001, building on the Foreign Intelligence and Surveillance Act (FISA):

Terrorism is an activity which:

1. *Intimidates or coerces the government or civil population,*
2. *Breaks criminal laws and*
3. *Endangers human life.*

According to the US Federal Bureau of Investigation:

Terrorism is the unlawful use of force or violence against persons or property to intimidate or coerce a government, the civilian population, or any segment thereof, in furtherance of political or social objectives.

According to the US State Department:

[Terrorism is] premeditated, politically motivated violence perpetrated against non-combatant targets by subnational groups or clandestine agents, usually intended to influence an audience.

UN academic consensus definition, written by terrorism expert A.P. Schmid and widely used by social scientists:

Terrorism is an anxiety-inspiring method of repeated violent action, employed by (semi-) clandestine individual, group or state actors, for idiosyncratic, criminal or political reasons, whereby – in contrast to assassination – the direct targets of violence are not the main targets. The immediate human victims of violence are generally chosen randomly (targets of opportunity) or selectively (representative or symbolic targets) from a target population, and serve as message generators. Threat- and violence-based communication processes between terrorist (organization), (imperilled) victims, and main targets are used to manipulate the main target (audience(s)), turning it into a target of terror, a target of demands, or a target of attention, depending on whether intimidation, coercion, or propaganda is primarily sought. (7)

UK Terrorism Act 2000:

It adopts a wide-ranging stance. Section 1 defines terrorism as:

1. *the use or threat of action*
2. *which (i) involves serious violence against any person, (ii) involves serious damage to property, (iii) endangers life, (iv) creates a serious health/safety risk to a section of the public, or (v) is designed seriously to interfere with or seriously to disrupt an electronic system*

3. *and which (i) involves firearms or explosives, (ii) is designed to influence the government, or (iii) is designed to intimidate the public or a section of the public*

4. *and is for the purposes of advancing a political, religious or ideological cause.*

How long has 'terrorism' been with us?

The term 'terrorist' itself dates back to the French Revolution of the late eighteenth century. It was coined during the French Reign of Terror in 1793–4, when the Committee of Public Safety, led by Maximilian Robespierre, justified a regime of terror to protect the newly installed revolutionary government and root out those opposed to its rule. More than 40000 people were guillotined in the course of the Terror.

However, extremists prepared to kill civilians to further their religious or political ends have been around for centuries. Among the earliest examples were Jewish Zealots, who in the first century AD would slit the throats of Roman occupiers of the eastern Mediterranean. The aim was to send an unambiguous message to the Roman authorities, and the Jews who collaborated with them.

Historians trace terrorism in more modern guises back to the nineteenth century, when the idea of using terrorism to deliver a message to an audience beyond the victim in order to draw attention to a political cause caught on. A group of Russian anti-tsarists called Narodnaya Volya (NV) were the first activists, though they scrupulously avoided causing 'innocent' deaths in their activities. Their efforts culminated in the assassination of Tsar Alexander II in 1881. NV's campaign created a blueprint which was adopted by other nationalist groups such as the Fenians/IRA fighting for an independent Ireland, and the Slavic nationalists, the Internal Macedonian Revolutionary Organization (IMRO).

The early twentieth century saw the emergence of state-sponsored groups. Officials in the Serbian Government and military were unofficially backing and training a number of Balkan groups. An activist from one of those groups, the Young Bosnians, assassinated Archduke Franz Ferdinand in 1914, setting in progress the chain of events leading to the First World War. Small-scale terrorist attacks and further assassinations during the inter-war years were overshadowed by the activities of totalitarian regimes including Stalinist Russia and Nazi Germany.

Israeli nationalists used terrorism against British forces policing the Palestine mandate, and through the 1960s and 1970s more groups using terrorist tactics for both nationalist and ideological ends emerged. They made good use of technology and the rapidly expanding media coverage available to them to attract the widest possible audience – the first example being the hijacking of a commercial aeroplane by the PLO in 1968. Since then, some have declined in strength while others, including the Northern Ireland, Basque separatist and Palestinian movements, have drifted towards more political activism.

State-sponsored terrorism, this time based primarily in Middle Eastern countries including Libya, Syria, Iran and Iraq and focusing on Western targets in the region, came to the fore once more in the 1980s, with atrocities such as the Libyan-sponsored bombing of the Pan Am jet over the Scottish town of Lockerbie in 1988.

At the same time, and increasingly taking centre stage internationally, there has been a re-emergence of religiously motivated attacks. Mark Burgess at the Center for Defense Information pins the new trend down to the Iranian revolution in 1979, which turned Iran into an Islamic republic 'prepared to use and support terrorism as a means of propagating its ideals beyond its own border'. The practice spread over the coming years, 'beyond Islam to every major world religion as well as many minor cults'. (8)

Since the attacks on the United States of September 2001, al-Qaeda and its offshoots have dominated terrorism on a global basis. But as Mark Burgess points out, it is important to remember that 'the citizens of countries such as Colombia or Northern Ireland (to name but two of those long faced with terrorism) are likely more preoccupied with when and where the next FARC [Fuerzas Armadas Revolucionarias De Colombia] or Real IRA attack will occur, rather than where the next al-Qaeda strike will fall.' (9)

TERRORIST FINANCING – COUNTERMEASURES AND FEATURES

What forms has the fight against the financing of terrorism taken?

Although much study has been made of the historical context of terrorism, analysis of how terrorist groups fund their activities has only moved to centre stage in recent years – and has only served to underscore the difficulties involved in attempting to shut down funding sources.

The simultaneous terrorist bombings of the US embassies in Kenya and Tanzania in 1998, linked to local members of the al-Qaeda network, marked a watershed in the issue of terrorist financing. Before those events, either state sponsorship or criminal activities were considered to underpin the flow of funds to terrorist groups, and such efforts as were made to staunch that flow focused on those two areas. Afterwards, however, as we shall see, attention shifted to the more nebulous world of sympathy funding and subscription and donation networks: and the task faced by the international community in countering the latter is much more challenging.

Suppression of state support amounts to putting pressure on countries seen to be providing financial help or other backing for terrorists. With moderate success, the UNSC authorized economic sanctions (and targeted military strikes) as a stick to dissuade countries like Libya and Sudan from supporting terrorist groups. They did not, however, have the desired effect on the Taliban in Afghanistan, who were economically cushioned by the substantial revenues they were harvesting in taxes on opium production.

United Nations Security Council (UNSC) Resolution 1269 in 1999 was the first to use the term 'terrorist financing', but it still focused on the role of states and its message was simple; those who actively supported terrorist groups or who did not take measures to suppress them would be answerable for any terrorist acts which those groups committed. The impact of UN sanctions was enhanced by the drying-up of funds from former Cold War sponsors. Indeed, the end of the Cold War helped to bring about a decline in state-sponsored terrorism, as countries like Syria, Iran, Libya and Sudan felt the effects of their international isolation.

As access to state funds diminished, terrorist groups made increasing use of other established sources of funding, both legal and illegal. However, it was only in 1999 that the international authorities started explicitly to make the connection between organized crime – including international drug trafficking and money laundering – and terrorism: it was UN Resolution 1333, passed in 2000 (not only imposing travel and arms sanctions on the Taliban but also freezing the assets of Osama Bin Laden himself), which really marked the start of a shift in international focus away from state sponsorship and towards the role of international criminal activities in terrorist financing. (10)

Then came 9/11. Within two weeks of the 9/11 attacks, the US Congress passed the USA PATRIOT Act, which not only radically overhauled the country's anti-money laundering legislation in general but also specifically targeted suspected transfers of terrorist money. The measures introduced by the PATRIOT Act have had a far-reaching impact not only on America's banks but also on any foreign bank dealing with them.

We look in more detail at the PATRIOT Act and at other national and international legal developments both before and since 2001 in Chapter 4. First, however, it is useful to consider the characteristics of terrorist funding and how it differs from money laundered in the aftermath of non-terrorist crimes.

What are the characteristics of terrorist financing?

The term 'terrorist financing' can apply to two distinct but connected types of activity. It may refer to the ongoing fundraising efforts by which a terrorist group supports its overall operations, arms acquisition, political activity (if relevant), propaganda output and basic training of recruits. These sums are generated from a wide variety of sources, some of which are unquestionably illegal, but many of which are completely legitimate at the point of donation. While individual amounts may be small, the total of the funds controlled may be very large. The general decline in state sponsorship since the end of the Cold War, and in particular since the international CTF regime was introduced since 9/11, has pushed groups to rely increasingly on funds from both sympathetic donors and criminal sources. And in respect of criminal sources of funding, says the FATF, there is little difference in the crimes committed by terrorist groups and those committed by organized crime groups: both make use of much the same criminal methods to raise money. (11) We use the term 'Type 1 terrorist financing' for this early-stage gathering of funds in relatively large quantities.

Terrorist financing in its other form, which we call 'Type 2 terrorist financing', refers to the money used to finance a specific terrorist operation. Funds are needed, for example, for the terrorist cell's food and accommodation, transport, safe houses, forged identity papers, and both legal and illegal bomb components (the Madrid train bombs, for instance, were detonated by mobile phones (12)). Most of these operations involve relatively small amounts: $400000 to $500000 for the 9/11 attacks, an estimated $10000 for the bombings of the US embassies in Kenya and Tanzania (13), less than $35000 for the 2002 bomb attacks in Bali (14), only £3000 for the IRA bombing of Bishopsgate in the City of London in 1993 (15). Moreover, although some money movements connected with such operations clearly constitute illicit transactions, many are perfectly legal – the kind of purchases that anyone might make. Unless they can be linked to a known criminal, or criminal operation, they are completely unremarkable and therefore almost impossible to detect within the vast turnover that takes place each day within the international financial system (16).

CASE STUDY

Illegal sources of terrorist funding: credit card fraud

A single individual fraudulently obtains at least 21 Visa and Mastercards (seven of which come from the same banking group), using two versions of his name. He runs up debts totalling over $85000 on the cards, some of which is spent on activities connected with terrorism. Another aspect of the scheme involves the 'skimming' of funds from innocent cardholders, by copying the details from the magnetic strip of their cards onto duplicate cards, and then using them for purchases or cash withdrawals on the account of the real cardholder. This activity continues until the fraud is discovered and transactions on the card are blocked. (17)

Criminal sources of financing may include drug and human trafficking, extortion and kidnapping, arms trading, fraud, robbery, gambling, smuggling and trafficking in counterfeit goods. For example, the FATF reports that one terrorist group derives the bulk of its funding from a combination of kidnap ransoms and the extortion from businesses of a special 'revolutionary tax' (a euphemism for protection money), while another relies on the trafficking of narcotics.

Regarding the funding of terrorism from legitimate sources – for example, takings from the sale of publications being donated to legitimate charities raising funds for humanitarian relief which are then directed for terrorist purposes – it appears that the importance of these sources varies from one terrorist group to another, according to various dynamics. Terrorist fundraisers supporting terrorist actions in their own home country may be able to tap into the sympathies (and perhaps the relative wealth) of an expatriate population on the other side of the world, by collecting donations, subscriptions or club membership fees, raising funds through social functions, or selling publications within the community. (18) Conversely, fundraisers for al-Qaeda have focused specifically on a certain geographical area (the Middle East) to secure financial contributions for a terrorist campaign which is global in nature, rather than confined to one country.

CASE STUDY

Apparently legal fundraising: place of worship used for collection of terrorist funds

Religious extremists in the United Kingdom persuade some wealthy foreigners living in Indonesia to pay for the creation of a place of worship there. These wealthy individuals are suspected of helping to conceal the activities of a terrorist group. It subsequently transpires that the building for the place of worship has been bought and renovated by a Mr Karnel, a businessman operating internationally in the building sector, and he has then sold the building on to Inter Group, a group of companies belonging to the wealthy foreigners.

The place of worship is intended for the use of the local community but is also used to lodge religious extremist 'travellers' and to collect funds. It starts to receive donations worth millions of dollars from other foreign businessmen. An Inter Group worker is said to have convinced his employers that a 'foundation' for collecting and using large sums of money would attract less attention from the authorities, and such a foundation is therefore set up.

Mr Karnel heads up a multi-purpose international financial network (investments allegedly stand at $53m for Indonesia alone, and include several companies based there), but it is believed that part of his empire provides support to a terrorist network. One of the companies located in Jakarta is allegedly a platform for collecting funds.

Mr Karnel also buys several other buildings in Indonesia, with the suspected collusion of a notary and a financial institution. The authorities block a property transaction on the basis of the country's foreign investment regulations, but a legal challenge is successful and the purchase is authorized. The funds held by the bank are then sent to another account with a bank based in a Non-Cooperative Countries & Territories (NCCT) jurisdiction, in order to conceal their origin. (19)

Note. This case study illustrates the difficulties of establishing a formal link between what are more-or-less legal activities (property purchases and money movement) and the financing of terrorist activities. Essentially, only hard evidence such as recordings of movements and meetings, testimony from credible witnesses and full documented transaction records can link events, relationships and motives in ways sufficient to make conviction likely.

Although terrorists may raise funds through a wide range of illegal or apparently legal routes, when it comes to laundering and transferring the proceeds of their fundraising activities they rely on much the same methods as non-terrorist criminal groups in their efforts to hide the source of illicit funds and move them to the country or region where they will be used. One FATF expert reported that the following range of processing techniques used for terrorist financial activity had been uncovered in his country: (20)

- front companies – genuine businesses where illegal profits can be blended with revenue from legitimate sources;
- shell companies – businesses without substance, incorporated to conceal the true beneficial ownership of the assets held;
- informal money transfer systems – funds outside the formal banking system, through systems such as *hawala*;

- nominees – use of family or associates, who are trusted within the community and will not attract the authorities' attention, to conduct transactions on their behalf in order to disguise the source and ownership of funds;

- structuring (smurfing) – cash deposits or bank draft purchases made at various institutions by several individuals; or transactions made below reporting levels; each deposit is small, but the total amount is substantial;

- credit cards (front-end loaded) – creating credit on a card by paying cash on the card, thereby enabling the credit to be converted back to cash;

- electronic funds transfer – use of wire transfer services to transfer funds to associates (see below);

- currency smuggling – physical movement of cash from one place to another in order to disguise its source and ownership.

Commonplace monetary instruments including travellers' cheques, bank cheques and money orders have also been used by various terrorist groups. (21)

The FATF report concludes that 'it would be difficult, if not impossible, to determine by the [processing] activity alone whether the particular act was related to terrorism or to organized crime.' Other factors, therefore, also have to be built into any examination of these activities if terrorist finances are to be positively identified. (22)

Several means of raising and/or moving money, including the use of 'informal' money remittance schemes, cash couriers, non-profit organizations (NPOs) and electronic fund transfers, have been specifically identified by the FATF in its Nine Special Recommendations on Terrorist Financing as posing real threats for exploitation by terrorists – and therefore as potential weak points in any effort to clamp down on terrorist financing. The use of wire transfers and the exploitation of customer charities and other non-profit organizations, in particular, are areas of concern with the potential to impact on financial institutions. How and why may they be misused by terrorists?

Wire transfers – the 'golden highway' of terrorist financing?

FATF's definition of the term *'wire'* or *'funds transfer'* involves 'any financial transaction carried out for a person through a financial institution by electronic means, with a view to making an amount of money available to a person at another financial institution.' Because a value of money, rather than the physical currency itself, moves from one bank account to another, wire transfer is both very swift and comparatively safe as a means of transferring funds around the world. (23)

The development of increasingly efficient interbank payment systems, such as SWIFT, offers both drawbacks and advantages for terrorists. On the one hand, the demand for greater security means that an electronic system generates electronic records that may be kept and transmitted with the transfer – records which can be and are used by the authorities and the banks in their investigation and detection activities. On the other hand, however, the sheer volume of trade and the fact that the money becomes available more or less instantaneously in the recipient's account, both work in the terrorists' favour. In addition, at the time of writing, consistent and enforceable international standards have yet to be fully embedded on issues such as recording key information on transactions, sending that information with the wire transfers, and maintaining records. This can hamper efforts by the authorities to investigate exactly who sent what to whom, and when.

There is a further complication in the fact that money transfers can also be carried out through non-bank enterprises such as bureaux de change and other money-transfer businesses, transferring funds either to banks or in some cases to similar non-bank businesses. Again, discrepancies in record-keeping requirements and the obligation to transmit information about the sender of the money may make it all the more difficult for the authorities to trace terrorist (or indeed other criminal) fund movements. As a FATF workshop on wire transfers in 2003 pointed out, a basic network for transmitting terrorist funds can be put into place simply by exploiting the fact that some countries monitor transfer details less comprehensively than others. For example, if records on the sender are not kept at the starting point of the wire, or if that information is not transmitted all the way to the end point via any intermediaries involved, then investigators attempting to find out more about the source of the funds in question are bound to come up against a brick wall. More complicated arrangements have also been observed, however. These may involve a series of wire transfers designed specifically to obfuscate the trail of financial movements. (24)

It is worth noting here that terrorists may go to some lengths to disguise the source of wired funds, for example by using false identities in transactions or sending funds via a number of separate financial institutions, so that the money arriving in the recipient account appears to have come from several different (apparently unrelated) sources. Despite these efforts, the size of individual transfers in comparison with typical wire transfer business is not

CASE STUDY

Wire transfers used to move terrorist money across borders

A terrorist organization based in Pakistan moves money via electronic transfers to the United Kingdom. This money is eventually used to rent safe houses, buy vehicles and purchase electronic components with which to make bombs. In order to move the funds between countries, the organization uses 'bridge' or 'conduit' accounts, whereby the accounts at either end are held in the names of people who have no obvious association with the terrorist group structure, and who could justify an exchange of funds if necessary because they are related to each other by blood or marriage.

In Pakistan, cash is deposited into bank accounts by the terrorist organization, and the transfers are made from those accounts. When it arrives in the UK some money is either left on deposit in the account or invested in mutual funds as a cushion against the organization's future needs. Other sums are transferred to different bank accounts managed by the organization's correspondent financial manager, where the money is used by the terrorists to pay for equipment and other day-to-day running expenses. (25)

noteworthy. Indeed, as FATF observes, 'the low value of the transfers when compared with the high overall volume of such transactions is an additional factor that further complicates detection of terrorist use of the financial system.' (26)

In Chapter 5 we will look further at the characteristics that may be linked with the movement of terrorist funds by wire transfer, and in Chapter 6 we consider how banks and financial establishments might consider operating wire-transfer business in the light of current best practice.

Vulnerability of charities and NPOs to abuse by terrorist financiers

The last two or three years in particular have seen increasing concern among FATF and other government bodies that charitable and other NPOs now play a much larger role in raising or moving terrorist funds than previously appeared to be the case.

Charities and NPOs can be set up in numerous legal forms and with differing levels of control on their operation according to the jurisdiction in which they are based, so it can be quite a challenge even to define the term. FATF defines NPOs according to their function rather than their legal form, to cover:

> *any legal entity that engages in the raising or disbursing of funds for charitable, religious, cultural, educational, social, fraternal or humanitarian purposes, or for the purposes of carrying out some other type of 'good works'. (27)*

Such a definition could cover organizations involved in almost any aspect of life, from sports and arts, to social justice and religion.

But beyond the broad range of their activities, there are several reasons why NPOs have proved so vulnerable to financial exploitation by terrorist groups. To name just a few:

- They tend to be trusted by the public.
- They have access to substantial sources of funds and considerable control over them.
- They are often cash-intensive.
- Many have a substantial international presence.
- Many have a focus particularly on those countries most in need of humanitarian support (which in many cases coincides with precisely those areas of conflict where terrorist groups are active). Many have both an international operational structure and an established financial framework geared to moving funds globally.
- Depending on the jurisdiction in question, there may be little or no regulation, with regard, for example, to registration, financial record-keeping, reporting or monitoring. (28)

CASE STUDY

CEO of charity uses charitable donations to support terrorist causes

An NPO is registered in the United States as a tax-exempt charity, with the stated purpose of carrying out humanitarian relief projects worldwide. Although its headquarters are in the US, it operates in various locations using slightly different names. Financial and business records are seized by the authorities from the head office, and also from the homes of the NPO's chief executive officer and another director; and on the same day the government also issues an order blocking its assets and records pending further investigation. Eleven months later, the authorities submit the NPO for a designation order under the UNSC resolution, on the grounds that it has supported a terrorist organization. The CEO is convicted for fraud and organized crime-related offences relating to the diversion of more than $315 000 of charitable donations to terrorist organizations. Before being sanctioned there is evidence that the charity has provided both direct and indirect support to terrorist groups. (29)

CASE STUDY

Fraudulent use of donations for a terrorist cause

An NPO based in Afghanistan solicits donations from local charities in Australia, Canada, the US and the UK, where there are established populations of supporters prepared to donate to the political and humanitarian causes which the NPO is supporting. It also raises funds from its headquarters in Afghanistan. The money is alleged by the NPO to be destined as support for widows and orphans. In fact though, the finance director of the NPO is also the head of organized fundraising for a worldwide Islamist militant organization, and instead of going to help widows and orphans some of the money is sent to the organization's operatives. (30)

There are several ways in which NPOs may be misused within the terrorist framework as noted below:

- *Deliberate fronts* In some cases, an NPO may be set up with a stated charitable purpose, but may from the beginning be nothing but a front, channelling all funds raised into the coffers of the terrorist group behind it. FATF's 2003 NPO Workshop noted that often these charities have a formal charitable or tax-exempt status, and also that they may use aggressive fundraising techniques, whether their target is the general public or a specific ethnic or religious group. (31)

- *'Cuckoo' charities* Other cases have been reported, where an existing charity with legitimate humanitarian aims is corrupted or infiltrated by terrorist supporters, who can then divert some of the funds raised by this 'cuckoo' charity (so called after the bird which lays its eggs in the nests of other birds and whose young then kill the other nestlings, to be fed by their unsuspecting parents) to illicit ends. The Islamic Red Crescent has in the past allegedly been infiltrated by al-Qaeda and other terrorists in this way. (32) Either way, donors and staff may or may not be aware of the organization's terrorist connections and the questionable uses to which their money may be put.

- *Laundering operations* Charities and NPOs may be used not only to raise money for terrorist purposes, but also for 'laundering' and transferring other funds (in the sense of disguising their points of origin) while shielding the ultimate end users from scrutiny. This is made easier by the fact that informal cash collection is a central feature of many ethnic or religious communities, and that these collections are not necessarily monitored. Illicit funds may, therefore, be integrated into the system and reported as legitimate cash collections.

- *Funds transfer specialists* In addition, as mentioned, charities with an international remit are likely to transfer funds from one region to another as a normal part of their operations and this is another aspect of their makeup that could be open to abuse by terrorist groups, particularly when the charity in question is subject to little external regulation or monitoring. So a charity could act as a conduit (wittingly or unwittingly) for the movement of funds, sending money internationally to an outpost branch or recipient service organization in the locality where the terrorists are based, at which point it is siphoned off. For example, as has been noted prior to their election as a government, funds raised internationally by the Palestinian group Hamas and wire-transferred might be traced to a specific Hamas-run charity in the West Bank, but the cash disbursements that could be taken from there and delivered by courier to Hamas operatives in the field for, say, a suicide bombing would be impossible to follow without very high-quality intelligence. (33)

The FATF's NPO workshop mentioned earlier identified cases where networks of related foundations have been established within ethnic communities in several countries and then apparently used as a conduit for illegal money remittances, collecting cash deposits through NPO bank accounts and then settling the accounts with their overseas contacts or offices. In some instances the suspicions of the authorities were aroused by the mismatch between the amounts handled by the NPO and the relatively modest incomes of the local community giving money to it. There was no clear evidence to link these schemes conclusively to terrorist financing, but the FATF drew attention to the potential for such abuse. (34)

At its heart then, the use of charitable organizations to fund terrorist activities is effectively a variation on standard criminal money laundering techniques. But despite the efforts made globally since 9/11 to clamp down on money laundering and terrorist financing, charities remain a preferred means for many terrorist groups to raise and move funds.

The flow of funds from donors to charities, from charities to aid groups and grassroots organizations, and from these organizations to the individuals on the ground is often not regulated or monitored in any coordinated fashion. As Matthew Levitt observes in a 2004 paper on terrorist financing: 'Without transparency and regulated audits, charities will remain an all-too-attractive means for terrorists to raise, launder and transfer funds.' (35) Crucially, he identifies Saudi Arabia as the biggest single source of charity abuse, and although in the wake of the May and November 2003 attacks in Riyadh, it is reported that the Saudis have 'reined in some two-thirds of the questionable charitable fundraising that was going on in the Kingdom', he believes there is still much to be done there. (36)

In the last analysis, however, we can assume that terrorist organizations are adept at evolving continually to sidestep new counter-terrorism and counter-terrorist financing measures. There is no exception to this as far as their exploitation of charities is concerned; clamp downs by the authorities and disruption to a group's known mode of operation may simply result in a different way of using a linked charity. We will look at this in more detail, and at possible indicators of charities' terrorist links, in Chapter 5.

DIFFERENCES BETWEEN MONEY LAUNDERING AND TERRORIST FINANCING

Although, as we have seen, some of the money raised to finance the activities of terrorist groups may be obtained and laundered in much the same ways as those used by non-terrorist criminals, there are at least a couple of key differences between the two.

Motive

The most fundamental difference is in the ultimate motive for the carrying out of criminal activity and the financial disguising activities which accompany it. Drug traffickers and other criminal groups carry out their crimes in order to make money, and go through the effort of converting that cash into something less traceable so that they can protect and make use of their ill-gotten gains. To these ends, they may be processing enormous amounts of cash. For narcotics and people traffickers the amounts may be in tens or hundreds of millions and for state-asset thieves, they may be in the billions. But whatever the activity, the essential principle is the same – the more the better. Terrorists, in contrast, are not primarily motivated by financial gain for its own sake, but usually as a means to a political or ideological goal. As we have seen, depending on the stage they are at, the amounts they process and the transactions they carry out may be quite small.

In his book *The Washing Machine*, Nick Kochan makes the observation that the financiers of terrorism 'tend to be outside the organization, as terrorist groups are primarily engaged in the business of ideological struggle rather than that of making money. Here, of course, these groups differ dramatically from the money launderer whose primary purpose is making, or at least protecting, his criminal funds.' (37)

Legitimate vs illegitimate source of funds

The second key difference is in the make-up of the money acquired, moved and spent by non-terrorist criminals and terrorist groups. The laundering of drug or other criminal profits, by definition, involves money that has been illegally acquired; but that is not necessarily so when it comes to the proceeds of terrorist fundraising. Certainly, they may have come from criminal activities; but they may equally have been generated from apparently legal sources such as charitable organizations. Nonetheless, says Nick Kochan, terrorists and their backers are keen to disguise the sources of their funds, because the money trail could lead investigators not only back to the origins of the money but also forward to the terrorist destination itself, and in particular those handling the money. (38)

Similarly, at the front end of the chain, money may be spent by terrorists on 'pre-crime' transactions – flying lessons for the 9/11 hijackers, say, or tube tickets for the London bombers – that are entirely legal unless they can somehow be linked to a known terrorist suspect and thereby to plans for a subsequent crime.

Countermeasures

In the less-than-optimistic words of the working party on terrorist finance at the 2005 Madrid Terrorism Summit: 'If confronting terrorists has challenged even the most sophisticated defences of modern nations, then confronting

Jihadist funding networks

The working party on terrorist finance at the Madrid Terrorism Summit in March 2005 reports that there is a long way to go before the finance networks supporting jihadist (militant Islamic) movements are properly understood.

The differing goals and perspectives of the various groups currently active are reflected in different sources of funding. For example, global terrorist organizations such as al-Qaeda or the Abu Nidal Organization are committed to suppressing Western influences on Muslim countries. They are believed to have been sponsored by several Middle Eastern states including Libya, Syria and Iran, and now draw on a broad range of supporters and constituencies.

Nationalist Palestinian groups such as the Palestine Liberation Front and the Popular Front for the Liberation of Palestine are backed by expatriate Palestinians, private donors in Saudi Arabia and the Gulf States, and Muslim and Iranian charities. They sometimes team up with Islamist groups such as Hamas (elected to government in 2006), which is fighting for an Islamic theocracy to be established in the disputed territory.

Shi'ite militants campaigning against Israel and Western influence in Lebanon, such as Hezbollah, obtain funding from Syria and Iran. In Southeast Asia, groups such as Jemaah Islamiyah are fighting for a fundamentalist Islamic theocracy in Indonesia, Singapore, Malaysia, Brunei, the Philippines and southern Thailand. They are funded by charities, ransom payments and the promotion of a regional Islamist economy.

But the report stresses that these funding networks are not formalised affairs in the Western sense. Instead, 'informal, personal initiatives are the bloodlines of terrorist funding', making Western efforts to stem the flow of funding 'an uphill struggle'.

'Only a quarter of the total amount of terrorist funds frozen since September 2001 has been seized in the Muslim world,' the report continues. 'The working group believes this constitutes a major failure, as jihadist groups appear to continue their funding efforts through the Islamic economic system, that is, by using financial entities based in the Muslim world.'

Indeed, 'economic and institutional weaknesses' in the financial systems of the Muslim world are pinpointed as key props in these networks. Issues of concern include:

- a lack of financial technology, institutions or financial regulatory systems, especially in nearly-failed states;
- a lack of independence and transparency in political, judicial and financial systems;
- 'the non-existence of accepted financial structures in the Muslim world'. (39)

terrorist funding networks and preventing funds from reaching terrorists has proven to be an almost impossible task.' (40)

Compared to trying to devise CTF activities, the steps necessary to combat money laundering are much more obvious and straightforward. The basic premise in anti-money laundering initiatives is that the bank has access both to its customers and to their accounts, and is best placed to notice irregularities that could signal money laundering activities. It is the bank's obligation (on pain of criminal penalties) to report any suspicious activities to the authorities by filing what is known as a Suspicious Activity Report (SAR) or Suspicious Transaction Report (STR). In the US and many other countries, banks are also required as a matter of course to report any cash transactions in excess of $10000 or an equivalent set amount.

Inherent in a bank's responsibility to report a suspicious transaction is the obligation to know enough about its customers and transaction patterns to recognize when something is suspicious. That in turn requires the bank to know its customer: who the beneficial owner of an account is, what the customer's likely transactions are, and what is the usual source of the customer's money. If the bank understands how a customer typically behaves, so the theory goes, it becomes possible to spot atypical behaviour. In addition, an understanding of the customer's probable transactions gives the bank an indication of the risk that the account will be used for money laundering, and will to some extent determine how closely that account is monitored by the bank. (41)

There are two points in the course of a transaction at which a bank may most easily spot something odd. First, at the 'customer interface' a trained bank teller who has direct contact with the customer may pick up unusual signals indicating that the transaction could be suspicious. Secondly, back-office analysis of financial transaction patterns using either specialist software or the more old-fashioned 'smell test' may throw up anomalies. The bank is able to narrow the field by focusing its efforts on 'high risk' customers and product lines, and on large transactions.

As the authors of the US Terrorist Financing Staff Monograph put it:

> *The key is to find those transactions that would be out of character for the customer's purported business activity. A large cash deposit would not be suspicious for a customer like Wal-Mart, but it would be for a customer whose only reported source of income is a Social Security cheque. (42)*

The aim of this regime is basically to deter criminals from trying to process large sums of illegally acquired cash through the formal financial system and to look to other routes instead. If they do use financial institutions, they have to break up the money and make many smaller transactions (below the reporting threshold, if it exists) across a number of different accounts, which takes longer and costs more.

Why existing AML methodologies are problematic for combating terrorist financing

When it comes to terrorist funds being moved in small amounts for seemingly innocuous purposes, however, as is the case, say, with Type 2 terrorist financing, banks generally simply aren't in a position to make any assumptions about it, because there is rarely anything out of the ordinary to alert them.

In the 2003 Hollywood movie *Minority Report*, Tom Cruise plays an officer in the recently formed 'Pre-Crime Department' of the LAPD. This unit, by harnessing the powers of three 'pre-cogs' (pre-cognitives who see future criminal events before they happen), is able to pre-empt serious crimes by arresting the 'perps' (perpetrators) before they commit the offences in question. Although clearly made purely for entertainment, the serious and obvious question posed by the film is 'How can someone be guilty of a crime before it has occurred?' – a very apposite query in relation to terrorist financing.

The answer, currently at least, is of course that they cannot be convicted of terrorist crimes; although if sufficient evidence of knowledge and intent is available (a crucial point for financial firms, to which we return later), they can be convicted of terrorist financing offences. But these in themselves can be very difficult to prove, particularly when faced with an enemy adept at disguising motive and method until the very last moment. The Terrorist Financing Staff Monograph points to the 9/11 hijackers' financial transactions as a prime example:

> *The 19 hijackers hid in plain sight: none of their transactions could have revealed their murderous purpose, no matter how hard the banks looked at them. (43)*

Two of the future hijackers – both of whom had US bank accounts – were suspected by the US Government of being al-Qaeda operatives; but their financial transactions gave absolutely nothing away, only living expenses, flying lessons and airline tickets. Hardly the stuff of conspiracy to murder.

But that, of course, will not always be the case. Bombs and bullets – and perhaps chemicals and other agents – are likely to remain the weapon of choice. In the context of 'pre-crime' transactions, the USA PATRIOT Act of 2001 (dealt with in greater detail in Chapter 4) introduces the idea of 'reverse money laundering'. Unlike conventional money laundering, reverse money laundering does not relate to serious crimes that have already taken place before the funds enter the financial system (such as fraud or counterfeiting), but to the criminal purpose for which the money is destined after it has passed through the system.

In his book *The Washing Machine*, Nick Kochan reports that Stefan Cassella, the deputy chief in the money laundering section of the US Department of Justice, believes that the same methods used in 'classic' criminal money laundering are also applied in reverse money laundering:

> *The money is disguised as legitimate funds for some lawful purpose when it really is to finance new crimes and new criminal enterprises ... The source*

of the money doesn't matter, it is what deadly purpose the money was intended to fund that matters.

Cassella apparently also argues that the conventional anti-money laundering arsenal – asset confiscation, bank regulation, prosecution – applies in the same way to reverse money laundering. (44) But such arguments do beg the question, once again, of how innocuous funds can be detected before a crime has been committed, unless they originate from a suspect source.

The unremarkable nature of pre-crime transactions at the dangerous front end of the terrorist finance chain means governments and financial authorities have had to think laterally in their efforts to come up with a system that will succeed in identifying terrorist finances where the money laundering methodologies may stumble. It has not proved an easy task. The New York Clearinghouse, a private consortium of major banks, apparently spent two years trying – and failing – to produce a financial profile for terrorist operatives in the US. Neither has it proved any easier to create a blueprint for recognizing terrorist fund-raising activities at the other, back end of the chain. An Islamist organization that collects funds from small donors, pools the money and then sends large wire transfers to Chechnya, Afghanistan or the West Bank each month could be a terrorist fund-raising operation; but it could be an entirely legitimate humanitarian operation striving to help civilians in impoverished and war-torn regions of the world. The government might have gathered information whereby it could distinguish between the two, but bank data alone would not. (45)

Without means of conclusively distinguishing either terrorist operatives or terrorist fund-raisers through their monetary transactions alone, in 2002 the US Financial Crimes Enforcement Network (FinCEN) published a report on patterns of 'suspicious activity' which might indicate terrorist financiers at work. It made use of suspicious activity reports (SARs) filed by US banks on 'nationals of countries associated with terrorist activity' (46). The FATF has also published guidance for financial institutions in their efforts to spot and clamp down on terrorist funding. (47) We have made extensive use of these resources in Chapter 5 ('What is Suspicious'?) and its associated training activities in Part 2.

Such reports, drawing on lessons learned from real-life suspicious transactions, do help to give bank staff some pointers to the kind of account activity or other features that should at least ring warning bells and which may trigger further enquiries. KYC – Know Your Customer – is just as important for an NPO account about which little is known, or for a very high cash turnover (VHCT) local shop within an ethnic community connected to a conflict zone, as it is for a shell company dealing with non-cooperative countries and terratories (NCCT's), or a correspondent bank with known business in a country known for the production or processing of narcotics. And as we have indicated in Chapter 1, we believe that it is essential for relevant staff to receive specific CTF as well as AML training. Many of the themes will be the same, but the context will be different and staff should be aware of it. Without heightened awareness of the whole picture, banks might start relying exclusively on ethnic criteria to identify terrorist financing. As the Monograph on Terrorist Financing points out such an approach would put the finances of many innocent people and organizations under the spotlight, generating bad will and wasting resources. 'Ethnic profiling – by itself – is both an unfair and an ineffective way for financial institutions to attack terrorist financing,' says the Monograph. (48)

Due diligence and record-keeping assume greater importance for CTF

Although financial institutions may have a reduced (though not negligible) capacity to spot terrorist funds moving through the system compared with non-terrorist criminal money, they can still make additional contributions to wider efforts to combat terrorist financing:

- by carrying out the requisite due diligence on every customer; and
- by making information on specific customers readily available to the authorities if they request it.

The first indication which a financial institution receives about the possible terrorist connections of one of its clients or customers may well be from the authorities. Acting on sensitive intelligence they may require information urgently regarding identity, beneficial ownership and transactions and it is vital that this is both comprehensive and immediately retrievable. This is a relatively new development, born of necessity in the US in the aftermath of 9/11, but adopted by other governments as best practice. As the Terrorist Financing Staff Monograph points out:

> *Before 9/11, the US government did not think in terms of financial tracking, certainly not systematically and on an urgent basis. (49)*

The US has developed two routes for the rapid retrieval of financial information on specific suspects. The first, developed by the FBI's Terrorist Financing Operations Section (TFOS), is based in the existing legal framework for obtaining financial information from banks and other financial institutions. But instead of taking the conventional (slow) route, the FBI makes use of a list of cooperative high-level contacts throughout the financial sector. When information on a particular individual is needed in an emergency, the FBI can call on its contacts and go through a speeded-up legal process to obtain what is needed. This system effectively enables the FBI to carry out almost real-time financial tracking of specific individuals, so that it can log the details and location of transactions more or less as they happen. This 'has enabled it to locate terrorist operatives in a foreign country and prevent terrorist attacks there on several occasions.' It has also 'proved very valuable in vetting potential threats.' (50)

The second route involves a regulation issued the USA PATRIOT Act, under which the Department of Treasury can put out a blanket requirement for financial institutions to carry out a check of their records for information on particular individuals. In an emergency they may be obliged to respond within as little as two days. As an alternative to a bank-by-bank enquiry – which would have been the only available option before 9/11 – this process can 'save an investigator hundreds of hours' in establishing whether or where a suspect holds an account in any one of the thousands of banks and other financial institutions around the US.

Clearly, the role of financial institutions in compiling and maintaining accurate customer files cannot be underestimated in such exercises. It is also important that they should be able to retrieve information promptly and provide it to the authorities in a useable format when it is required. We will look in more detail at the measures that currently constitute best practice in Chapter 6.

SOURCES

1. www.terrorism.com.
2. W. A. Tupman, 'Violent Business? Networking, Terrorism and Organized Crime', www.ex.ac.uk.
3. Brian Whitaker (2001), 'The Definition of Terrorism', *Guardian*, 7 May.
4. Ibid.
5. UN 60th General Assembly, press release 7 October 2005.
6. UN Proposals, outlined on BBC News website 26 July 2005.
7. www.unodc.org.
8. Mark Burgess (2003), 'A Brief History of Terrorism', July, www.cdi.org.
9. Ibid.
10. The information, above, on international counter-terrorist finance efforts before 9/11 is taken from Anne Clunan (2005), 'US and International Responses to Terrorist Financing', *Strategic Insights IV*, Issue 1, January.
11. Ibid., p. 240.
12. Clunan (2005).
13. National Commission on Terrorist Attacks in the United States (NCTAUS), *Monograph on Terrorist Financing* (2004), Chapter 4.
14. Zachary Abuza, 'Funding Terrorism in Southeast Asia: The Financial Network of Al Qaeda and Jemaah Islamiyah,' *NBR Analysis* 14:5.
15. HM Treasury/Home Office, 'Combating the Financing of Terrorism', October 2002.
16. Ibid.
17. FATF XIII Report on Money Laundering Typologies 2001–2002, p. 3.
18. Ibid.
19. Ibid., p. 4.
20. FATF Typologies, 2002–2003, p. 3.
21. FATF Typologies 2001–2002, p. 5.
22. FATF Typologies 2002–2003, p. 4.
23. FATF XV Report on Money Laundering Typologies 2003-2004, p. 4.
24. Ibid., p. 5.
25. Ibid.
26. Ibid., p. 6.
27. FATF Typologies 2002–2003, p. 4.
28. FATF Typologies 2003–2004, p. 8.
29. Ibid., p. 10.
30. FATF Interpretative Note to Special Recommendation VIII: Non Profit Organizations, October 2002, p. 7.
31. FATF Typologies, 2003-2004, p. 8.
32. Matthew Levitt (2004), 'Charitable Organizations and Terrorist Financing: A War on Terror Status-Check,' (paper presented at the workshop, 'The Dimensions of Terrorist Financing', University of Pittsburgh), 19 March, p. 3.
33. Ibid.
34. FATF Typologies 2003-2004, p. 9.
35. Levitt (2004), p. 5.
36. Ibid., p.6.
37. Nick Kochan (2005), *The Washing Machine: How Money Laundering and Terrorist Financing Soils Us* (Thomson), p. 65.
38. Ibid., p. 66.

39. Loretta Napoleoni and Rico Carisch, 'Terrorist Finance', *Confronting Terrorism* (Club de Madrid Series on Democracy and Terrorism, Volume II).
40. Ibid.
41. NCTAUS, 'Monograph on Terrorist Financing', Chapter 4.
42. Ibid.
43. Ibid.
44. Kochan (2005), p. 245.
45. NCTAUS, 'Monograph on Terrorist Financing', Chapter 4.
46. FinCEN, SAR Bulletin No 4, Jan 2002.
47. FATF, *Guidance for Financial Institutions in Detecting Terrorist Financing*, 24 April 2002; Chapter 5 draws on the contents of this paper.
48. NCTAUS, 'Monograph on Terrorist Financing', Chapter 4.
49. Ibid., p. 59.
50. Ibid., p. 60.

CHAPTER 3

Terrorist Finances Dissected

INTRODUCTION

For most people today, and certainly for a lot of Americans, terrorism since the attacks of 11 September 2001 has become more or less synonymous with high-profile attacks by militant Islamist groups. The best known and most global in its focus is al-Qaeda (or perhaps it is now more accurate to refer to 'al-Qaeda-affiliated groups'), but other Islamist organizations operate throughout much of Southeast Asia and in the Middle East.

It is certainly the case that Islamist terrorism is now the focus of the ongoing global war on terror, and that attacks including those in the US on 9/11, the two Bali bombings, the Madrid train attacks, and those in London on 7 July 2005, have been the driving force behind the measures introduced internationally to try and clamp down on terrorist financing networks. But it is worth remembering that many other groups with a more localized focus have (or have had) their own disruptive terrorist agendas, and their own complex financial arrangements. It is also worth remembering that with a rapidly changing world and a constantly shifting political landscape, new groups can emerge at any time to launch their own campaigns and financing methods. It makes sense, therefore, to cast the net more widely than just those Islamist groups which are currently in the news.

Before looking at the legal measures that have been taken to counter terrorist financing and the best practices that banks and other financial institutions can put in place, we have therefore considered it useful to examine in more detail the various ways in which a cross-section of terrorist groups have raised, moved and spent their money, both through the formal financial system and via a tranche of alternative routes from smuggling to '*hawala*'. Some groups' financial networks are better documented than others, and to an extent our choice has been shaped by the amount of information available in the public domain and from the valuable research conducted by others.

As well as being highly topical, al-Qaeda's financial setup has been studied in depth, so it is there that we start, reviewing not only the group's fundraising and money-moving activities in general, but also the detailed financial trails left by the hijackers in the run-up to the 9/11 plane attacks. We take a similar tack with the Bali bombers, Jemaah Islamiyah, following the money movements that preceded the 2002 attack in Bali.

We also examine two groups whose terrorist activities have been tempered in recent years by political recognition and negotiation – the Liberation Tigers of Tamil Eelam, also known as the LTTE or the Tamil Tigers, and the Provisional IRA. Both focus their attentions on a very specific geographical area, but draw (or have drawn) on an international support base for financial backing. The IRA provides an interesting study of how a terrorist group, whose raison d'être is in the process of being removed through the political process, may use its financial know-how and contacts simply to generate illicit wealth. As these words are written, the LTTE appears to be resuming its campaign in Sri Lanka.

The four case studies demonstrate that when it comes to making and moving money, terrorist groups are both creative and flexible. They also show how much overlap there may be between apparently legitimate business or charitable interests and illicit funds – and ultimately, how difficult it is likely to be for financial institutions to identify terrorist money with any certainty, unless they can link it somehow to a known operative or suspect.

AL-QAEDA ('THE BASE')

Background

The sources of al-Qaeda's wealth, and how it is moved between countries and distributed to active terrorist cells, are questions to which countless hours of effort have been devoted by intelligence agencies around the world.

The US Government has done a lot of work in trying to build a comprehensive picture of al-Qaeda's financial web and how it works. The image that emerges is of a decentralized, flexible system which draws money from many sources and distributes it in many different ways. Some are legal, some illegal; some are open, some covert; some involve paper trails, others do not. The complexity of these sources makes the job of detecting and intercepting those funds all the more difficult.

In the words of Lee Wolosky to the National Commission on Terrorist Attacks upon the US:

> *If al-Qaeda were financed only by Osama Bin Laden's personal inheritance, or only by a small number of state sponsors, and if it were only limited in scope to a small area of the globe, or weren't continuously replenishing its coffers, the problem would be much easier to solve. There is not one big pile of al-Qaeda's loot somewhere, waiting to be discovered and confiscated. (1)*

Methods of financing

So how does the organization raise money? According to a Council on Foreign Relations task force in 2002:

Al-Qaeda's financial backbone is built from the foundation of charities, non-governmental organizations, mosques, websites, fund-raisers, intermediaries, facilitators and banks and other financial institutions that helped finance the mujiheddin throughout the 1980s. This network extended to all corners of the Muslim world. (2)

Below are the main methods which have come to the fore.

Fund-raising

A main source of funding is through fund-raising. Donations come from sympathetic charities and non-profit organizations, mosques and individual fund-raisers, mainly in the Gulf region but also from further afield. Some donors know where their money is going; and what it is going to be used for; many others, it seems, may not.

Al-Qaeda taps into the religious obligation on all Muslims to give *zakat* – charitable donations to worthy causes – which are often collected by imams or other respected community leaders or institutions, and dispensed by them to suitable causes. Records are rarely kept, making it easy enough for supporters to divert cash to the terrorist coffers.

Legitimate businesses and criminal activity

There has also been speculation that al-Qaeda runs businesses with a legitimate front, and also raises money through illegitimate means, notably drug trafficking and so-called 'blood diamonds' mined by armed groups (see box). The US Terrorist Financing Staff Monograph believes that there is insufficient evidence that the organization has made use of either drug trade or blood diamonds. But Douglas Farah, a journalist who claims to have researched extensively into the links between terrorist financing and diamonds and other commodities, believes that gold, tanzanite and particularly diamonds play a central role in the terrorist finance structure:

There is strong evidence of al-Qaeda's ties to the African diamond trade, despite the reluctance of some in the US intelligence community to acknowledge the link,' Farah commented in February 2005. (3)

Blood diamonds

Blood or conflict diamonds are those that are mined in areas controlled by rebel or terrorist groups in Africa. They have been recognized by the General Assembly of the United Nations as an ongoing threat to peace in war-torn but gem-rich areas such as Angola and Sierra Leone, as they are sold in exchange for cash and weapons.*

Diamonds have been particularly valuable for al-Qaeda as a means of raising money, laundering funds and storing financial value in the face of a worldwide freeze on assets.

But they have also been widely used by Middle Eastern groups such as Hezbollah, which have long-standing access to West African diamonds.†

Their advantages for terrorist groups are several: they are easy to carry and are not picked up by metal detectors at airports, they hold their value, and when the time comes to sell they can be converted back to cash easily and anonymously. Blood diamonds are particularly attractive as they are outside the control of the national governments.

Douglas Farah, an investigative journalist who has become an authority on the close relationship of blood diamonds and other commodities to terrorist financing, reports that al-Qaeda appears to have bought around $20m of diamonds mined by the Revolutionary United Front (RUF) in Sierra Leone in the 14 months up to 11 September 2001. 'The evidence suggests a rapid, large-scale value transfer operation that allowed the terrorist group to move money out of traceable financial structures into untraceable commodities,' he comments.‡

* UN resolution (A/RES/55/56) adopted 1/12/2000, reported on www.un.org.

† Douglas Farah, 'Terrorist responses to improved US financial defenses', report to US House Subcommittee on Oversight and Investigations Committee on Financial Services, 16 Feb 2005.

‡ Ibid.

Moving the money

Formal financial system

Once the money has been raised, a variety of methods may be used to move it around to where it is needed. Before 9/11, al-Qaeda made good use of the global banking system. It focused on jurisdictions where it presumably considered that its financial activities had less chance of being disturbed – the Middle East and Pakistan. Indeed, as we shall see below, the 9/11 hijackers had US bank accounts, withdrew funds from ATMs and made use of international wire and bank transfers from the Middle East in the run-up to the attacks.

Alternative remittance systems

But even though transmitting money through the banking system has become more difficult since the tightening of the international AML and CFT regime in the aftermath of the 9/11 attacks, al-Qaeda has always had other options. The *hawala* system of money transfer (see below) is apparently central to their operation, especially since 9/11. It is ideal for the purpose, according to Lee Wolosky, because:

> *It is a cash business that leaves behind few, if any, written or electronic records for use by investigators in following money trails. It operates out of nondescript storefronts and countless bazaars and souks. It reaches both small villages throughout the region and large cities around the world. It is quick, efficient, reliable and inexpensive. It draws from a long tradition of providing anonymous services. It is staffed primarily by members of families that have been in this business for generations. And it is almost entirely unregulated around the world. (4)*

NB. See the Lessons Learned Ltd training film 'Follow The Money: How Terror is Financed' at www.lessonslearned.co.uk for a reconstruction of how the systems work.

Hawala

Hawala is a centuries-old means of moving money around the world, and is similar to various other regionally-based alternative remittance systems (ARS) including *hundi* and black market peso exchange. It is used by people who do not have access to banks in the developing world, and also by those who want to avoid the costs and bureaucracies of the formal system. In addition, it can be valuable for businesses looking to bypass their government's foreign exchange controls. Although many transactions involve perfectly legitimate funds intended for legitimate purposes, *hawala* is also wide open to abuse by money launderers and terrorists. In the light of that abuse, alternative remittance systems, including *hawala*, have been the subject of widespread research by organizations such as FATF.

Hawala is based on the trust existing between members of the same ethnic group – indeed, the word *hawala* means 'trust' in Hindi. The system is effectively unregulated, with little or no formal bookkeeping; records, such as they are, are in code indecipherable to outsiders. There are no regulations or training requirements to impede a *hawaladar* wanting to set up a business, and no identity checks are carried out on *hawala* customers, provided they are known within the community.

It works as follows. An Indian, say, living in Manchester and wishing to send money home to her family in Mumbai goes to the *hawaladar* (who is likely to run other business interests from the same premises) and pays him the money to be transferred, usually in cash, plus a small handling fee. He gives her a unique security code number, which she forwards to her family members. He then makes contact (by phone, internet or fax) with his link, another *hawaladar* in Mumbai, provides him with the code number and asks him to deliver that sum in Indian rupees to the family or arrange a pick-up, matching the specified code number to ensure security.

Money is not usually physically transferred between the two *hawaladars*; rather, just like the wire transfer sent by an international bank, *value* has been transferred. Because there are many such transactions taking place in both directions between the two over a period of time, the balance to be settled every so often is likely to be relatively small.

According to Nick Kochan in *The Washing Machine* (p. 214), larger-scale *hawala* transactions generally go through an intermediary, typically in Dubai, which is the centre of the international network. Some systems become quite complex once multiple currencies are involved, and mechanisms such as 'cash pooling accounts' have evolved to deal with the complexities in a flexible way. But the basic principles remain the same.

Physical transportation

Alternatively, couriers may be used to move cash physically. By using couriers recruited from within al-Qaeda, the movement of money can be kept completely 'within the family'. Cash smuggling – the simple transport of bundles of notes across borders in planes, ships, cars, motorcycles, bicycles, on foot or by pack animal – is made more attractive and highly effective by the relatively small amounts required for a terrorist operation.

Precious metals and stones

Value may also be transferred in the form of diamonds and other precious stones which are relatively easily converted into cash and are easily transportable. 'Blood diamond trading' has allegedly worked effectively for al-Qaeda in a number of ways. For example Zachary Abuza (one of the leading scholars on terrorism in Southeast Asia) claims that it has been used to raise funds for operational cells, to hide money targeted by financial sanctions imposed by the UN and US and to launder criminal profits. (5)

And Douglas Farah reports that al-Qaeda diamond purchases in West Africa gathered pace through 2001 until just before 9/11, with telephone calls from the middlemen handling the purchases to the organization's bases in Afghanistan right up to 10 September:

> *The available evidence points to al-Qaeda purchasing some $20 million worth of [blood] diamonds during the 14 months prior to 9/11. The evidence suggests a rapid, large-scale value transfer operation that allowed the terrorist group to move money out of traceable financial structures into untraceable commodities.' (6)*

Financing the 9/11 attacks

The original beneficial ownership of the funds used for the 9/11 plot is currently unknown, but the attack is estimated to have cost al-Qaeda only around $500000 in total, of which around $300000 is believed to have passed through US bank accounts opened by the hijackers. According to the National Commission on Terrorist Attacks upon the United States, on whose investigations and report this section is based, the money was used mainly for flight training, travel expenses and living costs (room, board and meals, vehicles, insurance, and so on) in America in the run-up to the attacks. The FBI believes that it was sufficient to cover all the hijackers' expenses (though they may have brought additional cash into the country and spent it without putting it into a bank account beforehand). (7)

Funds arrived in the US via three main routes as follows:

- international wire and bank-to-bank transfers;
- deposits of travellers cheques or cash brought in by the terrorists from overseas;
- some cash withdrawals from their overseas accounts through ATMs and credit card transactions.

All were apparently entirely legal money movements. Indeed, according to the 2004 US report, not only did the various financial institutions used by the hijackers not pick up any suspicious transactions, but even with the benefit of hindsight there was no reason why they should have done so. As the Monograph cites:

> *Neither the hijackers nor their financial facilitators were experts in the use of the international financial system. They created a paper trail linking them to each other and their facilitators. Still, they were easily adept enough to blend into the vast international financial system without doing anything to reveal themselves as criminals, let alone terrorists bent on mass murder. The money-laundering controls in place at the time were largely focused on drug trafficking and large-scale financial fraud and could not have detected the hijackers' transactions. The controls were never intended to, and could not, detect or disrupt the routine transactions in which the hijackers engaged. (8)*

So what did these 'routine transactions' amount to?

Wire transfers

The wire transfer funds totalling roughly $130 000 were sent to the hijackers' bank accounts in the US, mostly via wire or bank-to-bank transfers from Dubai in the United Arab Emirates (UAE) made by a Dubai-based plot facilitator, Ali Abdul Aziz Ali (Ali). He was given the money, he said, by the plot leader Khalid Sheihk Muhammad (KSM) (who is also his uncle) in 2000, some at a meeting in Pakistan and the balance via a courier. He kept the money at his house in Dubai rather than depositing it in his bank account there.

He sent the money in a series of six transfers. The first $5 000 went by wire from the Wall St Exchange Centre in Dubai (a money transmitter), but under the UAE Central Bank's regulations, in order to execute the payments he had to provide his work ID and address, and his mobile phone number – valuable clues in the FBI's subsequent search for him after the attacks.

Between 29 June and 17 September 2000, a further five transfers totalling almost $115 000 were sent from Ali using various aliases to the lead terrorists, Muhamad Atta and Marwan al-Shehhi, when they arrived in the US. On these occasions the money was dispatched from the UAE Exchange Centre (another money transmitter), which did not require identification. The first of these was another $5 000 wire transaction, and the other four were bank-to-bank transfers to a joint checking account opened by Atta and al-Shehhi at the SunTrust Bank in Florida. In each case he brought cash in UAE dirhams which were converted into dollars.

Ali used various aliases to make these transactions, but they were not the key to his security. Instead, 'he relied on the anonymity provided by the bustling financial centre of Dubai and the vast international monetary system. His employment as a computer wholesaler provided perfect cover.' Indeed, although Ali reported that KSM was concerned by the fact that the final transfer was for as much as $70 000, he himself wasn't worried: 'He knew that Dubai computer companies frequently transferred such amounts of money. Ali said he experienced no problems with … any transfer in aid of the hijackers.' (9)

Four wired transfers totalling more than $10 000 also came from the German-based cell member, Ramzi Binalshibh. A further $14 000 was wired on by him in two instalments, having been sent to him by wire from Mustafa al Hawsawi in the UAE. But again, none of the transfers aroused any suspicion among the billions of dollars' worth of international transfers going on each day.

Cash and travellers' cheques

The hijackers also brought cash and travellers cheques with them to the US. The first two to arrive opened a Bank of America account in February 2000 with a deposit of $9 900 in cash, but probably spent additional unbanked cash on living expenses. Al-Shehhi, the third to arrive, also apparently brought cash with him from his account in Germany, using it to purchase $2 000 of travellers cheques in a New York bank two days after his arrival in

May 2000. Similarly, hijacker Ziad Jarrah opened a bank account in Venice, Florida, with $2 000 in cash just after he arrived a month later. In both cases the authorities believe the men brought the cash with them into the US.

Between 23 April and 29 June 2001, a further 13 'muscle' hijackers arrived in the US, bringing more cash or travellers cheques with them each time; certainly there are records showing that six of them spent a total of $44 000 on travellers cheques in the UAE, which they subsequently made use of in the US. Some opened bank accounts on arrival. They may have received the funds directly from the plot leader, KSM, in Pakistan, though some may have been handed over in Dubai, on their way to the US.

Some cash was deposited by the muscle hijackers in bank accounts. More was apparently passed on to supplement the finances of some of the hijackers already in the US, as their bank accounts received deposits shortly after the muscle contingent arrived. For example, on 1 June 2001, $3 000 in cash or travellers cheques was deposited into Ziad Jarrah's SunTrust account and $8 000 was deposited into the al-Shehhi/Atta joint account.

The hijackers who made international trips after their arrival in the US also brought more funds into the country with them when they returned.

ATM withdrawals

Money was also brought into the US from overseas bank accounts using ATMs and credit cards. Hijacker, Hanj Hanjour used an ATM card in the US to access his accounts at the Saudi British Bank in Saudi Arabia and at Citibank in the UAE. The Citibank account was topped up by Ali to the tune of $5 000 while Hanjour was in the US.

Another hijacker, Fayez Banihammad, also used accounts set up at Standard Chartered Bank in the UAE in June 2001 to finances his activities in the US. He deposited about $30 000 in UAE dirhams, and drew down on the accounts when he reached the US, using both an ATM card and a Visa card. Among his purchases on the Visa card were tickets for the 9/11 plane for himself and one of the other hijackers.

Shortly before the flights, the hijackers actually returned around $26 000 to one of the al-Qaeda facilitators; a further $10 000, also destined for al-Qaeda, was intercepted by the FBI after the attacks.

Should the financial system have picked up on the hijackers' transactions? Contrary to many reports, the hijackers appear to have organized their funding legally within the established financial system. They all opened accounts in their own names, using passports and other ID. The National Commission concludes that there is no evidence of any of them presenting Social Security numbers, and no financial institution filed a SAR on any of them before the attacks, although reports were filed thereafter. Nor were the bank transactions in any way unusual. They generally amounted to occasional large-ish (but not remarkably large) deposits and frequent, relatively small withdrawals through ATMs, debit card transactions, cash withdrawals and occasional cheques. Such a pattern of account usage is commonplace.

The only occasion on which suspicion was aroused was in June 2001 at a SunTrust Bank branch in Florida, when al-Shehhi attempted to cash a cheque for $2180. He used ID with different addresses, and the bank staff were also concerned that his signature did not match that on file. The cheque was not accepted and the bank manager issued a routine internal alert to other SunTrust branches, warning them to keep an eye on the account for possible fraud. But the bank did not consider making a report to the government because there was nothing to suggest al-Shehhi had done anything illegal, let alone that he was a prospective hijacker.

The National Commission report concludes that:

> *even in hindsight there is nothing – including the SunTrust situation described above – to indicate that any SAR should have been filed or the hijackers otherwise reported to law enforcement. (10)*

Effect of the financing

It is worth reminding ourselves of what this innocuous stream of transactions actually led to. In the days before 11 September 2001, having returned the remaining money – $26000 in total – to Hawsawi in the UAE, the hijackers assembled in their various departure cities, ready to carry out arguably the most psychologically devastating attacks in American history. They were armed only with small knives, box cutters and cans of mace or pepper spray.

Atta and fellow hijacker Omari flew to Boston and spent their last evening shopping, eating pizza and making ATM withdrawals. Their three accomplices stayed in a hotel just outside Boston. Next morning they were among the 81 passengers who boarded American Airlines Flight 11, a Boeing 767 bound from Boston to Los Angeles. The plane took off at 7.59 a.m.; at 8.46 a.m., under the control of the hijackers, it ploughed into the North Tower of the World Trade Center in New York, the impact killing all the passengers, nine flight attendants and an unknown number of people in the tower.

Al-Shehhi and his team were also in Boston hotels the night before the attack. They took off from Boston on another Boeing 767, United Airlines Flight 175, an 8 a.m. departure for Los Angeles. There were 56 passengers and seven attendants on the flight, all of whom were killed instantly when the plane hit the South Tower of the World Trade Center at 9.03 a.m. Within 90 minutes both towers collapsed completely, killing more than 2600 people in total.

At 8.20 a.m., American Airlines Flight 77 – a Boeing 757 carrying 58 passengers and four attendants – left from Washington Dulles, again bound for Los Angeles. The five hijackers on board diverted the flight and at 9.37 a.m. flew it into the Pentagon in Washingon at 530 miles per hour. Everyone on the plane was killed. The death toll in the building was 125.

The fourth plane to be targeted was a Boeing 757, United Airlines Flight 93 from Newark to San Francisco. Unlike the other planes, Flight 93 was hijacked by only four terrorists, led by Jarrah and apparently destined for the White House. But in this case the 37 passengers fought back. After what must have been a desperate struggle, the plane came down in a field in Shanksville, Pennsylvania, about 20 minutes' flying time from Washington. Everyone on board was killed outright.

In total, 256 people died on the four planes.

When taken with those who lost their lives in the World Trade Centre buildings and the Pentagon, the final death toll was greater than that at Pearl Harbour in December 1941.

SOURCES

1. Lee Wolosky, statement to the National Commission on Terrorist Attacks Upon the United States, 1 April 2003.
2. Council on Foreign Relations, 'Terrorist Financing: Report of an Independent Task Force', October 2002.
3. Douglas Farah, 'Terrorist Responses to Improved Financial Defenses,' report to the House Subcommittee on Oversight and Investigations Committee on Financial Services, 16 February 2005.
4. National Commission on Terrorist Attacks upon the United States (NCTAUS), 'Monograph on Terrorist Financing', 2004.
5. Zachary Abuza, 'Funding Terrorism in Southeast Asia: The Financial Network of al-Qaeda and Jemaah Islamiyah', *NBR Analysis,* vol 14, no 5, December 2003, p. 43.
6. Douglas Farah, 'Terrorist Responses to Improved Financial Defenses'.
7. Details of the financial movements of the hijackers leading up to 9/11 were taken from Appendix A of the Monograph on Terrorist Financing cited above.
8. Ibid., p. 3.
9. Ibid., p. 135.
10. Ibid., p. 141.

JEMAAH ISLAMIYAH

Background

Jemaah Islamiyah (JI) was set up in Malaysia in 1993 or 1994 by two exiled radical Indonesian clerics, with the aim of creating an Islamic state throughout Southeast Asia. It apparently established close links with al-Qaeda at an early stage, and Professor Zachary Abuza (whose research on the funding structure of JI forms the basis of this section) comments that although it has a specific regional agenda rather than sharing the global jihadist goals of al-Qaeda, 'It should be seen as an integral part of the al-Qaeda network.' (1) Not only are a number of operatives members of both groups, but al-Qaeda provided JI leaders and members with training and funds; in addition some attacks were planned and executed by the two groups working together.

Although al-Qaeda did not target Southeast Asia for terrorist attacks, it had been active in the region well before JI started its offensive in the region in 2000. In the main, al-Qaeda's operations comprised fund-raising, recruiting, purchasing weapons and setting up front companies, attracted by the existence of Islamic charities and banks.

Notwithstanding its close affiliation with al-Qaeda, JI developed its own separate funding structure and has carried out some operations – including the Bali bombings of 2002 and, apparently, 2005 – on its own. It apparently generates a steady financial flow very effectively from a diversity of sources; for although more than 300 JI members, including many leaders, had been arrested as of October 2005 (2), the group has proved itself more than able to rebuild its network and plan further major attacks such as that in September 2004 on the Australian Embassy in Jakarta. Both exercises depended on continued funding. (3)

Methods of financing

At the 'back end' of the financial chain (farthest away from the terrorist operations), Zachary Abuza identifies eight main sources of income for JI.

1. Al-Qaeda cash donations

The most direct way is apparently through cash donations from al-Qaeda, delivered by personal couriers, who are often migrant Indonesian workers (though not necessarily JI members) returning home after periods of work overseas. Much cash has come from al-Qaeda in this way, but these funds appear to be earmarked specifically for attacks, and are not used for day-to-day expenses. (4)

2. Member donations

JI members themselves are also obliged to make financial donations to the organization, paying *zakat* amounting to 5 per cent of their income into the coffers of their cell. Many have modest lifestyles, but several are wealthier and give substantial sums to the cause. Active supporters of JI, notably in Singapore, have also apparently raised funds. (5)

3. Fundraising by clergy

JI members registered as Islamic clergy have also been able to raise voluntary donations from their congregations, from which they could then siphon off funds for the terrorist group.

4. Donations from expatriates

Donations by expatriate Indonesians, especially those living in Australia, are also believed to be important. (6)

5. Charitable donations

Much of JI's money is believed to come from the abuse of charitable funds. In some cases charities knowingly provide funds for terrorist groups; in others, apparently legitimate charities (cuckoo charities) are infiltrated by terrorist supporters who divert a proportion of funds, directly or indirectly, to their cause. In Indonesia 15–20 per cent of funds from Islamic charities are believed to be diverted into the coffers of political groups, including terrorist groups (7); in the Philippines it is estimated to be 50–60 per cent. (8)

In particular, Saudi-based charities have a well-established reputation for supplying funds to jihadists in other parts of the world: a UNSC report in 2002 noted that Saudi charities had passed between $300m and $500m to al-Qaeda and other militant Islamic charities, while an Indonesian official commented that 'The Saudi money has had a profound effect on extremist groups [in Indonesia], allowing some to keep going and inspiring others to start recruiting.' (9)

Professor Abuza has commented:

Although most of the [Saudi] donations to Islamic charities go to legitimate social work, a significant amount is diverted to terrorist and paramilitary activities ... It is doubtful that the central leadership of many of these charities has set out to assist terrorists, but there is a surprising lack of knowledge of what their branch offices are doing on the ground, and paltry oversight of how their funds are actually being used and allocated. (10)

But Saudi charities are by no means the only culprits and Abuza describes links between JI and allegedly charitable outfits based in Pakistan, the Philippines, Malaysia, Indonesia and Cambodia.

6. Business activities

Shell and front companies have also been used by JI. Some operate purely as shells to mask the purchase of materials for attacks; others, usually trading companies, have apparently been set up in Malaysia using al-Qaeda funds in order to generate 'clean' money from legitimate business. Several JI-run front firms have been discovered by the authorities, all of which were apparently donating 10 per cent of their profits to the JI jihad fund. In the words of one Swiss commentator cited by Professor Abuza:

The real problem ... is not freezing bank accounts. The bigger challenge is stopping the unknown number of apparently legitimate businesses set up to move money around the globe to terrorists. (11)

7. *Hawala*

It is also probable that long-established al-Qaeda controlled accounts and investments held in the Islamic banking sector itself are also used by JI. Comments Professor Abuza:

As Islamic banks were established to circumvent the practice of paying and charging interest, they often co-mingle funds to create investment vehicles, thereby creating ready opportunities for anonymous money transfers and settlements. (12)

8. Funds from crime

Finally, it seems that money from crimes such as robbery, kidnapping and extortion has a place in the treasury of JI. Professor Abuza points out:

There is a long tradition of 'fa'i' in Southeast Asia – using money from crime to support religious causes. Ideological purists often use criminals or find criminals who have found a religious calling, or are trying to atone for their sins. (13)

Indeed, as we shall see in more detail below, the Bali bombers part-funded their cell and its operations by robbing jewellery shops. Four of the 16 people arrested for the 2002 bombing had stolen some 2.5 kg of gold from the Elita Gold Store to help pay for the attack. One of the leaders of the plot, Imam Samudra, was also involved in online credit card scams, buying jewellery and other items using stolen cards and then reselling them. A plot to rob a bank was also uncovered by the Indonesian authorities in their investigation of the bombings.

Having looked at the different ways in which money may be raised by JI, we now look in more detail at the financial logistics uncovered behind the Bali attacks on 12 October 2002.

Financing the 2002 Bali bombings

If, at $500 000, the funding requirements of the 9/11 terrorists are considered modest in the context of international banking, then those of the Bali bombers were even smaller, coming in at less than $35 000. Funding for the attacks came from a number of sources and via several channels. It appears from the indictment of the leader of the JI cell responsible, Ali Ghufron (Mukhlas), that he had around $30 500 plus 200 000 baht (around £2 800 at current rates) for 'jihad operations'. This money apparently came directly from al-Qaeda's chief of operations, Khalid Sheikh Mohammed.

In March 2002, JI treasurer Wan Min Wan Mat transferred about $15 500 to Mukhlas 'for jihad activities'. About $2 000 was used by Mukhlas for travel, and the rest was earmarked for the Bali operation. In July 2002, Mukhlas had another $10 000 and 200 000 baht delivered to him in cash at his Indonesian home via an Indonesian labourer working in Malaysia. A further $5 000 was delivered to him from Malaysia via a personal courier in September. Mukhlas delivered money in rupiah to Jhoni Hendrawan, the logistical chief of the Bali plot, through a series of cash handovers totalling 350 m rupiah ($35 000) during August and September 2002.

In September 2002, Hendrawan handed out 23 m rupiah to the front-line bombers: 13 m rupiah for the chemicals used in the bombs and the rest for a down-payment on the minivan used to carry the bomb. A further 21.5 m rupiah was passed on four days later, to pay the balance on the minivan. The bombers received two further payments totalling 35 m rupiah from Hendrawan and Mukhlas, to cover the costs of hiring a car, buying a getaway motorbike and the rent of a house in Bali.

A second line of funding apparently came from the criminal activities of Imam Samudra, who (as mentioned above) robbed a gold shop in July 2002 in order to 'fund the jihad'. The haul comprised 2.5 kg of gold plus 5 m rupiah in cash, which was delivered to JI members; the bombers received an additional 20 m rupiah ($2 000) via a bank account belonging to another JI member.

As can be seen from the above, most of the money for the attack appears to have come directly from al-Qaeda; only a small proportion was generated by JI itself through the gold shop robbery. Al-Qaeda were apparently so pleased with the outcome of the attack that Khalid Sheikh Mohammad subsequently sent Hambali, the head of JI's operations, a further $100 000 for use at his own discretion.

Effect of the financing

The Bali bombings began just after 11 p.m. on 12 October 2002, when an explosive device was electronically detonated in Paddy's Irish Pub, a crowded bar at the heart of Bali's entertainment district, near Kuta Beach. It seems that one attacker wore a bomb vest or carried a bomb into the bar. Seconds later, as victims ran from the scene of the explosion, a second bomb – this time a Mitsubishi minivan packed with around 1 000 kg of explosives – was detonated outside the Sari Club, again, apparently by a suicide bomber. About a minute later, a third bomb packed with excrement exploded a few miles away outside the US Consulate, but no one was hurt there.

In all, 202 people of different nationalities were killed, including 38 Indonesians; hundreds more were injured, mostly holidaymakers and backpackers and a number of rugby players taking part in a tournament on the island. The local hospital was unable to cope with the number of casualties, particularly burn victims with terrible injuries, and many were flown to hospitals in Australia.

The bombing was condemned by the Indonesian chief of police General Da'i Bachtiar as 'the worst act of terror in Indonesia's history'. Several suspects were later rounded up and tried, including Mukhlas, his brother Amrozi, who bought the van and the explosives used, and Imam Samudra; all three were sentenced to death but have appealed. Ali Imron, another brother of Mukhlas, was jailed for life, as was Sarjiyo, who mixed the chemicals used in the attack and packed the bombs into the back of the van. Hambali was arrested in Thailand on 15 August 2003, and is now held by the Americans in an undisclosed location.

Zachary Abuza believes that despite the fact that many of JI's members and leaders have been picked off, the whole financial network remains largely intact.

SOURCES

1. Zachary Abuza, 'Funding Terrorism in Southeast Asia: The Financial Network of al-Qaeda and Jemaah Islamiyah,' *NBR Analysis* 14:5, December 2003, p. 12.
2. Zachary Abuza, 'The killers' new tactic: smaller bombs, more often', *Sydney Morning Herald* online (www.smh.com.au), 3 October 2005.
3. Ibid., p. 20.
4. Ibid., p. 21.
5. Ibid., p. 44.
6. Ibid., p. 47.
7. YeoWei Meng, 'Bali in the shadow of terror', *Asia Times Online*, 12 October 2004.
8. Abuza, 'Funding Terrorism in Southeast Asia', p. 22.
9. Ibid., p. 24.
10. Ibid., p. 25.
11. Ibid., p. 35.
12. Ibid., p. 48.
13. Abuza, 'Funding Terrorism in Southeast Asia', p. 50.

LIBERATION TIGERS OF TAMIL EELAM

Background

The Liberation Tigers of Tamil Eelam (LTTE), also known as the Tamil Tigers, is a separatist nationalist group fighting for an independent state in those parts of Sri Lanka inhabited substantially by ethnic Tamils. It is worth recording that the Tamil Tigers were among the pioneers of suicide bombing: since its inception in 1976, the group has carried out more than 200 suicide bomb attacks, including that which killed the Indian Prime Minister Rajiv

Ghandi in May 1991. The civil war in Sri Lanka between the LTTE and the Buddhist Sinhalese majority has claimed more than 60 000 lives and at the time of writing looks set to reignite after several years of political discussions. (1)

Although its local sphere of operations is confined almost entirely to Sri Lanka, the LTTE's fund-raising activities and support base are global. However, because it is terrorist attacks rather than terrorist infrastructure that tend to attract media coverage, interest in the LTTE's operations has tended to be concentrated in the Indian subcontinent rather than in the West as a whole. Indeed, until 1999, the countries most central to the group's international support base – the UK, Australia and Canada – took the view that the LTTE was engaged in a 'legitimate sub-state insurgency'. Following the suicide bomb attack on the Central Bank Building in Columbo, however, which made headlines worldwide in January 1996, the LTTE was designated a foreign terrorist organization by the US State Department – making it a crime to belong to or raise funds for the group. Canada joined the US in 1999, and other countries, including India, the UK, Australia and South Africa, have subsequently followed suit.

In the 1990s, the LTTE was considered 'arguably the most lethal and well-organized terrorist group in the world.' (2) As the war on terror gained momentum in the wake of the attacks of 9/11, the LTTE maintained a ceasefire agreed with the Sri Lankan Government in December 2001; but the peace process has effectively been stalled since April 2003 (3), and LTTE gunmen were blamed for the assassination in August 2005 of the Sri Lankan Foreign Minister. In the wake of that killing, the EU has announced that it is considering formally designating the LTTE a terrorist organization.

According to the Council of Foreign Relations (CFR), the group's relatively conciliatory stance since 9/11 was influenced by various factors, including international initiatives against terrorist funding (which we will examine below), as well as 'a widespread post-September 11 disdain for suicide terrorism, and dwindling support for terror among many Tamils'. (4) Nonetheless, the LTTE is widely considered 'to have one of the best-organized financial infrastructures of any terrorist group worldwide, with wealth generated through a variety of sources. It is estimated that these may yield up to $50 m a year. (5)

Methods of financing

How do the Tamil Tigers raise their money? There appear to be various sources:

1. The Tamil diaspora – voluntary payments

The primary source appears to be the various Tamil diasporas around the world. They are integrated into a single support system for the terrorists through the group's financial infrastructure, coordinated through its 'International Secretariat' (based in London until the UK prohibited the LTTE in 2001). As of 2001 there were expatriate Tamil groups in 54 countries worldwide (6), but the main areas are the US, Switzerland, India and the Scandinavian countries, and in particular the UK, Canada and Australia.

It is estimated that up to $2 m per month is raised from the diaspora, of which as much as a quarter comes from Canadian Tamils. The Tigers have an effective propaganda machine, and many contributions – from established expatriate Tamils who believe in the terrorists' cause and methods, and from illegal immigrants who rely on the LTTE to provide them with forged documents, jobs and housing in the host country – are made on a voluntary basis.

2. The Tamil diaspora – extortion

But in other cases contributions are raised through extortion. (7) For example, technically illegal Tamil immigrants can be coerced into making payments under threat of exposure to the immigration authorities. 'The LTTE makes much of its money from 'protection', or from threatening the lives of the relatives of potential donors "back home",' according to Nick Kochan in his study of money laundering and terrorist financing, *The Washing Machine.* (8)

The size of this 'tax' is apparently determined by the income of the Tamil family: in 2004 it varied from $40 to $80 per month. (9) Funds are allegedly collected through front organizations such as the United Tamil Organization (UTO) in the UK and the Federation of Associations of Canadian Tamils (FACT) in Canada. It appears that in order to sidestep international legal and political counter-terrorism measures, the money is usually sent back to Sri Lanka via pro-LTTE Tamil cultural, human rights or humanitarian agencies. As one commentator observes, and as we have commented before, 'The main problem in checking financial flows to terrorist organizations by individual governments is the difficulty in proving that the funds collected are being used for terrorist activities' (10) – the so-called 'pre-crime' problem.

3. Diversion of funds from NPOs and charities

The LTTE also raises money by diverting donations to non-government and aid organizations involved with Tamil social services and development programmes in Sri Lanka. In some places, particularly where NPOs are not closely monitored by the authorities, the LTTE appears to be fairly open in its operations. For instance, the group seems to make profitable use of the fact that Norwegian NPOs apparently do not need to register with the government in order to raise money for their cause. (11)

4. Profits from legitimate businesses

In addition, the organization has made use of a broad base of apparently legitimate commercial ventures worldwide, ranging from the operation of ocean liners and restaurants to fruit canning, petrol retail, travel agencies and jewellery. In 2001, Lord Michael Naseby, Joint Chairman of the All Party Sri Lanka Group, reported to the UK House of Lords that 'some twenty thousand illegal Tamil immigrants in London alone run LTTE front companies'. (12) It seems that the organization will provide start-up capital for new businesses run by trusted people, and subsequent profits are then split on an agreed basis. (13) MLROs will recognize this as being similar to the front 'company' operations run by some criminal, but non-terrorist, money launderers.

In the mid 1980s the LTTE apparently built up a fleet of around ten ocean-going freighters, owned by front companies and registered in Liberia, Honduras or Panama, and used not only to carry Southeast Asian timber and goods around the world for profit, but also to carry arms to the LTTE base in northern Sri Lanka. (14) The ships were also used for a more recent fund-raising exercise: the smuggling of refugees out of Sri Lanka and India and into Western countries, for which anything between $18000 and $32000 per person may be charged. (15)

5. Criminal activities

The LTTE's fleet and established clandestine international network means it is also ideally placed to smuggle narcotics (mainly heroin), raw or processed, from the production areas of Cambodia and Myanmar to the rest of the world, and there are apparently strong links between the LTTE and various international narcotics cartels. As well as using its own transport system, however, the group apparently also moves drugs internationally via migrants and asylum seekers. (16) Money is generated indirectly from other illegal activities, such as passport and visa counterfeiting as well as arms smuggling, carried out by Tamil criminal gangs supportive of the LTTE cause. (17)

Raising money is one thing; protecting it and making it available for the purchase of arms and explosives is another. When it comes to moving money around, the LTTE is apparently well served by the plethora of legitimate businesses and Tamil aid organizations from which it receives funding. As well as finances, these organizations may enable the group to access the sophisticated and efficient methods of money transmission used by the commercial world. (18) Similarly, they will inevitably provide access to conventional storage options such as bank accounts, as well as to investment opportunities in real estate and other assets through intermediaries in the Tamil diaspora. They may also hold funds on behalf of the LTTE in their own accounts, which can be drawn down, as and when cash is needed by the group. (19)

It can be seen from the above that the LTTE does not rely on state sponsorship with most of its funds generated through sources largely under its control. However, its dependency on access to funds from the Tamil diaspora leaves it potentially vulnerable to international counter-terrorism measures. The group is now listed as a terrorist organization in many large countries, making it much harder to fund-raise openly among expatriates. In addition, Sinhalese expatriates have been lobbying their host governments to impose tight restrictions outlawing the LTTE's financial networks. (20)

According to N. Manoharan writing in 2004, 'All these measures have affected external financial flows to the Tigers, but only to some extent. The LTTE's continued economic prosperity indicates that these countermeasures are not adequate.' (21)

SOURCES

1. Council of Foreign Relations (CFR), LTTE briefing (www.cfrterrorism.org).
2. Joseph Brewda and Madhu Gurung (1995), 'Southern India, Sri Lanka Terrorism', *Executive Intelligence Review*, 13 October.
3. Amantha Perera (2005), 'Sri Lanka – a Government on the Edge', *South Asia Intelligence Review*, 20 June (South Asia Terrorism Portal www.satp.org).
4. CFR, LTTE briefing.
5. Steve Kiser (2004), 'Financing Terror – An Analysis and Simulation for Affecting al-Qaeda's Financial Infrastructure,' dissertation published September, p. 34 (www.rand.org).
6. Ibid.
7. N Manoharan (2004), 'Financial Fodder – External Sources of LTTE Funds', Institute of Peace and Conflict Studies, 20 October.
8. Nick Kochan (2005), *The Washing Machine: How Money Laundering and Terrorist Financing Soils Us* (Thomson), p. 99.
9. Ibid.
10. Ibid.
11. Kiser (2004), p. 35.
12. Kochan (2005), p. 99.
13. Manoharan (2004).
14. Kochan (2005), p. 98.
15. Kiser (2004), p. 36.
16. Manoharan (2004).
17. Ibid.
18. Kiser (2004), p. 36.
19. Ibid., p. 37.
20. Manoharan (2004).
21. Ibid.

IRISH REPUBLICAN ARMY

Background

The Irish Republican Army (IRA) was the product of resentment felt by the minority Northern Irish Catholics at the creation by the British of a Protestant-controlled Northern Ireland in 1920, and its *raison d'etre* was to remove the British Crown, and reunite the island of Ireland as a single, 32-county republic under a Catholic majority.

The Provisional IRA (PIRA) – the main paramilitary group fighting for the republican movement, and essentially the modern IRA – was born out of the riots between Catholics and Protestants in the summer of 1969 (the beginning of 'the Troubles'), when it split from the Official IRA. The latter were arguing for a more peaceful political solution but gradually lost ground to the Provisionals or 'Provos'.

By the mid-1990s, the violence in Northern Ireland had reached a stalemate, a ceasefire had been declared and moves were afoot for a more permanent political settlement.

The Provisional IRA's political wing, Sinn Fein, signed the Good Friday Accords with the British Government in April 1998. The agreement was the spearhead of a serious effort to disarm the various paramilitary groups; it also created a democratically elected governing body for the people of Northern Ireland. Since then, despite various setbacks including the suspension of the Northern Ireland power-sharing government, political measures rather than terrorist attacks have dominated the agenda. The US State Department no longer considers the PIRA to be a terrorist organization, although it was actually classified as one up to 2000. However, two splinter groups – 'The Real IRA' and the 'Continuity IRA' – still carry out occasional terrorist attacks.

But as we shall see, just because politically motivated terrorist activities have largely ceased, does not necessarily mean an end to fund-raising activities on the part of the Provisionals. For as Nick Kochan has observed:

> *Peace (or what passes for peace in a society riven by low-level sectarian violence) has fomented an outbreak of commercial crime and money laundering that threatens the society's harmony in quite a different way than [did] terrorism. (1)*

PIRA fund-raising

It was only with the escalation of violence in 1969 that external funds began to be generated on any substantial scale. Before that, the IRA had existed on a pretty much hand-to-mouth basis, relying mainly on donations from members and petty crime. (2) Thereafter, however, the fund-raising network rapidly developed, drawing on both external and internal sources. Estimates of annual budgets for the PIRA ranged at the height of its activities during the 1980s from £6.5 m to £15 m, though it is now believed to need only around £5 m or so to meet its costs each year. (3) However, it is still believed to have the capacity to raise funds considerably above that level – an estimate of £7.7 m was put forward by the Police Services of Northern Ireland in 2002. (4)

Like the LTTE, the group had a very specific focus of operations, carrying out attacks almost exclusively in Northern Ireland and mainland Britain – but as we shall see, its fund-raising network was international in its scope, stretching from the US to Libya.

In part because the campaign was relatively local, few sophisticated or complex outgoings were involved: the money that was raised for the 'cause' was used mainly for weapons and munitions, wages, training of paramilitaries, payments to the owners of safe houses and welfare payments for the families of activists serving prison sentences, as well, as for supporting the political activities of Sinn Fein. (5)

Incoming funds, in contrast, were generated from a broad spectrum of sources, which we discuss below.

The United States

The nine-million strong self-identified Irish Catholic diaspora in the United States constituted a major source of revenue for the PIRA throughout the Troubles. Around 70 per cent of this group live in the north-eastern states, where it is easy to move within well-defined Catholic-Irish circles. As Steve

Kiser explains, 'Organizations sympathetic to the Irish cause (such as Clann na Gael, the US branch of the Irish Republican Brotherhood,) provided a ready structure and organization that enabled fundraising.' (6)

This diaspora included former IRA members, who were able to make good use of burgeoning Irish republican sentiments after the Troubles flared in 1968. In 1970 ex-IRA man Michael Flannery helped set up the Northern Aid Committee – Noraid – specifically to raise money for the Provisionals. As well as generating funds from Noraid members, he targeted members of other working-class Irish Catholic clubs such as Friends of Ireland and the Irish National Caucus. (7) They were more likely to make donations after a terrorist attack, or some other high-profile event such as the death of hunger striker Bobby Sands, had taken place.

Official documents provided by Noraid for the US Department of Justice show that a total of $3 m was raised by the organization and sent to Northern Ireland between 1970 and 1986, and a further $600 000 between 1986 and 1999. But because some money may have been sent directly to individuals and groups considered criminal by the Department of Justice (and therefore would not have been declared in the official report), those figures are probably well below the real amounts raised by Noraid for the nationalist cause. (8)

European Union fraud

The PIRA was able to exploit European Economic Community (EEC, as it was then called) financial subsidies made to southern Irish farmers in order to help them export produce to the UK. PIRA members posed as legitimate farmers and took their EEC money for exports of livestock and grain to Northern Ireland; then they smuggled them back into southern Ireland and re-exported them. The PIRA apparently raised an estimated £8 000 per week this way during the 1980s. (9)

Libya

Libya acted as a state sponsor to the PIRA. The Libyan leader Muammar al-Qadhafi was a bitter opponent of British Prime Minister Margaret Thatcher and it is estimated he may have provided the group with as much as $20 m from 1968 to the mid-1980s, as well as small arms and explosives. (10)

Legitimate business activity

As well as external income sources, the PIRA also generated money internally; indeed, since Libyan funding dried up in the early 1990s and Noraid cash flows shortly after, PIRA finances have been largely internally funded. (11) The 1980s saw a series of acquisitions of public houses and other leisure facilities across Ireland, and an estimated $30 m is tied up in real estate in southern Ireland alone; Nick Kochan reports a police commentator observing that: 'The Provisionals supposedly have 20 pubs in the Republic of Ireland. In Northern Ireland, it is likely that they control, or at least have influence over, many more.' (12)

The PIRA's portfolio of commercial assets extends beyond pubs to include taxicab services in Dublin and Belfast, estimated even in 1994 to generate an annual income getting on for $1 m. And they appear to have been adept at 'synergizing' (to coin a business phrase) their financial and political/military objectives. As Steve Kiser wryly observes: 'The success of these cab operations is due in no small part to the PIRA leadership's decision to eliminate the competition to taxis, most notably in the sustained fire-bombing campaign of the city-run bus systems.' (13)

Video stores, guest houses, a security firm and courier services are among the other front businesses owned by the PIRA. 'All of these firms pursue legal business interests and report their income to British taxation authorities; their profits, however, go to activities inimical to the British government's interest,' comments Kiser. There are others, however, that operate on a less legitimate basis, for example producing counterfeit DVDs and CDs. (14)

Criminal activities

The PIRA also had a raft of criminal money-making activities. These include kidnapping for ransom (generally of humans but a notable exception being the case of Shergar, a renowned racehorse for which $2 m was demanded in ransom money) and armed robbery (the most recent in December 2004, when a group believed to have close links with the PIRA stole more than £26.5 m from the Northern Bank in Northern Ireland). It is believed that the PIRA has been behind some of the most high-value and well-organized robberies in Ireland since the early 1970s. (15)

'Protection' sold to local businesses is another long-standing source of income. Originally it was a pretty rough and ready affair, amounting to demands for cash from armed men, but it metamorphosed over the years into a much less direct arrangement. New businesses are approached by representatives of an apparently legitimate security company. Writing in 1999, Horton and Taylor noted that extortion had become an increasingly popular form of fund-raising for Irish terrorists: 'The Belfast *Yellow Pages* in 1970 lists only six security firms, but today there are more than 60.' (16)

Common theft, burglary, income tax frauds, and the smuggling of various products, notably fuel and cigarettes, have also played a part in raising money for the PIRA's funds. There is evidence that drug money comes to the PIRA, but it appears to be generated by extortion from drug dealers rather than through direct involvement in the trade. (17)

The PIRA has not been involved in all these activities simultaneously; indeed, in some cases it may have made use of them for a relatively short length of time. Moreover, a considerable element of specialization is apparent within the organization, thereby increasing its effectiveness. It seems that these factors have been responses to changes within the PIRA (for example, its increasing politicization) and new opportunities to exploit in the wider environment – evidence of 'an opportunistic, almost entrepreneurial quality to this aspect of the organization', according to one commentator. (18)

Since the Good Friday Accords, the paramilitaries' preoccupation with their original republican aims and terrorist pursuits to that end has receded. At the same time, some earlier sources of funding are drying up, notably donations from American Irish Catholics who, in the words of Nick Kochan, have generally been 'roused to dig deep by news of high-profile terrorist acts' (of which, of course, there have been very few since the ceasefire). (19) Again demonstrating its capacity for flexibility and the exploitation of new financial opportunities, the PIRA apparently started looking for other sources of income, and to that end has sold its skills in terrorism and bomb making to the Revolutionary Armed Forces of Columbia (FARC) and also to Palestinian groups in Israel and Palestine. (20)

PIRA money laundering

How has the PIRA moved and laundered its various sources of funding over the years?

Physical cash movement

Noraid money was officially sent to the offices of the Northern Aid Committee in Belfast. In the early days funds were transmitted to Ireland via messengers and couriers (many of whom were thought to be police officers of Irish descent taking holidays back to the old country and carrying bulk cash at least twice a month to the Noraid offices). Subsequently, wire transfers and deposits in US banks with Irish branches were used, enabling PIRA members to access the cash via ATM withdrawals. (21)

Front companies

Laundering was required for local criminally derived income, and here the commercial businesses operated or funded by the PIRA proved most useful. Horgan and Taylor provide a couple of examples of how the PIRA has lent funds to local businesses, with the aim of both laundering the proceeds of armed robberies and other crimes into a legitimate company, and making a sound profit on the investment. (22)

Use of professional services

The journalist Veronica Guerin reported in 1996 that such ventures (that is, the ownership of front companies) provide a regular cash income and are an ideal cover for laundering stolen cash. The true ownership of these businesses is concealed in a myriad of holding companies in a complex scheme devised by an accountant well known to the Gardai (the police force of the Republic). The accountant operates from an office in Dublin's northside … [According to a source] 'All his work is legal, except that it is done on behalf of an illegal organization.' (23) These types of activity would again be familiar to MLROs in a criminal, but non-terrorist, AML context.

In a wider context, Horgan and Taylor emphasize the fact that PIRA fund-raising activities involve 'considerable and influential resources and contacts in the non-terrorism world'. For example, the purchase of a hotel using PIRA illicit money involved the services of an accountant acting for the group, as well as false references from a bank manager and false mortgage valuations from an auctioneer. (24)

Challenges in combating PIRA money laundering

The authorities' response to terrorist fund-raising in Northern Ireland has been seen by many as weak and ineffective. In 2002, Raymond White, Assistant Chief Constable in the Customs and Excise Department of the Police Service of Northern Ireland, sketched out the problem to the House of Commons Select Committee on Northern Ireland:

> *The money does not rest in any financial institution such as a bank or building society under a recognized title which is 'Provisional IRA'. The money that they raise is actually given to people who are in business. They are still one step ahead of us in the sense that the money is outsourced to legitimate businesses. So rather than walking in through the bank door, they are walking ... into somebody's business premises and money's deposited there. It can be put into the individual's personal account; it can go into the company account. It just sits there and they can draw down or hide it as part of the profits of that business for the years, so it is tremendously difficult financially to detect. Obviously there must be bankers or accountants or other financial institutions that must be aware of these large transactions. (25)*

Once again, says Nick Kochan:

> *The challenge to the authorities in every case is to distinguish terrorist money, which is money destined to fund terror, from criminal money, which is money acquired from crime or destined to be part of a financial scheme. (26)*

In February 2003, a new UK Government initiative designed to break the loop between organized criminal enterprises and their assets was introduced to Northern Ireland. The aim of the Assets Recovery Agency (ARA) is to disrupt organized criminal empires – and PIRA would now be included within such a definition – by specifically targeting and reclaiming their ill-gotten assets. This demands a multi-agency approach, and the ARA works in partnership not only with a wide range of other government departments and agencies in the UK and Northern Ireland, but also with the Criminal Assets Bureau in the Republic of Ireland to tackle cases with a cross-border dimension.

Over £6 m in assets were frozen in the first two years, but such a task remains fraught with difficulty. A major expansion is under way: the aim for 2005 for example was to initiate 25 cases – double the number initiated in 2004. In June 2005, there were almost 90 properties in Northern Ireland with restraint orders on them, and more than 100 bank and other financial accounts.

In some cases there may be links to paramilitary groups: for example, a defendant whose assets were frozen by the ARA in Belfast in September 2005 was alleged to have been involved in armed robbery, drug trafficking and firearms offences, and to have links with other criminal groups linked to both Republican and Loyalist paramilitaries. (27)

SOURCES

1. Nick Kochan (2005), *The Washing Machine: How Money Laundering and Terrorist Financing Soils US* (Thomson), p. 81.
2. Steve Kiser (2004), 'Financing Terror – An Analysis and Simulation for Affecting al-Qaeda's Financial Infrastructure,' dissertation published Sept, p. 59.
3. Kochan (2005), p. 82.
4. Richard Evans (2002), 'Organized Crime and Terrorist Financing in Northern Ireland,' *Jane's Intelligence Review*, 1 September.
5. Kiser (2004), p. 52.
6. Ibid., p. 53.
7. Ibid.
8. Ibid., p. 54.
9. Ibid.
10. Ibid., p. 55.
11. Ibid., p. 60.
12. Kochan (2005), *The Washing Machine*, p82.
13. Kiser (2004), 'Financing Terror', p55.
14. Ibid.
15. John Horgan and Max Taylor (1999), 'Playing the Green Card – Financing the Provisional IRA, Part I', *Terrorism and Political Violence*, Summer.
16. Kochan (2005), p. 81.
17. Ibid., p. 82.
18. Horgan and Taylor (1999).
19. Kochan (2005), p. 85.
20. Ibid.
21. Kiser (2004), p. 59.
22. John Horgan and Max Taylor (2003), 'Playing the Green Card – Financing the Provisional IRA, Part II', *Terrorism and Political Violence*, Summer.
23. Veronica Guerin (1996), 'IRA used ceasefire to plan bomb campaign,' *Sunday Independent*, 23 June.
24. Horgan and Taylor (2003), p. 40.
25. Quoted in Kochan (2005), p. 86.
26. Ibid., p. 87.
27. www.assetsrecovery.gov.uk (2005), 'ARA freezes assets of alleged Belfast organized criminal', press release, 30 September.

CHAPTER 4

International and National Legal and Quasi-Legal Requirements

The CTF legislation put into place by individual countries is a reflection of broader requirements and approaches agreed by international bodies, in particular the United Nations and the Financial Action Task Force on Money Laundering (FATF). Whilst the FATF requirements and those of their affiliated regional groups are not strictly legal requirements in the sense that UN treaties (when ratified) and national legislation are, nevertheless the overall effect is to create a framework of legal and quasi-legal requirements which we have attempted to summarize here, and which should be read in conjunction with Chapter 6 ('Best Practice') which deals with guidance issued by various industry-specific bodies.

We have concentrated on what we believe to be the main points to be considered for appropriate treatment in CTF training sessions; the summary is not intended to be exhaustive and organizations should seek specialist legal advice for specific operational issues.

We work from the general to the particular, and look first at the requirements issued by international organizations before moving on to national legal requirements in some of the major financial centres. Where relevant, we have included reference to anti-money laundering material as well.

INTERNATIONAL AUTHORITIES

United Nations

The UN has built up a network of interlocking conventions and resolutions in the light of various acts of international terrorism.

International Convention for the Suppression of the Financing of Terrorism, 1999

Following a series of resolutions condemning terrorist action during the 1990s, the UN adopted this Convention at the General Assembly held in New York in December 1999. The resultant treaty came into force in April

2002; as of November 2005, it had been signed by 147 countries and ratified by 132. The treaty requires countries to criminalize the act of providing or collecting funds with the intention or knowledge that those funds will be used to carry out a terrorist attack. It goes so far as to assert that 'financing is at the heart of terrorist activity' and lays the foundations for closer cooperation between law enforcement agencies, financial authorities and individual countries.

Countries that have ratified the treaty (known as State Parties) are required to put into place mechanisms to identify, detect and freeze or seize assets used or earmarked for terrorist activities, and financial institutions are called upon to be vigilant with regard to unusual transactions and to report to the authorities anything that they suspect may have links with terrorism or terrorist activities. They are also obliged to prosecute or extradite offenders, and to cooperate with other countries' investigations. A State Party cannot, for example, turn down a request for mutual legal assistance on the grounds of its own banking secrecy laws.

UNSCRs 1267 and 1333

The UNSC issued resolution UNSCR 1267 in 1999, aimed at blocking the finance network of the Taliban in Afghanistan, and UNSCR 1333 in 2000, focusing on that of al-Qaeda.

UNSCR 1373

Following the attacks on the World Trade Center in September 2001, the UNSC passed UNSCR 1373 for the Suppression of the Financing of Terrorism. This is one of the lynchpins of international action against terrorist financing, and includes a range of steps and strategies to combat the financing of terrorism generally.

Resolution 1373 reconfirms that all states should prevent or suppress terrorist financing, criminalize fund-raising or the provision of economic resources for terrorism, and freeze the financial assets of terrorist groups. Terrorist acts should be established as serious criminal offences and anyone involved in their financing, planning or perpetration should be denied any kind of support and brought to justice. Particular emphasis is placed on the exchange of information between countries, not only with regard to terrorist actions and movements but also in the light of the close links between terrorist acts and other types of organized crime and money laundering. And it was UNSCR 1373 which extended the notification and sanctions regime to individuals and organizations suspected of connections with terrorism.

Resolution 1373 also established the Counter-Terrorism Committee (CTC) as a monitoring body to try to ensure the resolution is effectively implemented and to provide assistance for countries that need help in this regard.

UNSCR 1390

A further resolution, UNSCR 1390, was passed in 2002 after the defeat of the Taliban, strengthening the sanctions against remaining elements of both that group and al-Qaeda. The UN listed 293 individuals and organizations whose assets were to be frozen under the three resolutions; the UK alone froze more than $100 m in response, though in the aftermath of the taking of Kabul, most has been unfrozen and made available to the new Afghan Government.

UNSCRs 1456 and 1617

Other subsequent resolutions on terrorist financing passed by the UNSC include UNSCR 1456, which reaffirms the need to suppress all active and passive support to terrorism, and also provides guidelines for the CTC to intensify its efforts to encourage member states to implement UNSCR 1373 and UNSCR 1617 (July 2005) which effected a further clampdown on Osama bin Laden, al-Qaeda and any splinter groups.

UNSCR 1624

The UN 50-year anniversary in September 2005 saw the adoption of UNSCR 1624, which among other things stresses that countries should criminalize *incitement* to commit terrorist acts and calls upon states to strengthen international border security. This development was largely occasioned by the open preaching of overtly violent and aggressive teachings by a number of high-profile Islamic clerics and scholars, such as Abu Hamza in the UK.

The Council of Europe

Europe's oldest multi-nation political organization has 46 member states, including 21 Central and Eastern European countries. It has drawn up a series of conventions against money laundering and terrorism, aimed at suppressing criminal concerns and terrorist movements and reducing their ability to operate in Europe.

The Convention on Laundering, Search, Seizure and Confiscation of the Proceeds from Crime [ETS 141]

Also known as the Strasbourg Convention, this was signed in 1990 and entered into force in September 1993. The Convention aimed to counter the laundering of the proceeds of all types of crime (not just drug trafficking) and to improve international cooperation, both between Council of Europe member states and with other states including the USA, Canada and Australia.

For example, when criminal assets have been transferred abroad into overseas bank accounts, states which are parties to the convention (including the UK) are then required to cooperate with each other in order to freeze and seize them. Provision is also made for mutual assistance in investigations into money laundering, including the lifting of bank secrecy, the forwarding of information to another state without a prior request, and the adoption of common investigative techniques.

The Convention on the Laundering, Search, Seizure and Confiscation of the Proceeds from Crime, and on the Financing of Terrorism

Updating and expanding on the Strasbourg Convention, the Convention was adopted by the Committee of Ministers in May 2005 and was firmly grounded in the 1999 UN International Convention for the Suppression of the Financing of Terrorism (discussed above). Crucially, the 2005 Convention focuses not only on the laundering and confiscation of criminal proceeds, but also on the interdiction of 'clean' money generated through legitimate sources but destined for criminal purposes – a key activity for financiers of terrorism, as we have seen.

The text addresses the fact that quick access to financial information or information on assets held by criminal organizations, including terrorist groups, is key to the successful implementation of preventive and suppressive measures against them.

Financial Action Task Force

The FATF is an inter-governmental body currently comprising 33 members. It was set up by the then G-7 Summit held in Paris in 1989 in response to the growing threat posed by international money laundering, and was given the task of examining money laundering techniques and trends, setting out measures to combat them and then reviewing the action taken at both the national and international level. As terrorist financing has risen up the international agenda, the FATF's role has naturally extended to encompass CTF as well. It works in close cooperation with various other international bodies, including the IMF, the World Bank and the United Nations.

The FATF effectively has a manifold role at the heart of the overall AML and CTF regime:

- To monitor the progress of countries in introducing AML and CTF measures, using self-assessments and more detailed mutual evaluations. Non-cooperative governments have found themselves under heavy moral, political and economic pressure to toe the line through the reviews: for example, Austria eventually agreed to prohibit anonymous savings accounts as a result of pressure from the FATF, and the countries of Eastern Europe and the former Soviet Union (including Russia) have embarked upon urgent national legislative programmes in a very short space of time.
- To review trends, techniques and innovations in money laundering (which has led to the annual money laundering typologies reports, on which many of the case studies and training exercises in this book are based), and to keep member states abreast of the findings.
- To build a global AML and CTF network by extending the reach of FATF principles. This has resulted in new member countries joining the group; it has also led to the formation of regional FATF-style groups such as the Caribbean and East Asia Groups.
- At the heart of FATF's activities are their recommendations on measures for the combating of money laundering and, latterly, terrorist financing. As MLROs will know, 'The Forty Recommendations' address AML and the

'Nine Special Recommendations' address CTF. Even though this book is on countering terrorist financing, given the relevance of many of the initial Forty Recommendations to CTF as well, we have felt it appropriate to summarize all of the recommendations here.

The FATF Forty Recommendations on anti-money laundering

The Forty Recommendations were first published in 1990, revised in 1996, and comprehensively updated in 2003. They were designed to provide a comprehensive plan of action needed to fight money laundering, encompassing:

- criminal justice and law enforcement
- the financial system and its regulation
- international cooperation.

Countries have diverse legal and financial systems and therefore all cannot take identical measures. The FATF Forty therefore lay out broad principles for countries to implement according to their particular circumstances and constitutional frameworks. They are not a binding international convention, but many countries around the world have made a political commitment to fight money laundering by adopting and implementing them and face censure and reprisals if they refuse to do so.

Legal definitions and asset confiscation

- The recommendations cover steps for countries to take to define the scope of the offence of money laundering, and to give their authorities the power to confiscate laundered assets and freeze or seize accounts of suspects. (R1–R3)

Banking secrecy

- Countries need to ensure that their banking secrecy laws do not work against implementation of the recommendations. (R4)

Due diligence – circumstances

- Financial institutions are to have obligations regarding customer due diligence and record keeping (R5): they are not to keep anonymous accounts or accounts held in obviously fictitious names, and they are to undertake due diligence measures when:
  - establishing a new business relationship;
  - carrying out occasional transactions, either above a designated threshold or via wire transfer in certain circumstances;
  - there is a suspicion that money laundering or terrorist funding may be going on; or
  - there are concerns over the original customer ID.

Due diligence – basic requirements

- The requirements for customer due diligence are also spelt out:
  - carrying out thorough customer identification;
  - identifying the beneficial owner of the assets;
  - obtaining information on the purpose and nature of the business relationship; and
  - monitoring that relationship on an ongoing basis to ensure that the transactions carried out are in keeping with what is known about the business and its usual transaction patterns and fund sources.

Due diligence – risk assessment

- Due diligence should be applied not only to all new customers, but also to existing customers 'on the basis of materiality and risk'. If the financial institution cannot obtain the information it needs, it should not open the account or perform the transaction, and should consider filing a suspicious transaction report. Guidance is also given for additional due diligence for 'politically exposed persons' (PEPs – those holding prominent political or government positions in the country and those related to them). (R6)

Correspondent banking

When it comes to cross-border correspondent banking, financial institutions should be instructed, among other things, to:

- carry out additional checks on the reputation and quality of supervision of the bank or other organization they are dealing with;
- assess its money laundering and terrorist financing controls; and
- get clearance from senior management before establishing new correspondent relationships of this sort. (R7)

Non-face-to-face transactions

- Financial institutions are also warned to be vigilant with regard to the opportunities for money laundering that may arise as a consequence of new technology. In particular, R8 stresses that they should 'have policies and procedures in place to address any specific risks associated with non-face-to-face business relationships or transactions' – of particular importance in the development of telephone, mobile and Internet-based products and services.

Financial intermediaries

Where financial intermediaries are involved in bringing business to institutions, the intermediaries may perform the due diligence measures, but the financial institution needs to:

- double-check the identification documents; and
- satisfy itself that the intermediary itself is properly regulated and supervised.

It is left to each country to decide in which other countries intermediaries may be based, but they need to consider whether or not countries comply sufficiently with the FATF Recommendations. (R9)

Record-keeping

Record-keeping is also addressed (R11): financial institutions should maintain all transaction records for at least five years from the date of the transaction so that they can assist the authorities with information on individual transactions if required. They should also keep records of the identification data collected through the due diligence process, for at least five years after the business relationship has ended.

Suspicion reporting

As well as due diligence, the recommendations address the issue of what happens if a financial institution suspects that funds are related to money laundering or were criminally obtained. It should be under a legal or regulatory obligation to make a prompt report of its suspicions to the relevant Financial Intelligence Unit (FIU). (R13)

Internal policies and controls

To ensure that anti-money laundering measures are thoroughly embedded within the organization, financial institutions should create internal policies and controls, including:

- screening measures when new staff are being hired;
- compliance management arrangements; and
- ongoing staff training programmes. (R15)

Customer confidentiality and 'tipping-off'

If a suspicious transaction report is filed in good faith by a bank or other financial institution, the directors and staff should not be liable for breach of confidentiality, even if they do not know exactly what criminal activity took place, and also even if it transpires that in fact no crime was committed.

The staff and directors should also be prohibited by law from disclosing to the customer the fact that such a report has been filed with the FIU. (R14)

Sanctions

Countries should put in place 'effective, proportionate and dissuasive sanctions' against individuals or organizations that fail to comply with AML requirements. (R17)

Non-financial services 'gatekeepers'

R12 and R16 set out the customer due diligence, record-keeping and reporting requirements as they apply to other businesses, including casinos, estate agents, dealers in bullion or gems, lawyers, notaries and other legal professionals, accountants, and trust and company service providers.

Shell banks

R18 recommends that countries should not allow the establishment or continued operation of shell banks ('nameplate' banks with no premises, staff and banking operations); nor should financial institutions have dealings with shell banks, *or* with foreign banks which themselves do business with shell banks.

Border currency controls and threshold reporting

Further suggestions include the idea that countries should introduce measures to monitor the physical transportation of currency and bearer negotiable instruments across borders; and the implementation of a scheme whereby financial institutions report designated transactions above a fixed level to a central agency as a matter of course, for use in money laundering or terrorist financing investigations. (R19)

Use of international findings

Financial institutions are warned to pay particular attention to business dealings with individuals, companies or other financial institutions based in countries that fail to comply with the FATF Recommendations. If they come across a questionable transaction, they should gather as much information as possible about its background and purpose and make the information available to the relevant authorities. (R21)

Parents, branches and subsidiaries

With regard to overseas branches and majority-owned subsidiaries of financial institutions, the parent companies are expected to apply the FATF principles as far as local laws and regulations allow them to – especially in countries that are not themselves fully committed to FATF's recommendations. (R22)

Effective regulation

It is the responsibility of each country to create an adequate regulatory and supervisory environment, and to ensure that its financial institutions are complying with the FATF Recommendations. (R23) Countries also need to provide guidance and feedback to assist regulated organizations – in particular with regard to detecting and reporting suspicious transactions. (R25)

Systems

A number of the FATF 40 Recommendations focus on the obligations of countries to set up 'systems' to combat money laundering. These include:

- the establishment of a Financial Intelligence Unit (FIU) to act as a central information and analysis point in respect of information reports filed by gatekeepers; (R26)
- the need for designated specialist law-enforcement agencies to investigate cases and where necessary work with their equivalents in other countries; (R27) and
- powers for investigators and supervisors within the system to obtain the information which they need in order to do their jobs, and to impose sanctions where they do not get full cooperation from banks or individuals. (R28–29)

Beneficial ownership and international cooperation

Transparency in the issue of beneficial ownership is also addressed (R33–34) – a very important requirement. Finally, a number of recommendations are made that countries should cooperate with international requests for legal assistance, to seize or freeze assets, to extradite suspects, and in general to 'provide the widest possible range of international cooperation with their foreign counterparts'. (R35–40)

Extending the FATF's scope

Widening the net

Over the past decade or so, the FATF has pushed its remit steadily wider, geographically, functionally and in terms of the kinds of businesses affected, reflecting the way in which criminal networks have responded to the countermeasures taken in the banking sector by utilising other types of financial institutions, such as insurance companies and bureaux de change. In 1996, money laundering crimes were expanded to include other predicate offences beyond drug trafficking, and non-bank financial institutions as well as banks were brought under the influence of the FATF Recommendations. More recently, as we have seen, the focus has spread beyond the financial services industry to encompass businesses such as auctioneers, casinos, car-dealerships, company formation agents, lawyers, accountants and tax advisers.

The NCCT regime

In 2000, the FATF took perhaps its most dramatic new initiative to 'name and shame' what it designated as 'Non-Cooperative Countries and Terroritories' (NCCTs). These were jurisdictions not participating in the general move towards stricter financial regulation and greater international cooperation, which were instead offering financial services under strict banking secrecy and without sufficient control or regulation by the authorities.

Despite the fact that, over time, the list has been emptied as countries have taken the necessary measures, the NCCT mechanism still exists and is a weapon which these authors believe is likely to be used again in the future, but with the 'trigger' set at a more demanding level. Offending countries and territories are encouraged by advice and technical assistance from FATF or its regional equivalent, or other international bodies. Those that prove unwilling to take constructive action to improve their financial system to bring it into line with FATF standards may be subject to a regime of inspections and assessments culminating in the appearance of the country on the NCCT list – an action with extremely negative reputational and economic consequences. For example, financial institutions in FATF member states could be required to carry out additional due diligence checks on any transactions involving the NCCT. Or they could be asked to restrict or even prohibit financial transactions with the NCCT in question.

The NCCT initiative has proved a successful one – at least in getting countries to address the issues through legislation and infrastructure. Of the 47 countries whose systems were initially reviewed by the FATF in 2000 and 2001, a total of 23 countries were listed as NCCTs – 15 in 2000 and a further eight in 2001.

The Nine Special Recommendations

In the wake of the terrorist attacks on the United States of 11 September 2001, the FATF issued eight additional recommendations relating specifically to terrorist financing. A ninth was added in October 2004. Used in conjunction with the original FATF Forty, they 'set out the basic framework to detect, prevent and suppress the financing of terrorism and terrorist acts' and we précis them below.

I. Ratification and implementation of UN instruments
Each country should take immediate steps to ratify and to implement fully the 1999 UN International Convention for the Suppression of the Financing of Terrorism (see above), and also the UN resolutions relating to the prevention and suppression of terrorist financing, particularly UNSCR 1373.

II. Criminalizing the financing of terrorism and associated money laundering
Each country should criminalize the financing of terrorism, terrorist acts and terrorist organizations, designating these offences as money laundering predicate offences (that is, as offences which attract the application of AML laws; other predicate offences refer to crimes by which funds are generated for laundering, such as theft, fraud or smuggling and, of course, drug trafficking).

III. Freezing and confiscating terrorist assets
Countries should put in place measures to freeze funds or other terrorist assets, in accordance with the UN resolutions referred to above. Countries should also introduce a legal framework and other measures enabling the authorities to seize and confiscate property which is used or allocated for use in terrorist financing.

IV. Reporting suspicious transactions related to terrorism
If financial institutions, or other organizations subject to AML obligations, suspect that funds are somehow linked to or earmarked for terrorist acts or terrorism, they should be required promptly to report their suspicions to the relevant authorities.

V. International cooperation

On the basis of treaties, arrangements or other mechanisms for mutual exchange of legal information, countries should give each other as much assistance as possible with investigations and proceedings relating to terrorist financing. Countries should also take every precaution to ensure they do not provide safe havens for anyone charged with financing terrorism, and should have procedures in place to extradite them if necessary.

VI. Alternative remittance

Countries should take action to ensure that individuals or businesses providing money transmission services, including those operating through an informal money or value transfer scheme (such as *hawala)* are licensed or registered and are subject to the same FATF recommendations that apply to banks and other financial institutions. Illegal money transfer operators should be subject to sanctions.

VII. Wire transfers

Financial institutions, including money remitters, should be required to include accurate and meaningful details of the originator (including their name, address and account number) with any wired fund transfers, and this information should remain with the financial transfer throughout its journey through the payment chain. Financial institutions should look for suspicious activity and monitor any funds transfers that do *not* contain all the relevant sender information for potentially suspicious activity.

VIII. Non-profit organizations

Countries should review their laws and regulations insofar as they apply to organizations which may be open to abuse for the purposes of terrorist financing. Non-profit organizations (NPOs) are particularly vulnerable, so countries need to ensure that their system of NPOs cannot be easily misused. (As we have seen in Chapter 2, this may happen when terrorist organizations pose as legitimate entities, or if a legitimate organization is exploited for use as a conduit for terrorist funds, or if NPO funds intended for legitimate purposes are siphoned off to the coffers of terrorist organizations.)

IX. Cash couriers

Countries should put into place measures to detect the physical movement of cash and bearer negotiable instruments across international borders. These measures should include a declaration system or other disclosure arrangement. The authorities should have the authority to stop such currency movements if they are falsely declared, or if they are suspected of having links to terrorist financing or money laundering. Appropriate sanctions should be put in place to deal with people who make false declarations, and currency linked to money laundering or terrorist financing should be confiscated under measures consistent with Special Recommendation III above.

What do the Special Recommendations mean for financial institutions?

The thrust of most of the Special Recommendations is towards ensuring that *countries* themselves are taking the necessary legislative and regulatory steps to recognize and clamp down on terrorist financing. But there are certain aspects in which the onus is on *individual financial institutions* to take action. (See Chapter 6 for a more detailed examination of best practice guidelines for financial institutions.)

The key recommendation in this respect is Special Recommendation IV 'Reporting suspicious transactions related to terrorism', which underscores the need for banks both to be vigilant in monitoring transactions and to file a report promptly if their suspicions are aroused.

Special Recommendation III 'Freezing terrorist assets' also has clear implications for banks and other financial institutions along the same lines. The FATF guidelines of October 2003 on best practice for Special Recommendation III, backing up this Special Recommendation, point out that:

> *Active participation and full support by the private sector is also essential to the success of any terrorist financing freezing campaign. Consequently, jurisdictions should work with the private sector to ensure its ongoing cooperation in developing and implementing an effective [counter-] terrorist financing regime.*

Best practice outlined in the guidelines includes requirements for:

- jurisdictions to develop a process for banks to provide information (including names, accounts, amounts) on frozen accounts to the authorities or courts, modifying the existing banking secrecy laws as necessary to do so; and
- public indemnity laws with which to shield financial institutions and their staff, among others, from legal liability when they act in good faith to freeze what they believe to be terrorist-linked funds.

Information needs to flow two ways, however, and the guidelines also emphasize that a key best practice requirement in asset freezing involves facilitating communication with the private sector. This includes, among various other issues:

- the publication and prompt updating of a designated persons list in a user-friendly format, including different entries for different aliases or name spellings; and
- notification of pending designations to those financial institutions where the listed targets are believed to have accounts, so that they can act immediately when the designation is announced. (NB: This is arguably the single most important practical measure which can be taken from an operational banking perspective; it is one of the measures which really can prevent a syndrome of 'shutting the stable door after the horse has bolted'.)

Jurisdictions also need to work with financial institutions to ensure that they have procedures in place to prevent listed targets from carrying out transactions with or through them; to encourage them to examine past financial activity by any listed customers; and to help them tighten up on customer identification rules and improve on record-keeping.

Finally, it is stated that jurisdictions should make sure that the information provided by banks and other financial institutions is made available and fully utilised by law enforcement agencies, with feedback from those agencies to indicate how the financial intelligence received is being used by them in their investigations of terrorist financing. MLROs will be aware that this has been a particular source of friction, with a real perception in many countries that reporting is one-way traffic, with in fact, very little feedback from the authority to the regulated sector.

FATF-style regional bodies (FSRBs)

Several regional organizations have been established to carry forward the principles and practices set out by FATF on a more localized basis. They include:

- the Asia/Pacific Group on Money Laundering (APG), which produces annual reports on money laundering and terrorist financing trends and techniques in the region;
- the Caribbean Financial Action Task Force (CFATF);
- the Eastern and Southern Africa Anti-Money Laundering Group (ESAAMLG);
- the Grupo de Accion Financiera Sud America (GAFISud);
- the East Asia Group (EAG), the membership of this last one spreading slightly further west than its name implies, consisting as it does of Russia, Belarus, Kazakhstan, Uzbekistan, Tajikistan and China.

International Monetary Fund (IMF)

The IMF has long been involved in international efforts to combat money laundering at a national level, and after the events of 9/11 it intensified and extended the remit of these activities to include combating the financing of terrorism. As a collaborative institution with a near-universal membership of countries (it has 184 members), the IMF is perhaps a natural forum for countries to share information and develop common approaches and appropriate policies to deal with such issues.

The IMF has also brought to bear its capabilities in the assessment of member states' financial sectors, and the provision of technical assistance to help countries strengthen their financial sectors. In March 2004, the IMF Executive Board agreed to make AML and CTF assessments and technical assistance a regular part of IMF work, and to expand this work to cover the full scope of the FATF recommendations.

The resulting Financial Sector Assessment Programme (FSAP) is a joint effort with the World Bank; it is designed to provide member countries with a comprehensive evaluation of their financial systems as a whole, rather than those of individual financial institutions. The FSAP aims to alert the national authorities to weaknesses in their systems, and to help them design countermeasures to reduce those weaknesses. By the end of June 2005, about 120 countries (or about two-thirds of the IMF's membership) had participated in the programme.

The IMF and World Bank are also involved in policy development in the CTF arena. IMF publications include

- a reference guide on AML/CFT issues;
- handbooks on Financial Intelligence Units (most recently 2004);
- *Suppressing the Financing of Terrorism: a handbook for legislative drafting* (August 2003);
- a number of works on remittance systems, the most recent being *Regulatory Frameworks for Hawala and Other Remittance Systems* (2005);
- working papers on many topics including 'The Impact of Terrorism on Financial Markets' (March 2005).

European Union

Much of the EU's anti-terrorist regulation is aimed at bringing the legislation of individual member states better into line and improving cooperation between them.

Council Recommendation of 9 December 1999

With regard to countering terrorist finance, this Council Recommendation of 9 December 1999 was brought in to boost cooperation between the member states; it recommended that member states should exchange information regularly on the structures and methods used to finance terrorist groups, and particularly those identified as posing a specific threat to EU countries.

EU Second Money Laundering Directive December 2001

Although planned long before 9/11, the Second Money Laundering Directive, a wide-ranging deepening and strengthening of the EU's existing First Money Laundering Directive of 1991, widened the definition of criminal activity capable of giving rise to money laundering by including not only all organized crime but also a wide range of serious crimes and, crucially, offences relating to terrorism.

In a wider context, the other key provisions of the Second Directive were:

- the addition of lawyers, accountants, tax advisers, real estate agents, casinos and dealers in 'high value goods' (such as auctioneers and car dealerships) as 'gatekeepers' bound by AML/CTF legislation;
- enhanced identification requirement for non-face-to-face customers and transactions.

Council Common Position (2001/931/CESC)

December 2001 also saw the implementation of this Council Common Position in drawing up a list of individuals, groups and entities involved in terrorism whose assets were to be frozen. The list time included ETA (Basque Fatherland and Liberty), the IRA (Irish Republican Army), GRAPO (the First of October Anti-Fascist Resistance Group), Hamas, Palestinian Islamic Jihad and other revolutionary activist groups, as well as the names of individuals belonging to such groups. (Al-Qaeda, Osama bin Laden and his associates were already designated in a separate Council Common Position of February 2001.)

Council Framework Decision (2002/465/JHA)

This Framework Decision was an attempt to make the fight against terrorism within the EU more efficient. Beforehand, only seven countries – France, Germany, Italy, Portugal, Greece, Spain and the UK out of the then 15 member states – had specific laws to fight terrorism, and these varied from one country to another. In the other member states, where no such legislation existed, terrorist acts were judged on the basis of common criminal offences. The thrust of the Framework Decision was, therefore, to urge member countries to align their anti-terrorism laws.

Council Framework Decision (2002/475/JHA)

This decision was taken at the same time and obliged member states to criminalize actions related to terrorism, including the provision of any form of funding for terrorist activities.

Council Framework Decision (2003/577/JHA)

A third decision, in July 2003, saw the introduction of the principle of mutual recognition of judicial orders to freeze property and evidence – in other words, that one member state must act on a judicial order to that effect issued by another member state.

Regulation on Cash Control 2005

In July 2005, the EU adopted its regulation on cash control in and out of the EU on a Community-wide basis. Under the new regulation, travellers carrying more than €10000 (or its equivalent in currency or easily convertible assets) would be obliged to declare it when they pass through customs controls on the way in or out of the EU. The level was originally set at €15000, to complement that set for transactions through financial institutions in the Third Money Laundering Directive (see below), but was reduced on the basis that money can be more easily transferred as cash across borders and therefore controls need to be tighter.

Third Anti-Money Laundering Directive June 2005

Adopted by the European Commission in June 2005, among other things (see below) the Directive applies when cash payments of more than €15000 are made, and covers not only the financial sector but also lawyers, accountants, estate agents, casinos, trust and company service providers, and anyone selling goods for which €15000 plus is tendered in cash.

When such instances occur, the Directive requires the organization in question to check and verify the identity of the customer and the beneficial owner of the money, and to monitor the business relationship between the two. Any suspicions of money laundering or terrorist financing need to be reported to the national FIU. Organizations subject to the Directive also need to make sure they have the necessary policies and procedures in place, such as training for staff and internal compliance checks.

As far as terrorist financing is concerned, when taken in conjunction with the 2005 Regulation on Cash Control, this emphasis on cash at quite a low threshold, does constitute, perhaps, a stark warning about the way in which the lethal front end of the terrorist's operations are conducted.

In a wider context, other key provisions of the Third Directive are:

- the adoption of a 'risk-based approach' to customer due diligence, with simplified due diligence for 'lower risk' customers and enhanced due diligence for 'higher risk' customers;
- a requirement for ongoing due diligence 'to ensure that the transactions being conducted are consistent with the ... business and risk profile, including ... the source of funds ...';
- a prohibition on anonymous accounts and those in fictitious names;
- the addition of life insurance and investment intermediaries as gatekeepers bound by AML/CTF legislation.

Forthcoming EU measures

Other measures will include a Regulation on Wire Transfers, which will implement the FATF Special Recommendation VII. The Regulation will detail the information to be obtained by the money transfer service from anyone wiring funds, and will stipulate that the information must be sent with the wire transfer and must be received by the recipient service.

Also in the pipeline is a Code of Conduct aimed at preventing the misuse of charities by terrorists. (See Chapter 6 for a more detailed summary of current perceived CTF best practice for charities and other NPOs.)

OTHER ORGANIZATIONS

Basel Committee on Banking Supervision

The Basel Committee was established at the end of 1974, and comprises central bank (or banking supervision authority) representatives from 13 countries including the US, the UK, Japan and a number of EU states. The Committee formulates broad supervisory standards and guidelines and recommends statements of best practice in the expectation that individual authorities will take steps to implement them through detailed arrangements – statutory or otherwise – suited to their own national systems. Its main guidance documents including the following:

Customer Due Diligence for Banks, October 2001

In the context of CTF, in October 2001, and coincidentally straight after the 9/11 attacks, the Basel Committee issued guidance for banks and banking supervisors on due diligence processes. The publication *Customer Due Diligence for Banks* sets out minimum standards for banks to follow (see also Chapter 6 on best practice). Further know-your-customer guidance, *Consolidated KYC Risk Management*, was published in October 2004.

Other documents

The Committee has also produced a report on the 'Sharing of financial records between jurisdictions in connection with the fight against terrorist financing' (April 2002) and 'Initiatives by the BCBS, IAIS (International Association of Insurance Supervisors) and IOSCO (International Organization of Securities Commissions) to combat money laundering and the financing of terrorism' (June 2003).

Egmont Group

The Egmont Group was set up to support the growing number of FIUs set up by various countries since 11 September 2001. Its purpose is broadly to provide a forum through which FIUs can improve their national AML and CTF programmes.

LEGISLATION INTRODUCED BY INDIVIDUAL COUNTRIES

As we have seen, countries' CTF legislation is shaped partly by international initiatives, and particularly the need to comply with key Regulations, notably:

- 1999 UN International Convention for the Suppression of the Financing of Terrorism
- UNSCR 1373 on the Suppression of the Financing of Terrorism
- FATF Forty Recommendations on Money Laundering and Nine Special Recommendations on Terrorist Financing.

But individual countries also deal with their international obligations in the light of their own circumstances, and may also take additional steps to clamp down on the movement of terrorist funds. Below, we summarize key legislation enacted against terrorist financing by a selection of countries containing important financial centres. Contained on the CD-ROM which comes with this book are examples of quiz-based training tools which can be used for introducing staff to key requirements.

United Kingdom

Principal legislation:

- Proceeds of Crime Act 2002 (POCA) (as amended)
- Terrorism Act 2000 (as amended by Anti-Terrorism, Crime and Security Act (2001))
- Money Laundering Regulations 2003 (for replacement in December 2007).
- Terrorism Act 2006

Proceeds of Crime Act 2002 (as amended)

- Consolidates and extends existing UK AML laws.
- Replaces money laundering provisions in Drug Trafficking Act 1994 and Criminal Justice Act 1988.
- Creates criminal offence of money laundering in respect of *all* criminal property.
- Includes criminal property derived from overseas crimes if they would have been a crime if committed in the UK.
- No *de minimis* value threshold of property concerned.
- Establishes Assets Recovery Agency, which has power to investigate whether a person holds criminal assets/money, to recover criminal assets/money and to require forfeiture of money that is intended to be used for criminal purposes.
- Creates investigative powers in form of:
  - production order
  - search and seizure warrant
  - disclosure order
  - customer information order
  - account monitoring order.
- Creates criminal offence if a firm fails to comply with requirements under a disclosure order or a customer information order, or knowingly or recklessly makes a statement in purported compliance with such an order that is in fact false or misleading in a material respect. The offence is punishable by up to 6 months' imprisonment and/or a level 5 fine.
- Creates criminal offences of:
  - money laundering;
  - entering into an arrangement or becoming concerned in an arrangement which a person knows or suspects facilitates the acquisition, retention, use or control of criminal property by or on behalf of another person;
  - acquiring/using/having possession of property which a person knows or suspects constitutes or represents the proceeds of crime.

- Offences are punishable by up to 14 years' imprisonment and/or an unlimited fine.

- Defence to these offences includes if person involved discloses the money laundering, either to the authorities or in accordance with an approved internal disclosure procedure, either before the prohibited act is carried out or as soon as is reasonably practical afterwards or if the person had a reasonable excuse for not making the disclosure.

- Creates criminal offence of failing to report if a person knows or suspects or has reasonable grounds for knowing or suspecting that money laundering is taking place, where:

  - the information giving rise to the person's knowledge/suspicion/ reasonable grounds for knowledge or suspicion came to them in the course of conducting a business in the regulated sector;

  - they can identify the person involved in money laundering or the whereabouts of any laundered property or they believe or it reasonable for them to believe that the information they have may assist in identifying the person involved or the whereabouts of laundered money;

  - the disclosure is not made as soon as is practical after the information came to them.

- In determining whether an offence of failing to report has been committed, courts are required to take into account whether industry guidance has been followed.

- Offence of failing to report is punishable by up to five years' imprisonment and/or an unlimited fine.

- A defence to the offence of failing to report exists if the failure is by an employee and they can show that they did not know/suspect that money laundering was taking place *and* their employer has not provided them with AML training.

- Creates criminal offence of 'tipping-off' (disclosing that a report has been or will be filed), punishable by up to five years' imprisonment and/or an unlimited fine.

- Creates criminal offence of prejudicing an investigation by destroying or disposing of documents relevant to that investigation, punishable by up to five years' imprisonment and/or an unlimited fine.

Terrorism Act 2000 (as amended by Anti-Terrorism, Crime and Security Act (2001))

- Introduces measures which include those to cut off terrorist funding. Initial focus was on terrorism in Northern Ireland. Amended following September 11 attacks.

- Establishes list of proscribed organizations with which financial institutions are prohibited from dealing.

- Creates criminal offence of belonging to/professing to belong to a proscribed organization, punishable by up to ten years' imprisonment and/or a fine.

- Creates criminal offence of supporting or inviting support for a proscribed organization, punishable by up to 10 years' imprisonment and/or a fine.
- Creates criminal offences of fund-raising for terrorist purposes, of using money for terrorist purposes, and of funding terrorist activity, punishable by up to 14 years' imprisonment and/or an unlimited fine.
- Creates criminal offence of money laundering in relation to terrorist property: it is an offence if a person enters into an arrangement which facilitates the retention or control of terrorist property *unless* the person did not know and had no reasonable cause to suspect that the arrangement related to terrorist property. Offence is punishable by up to 14 years' imprisonment and/or an unlimited fine.
- Creates criminal offence of failing to report if a person knows or suspects that any property is terrorist property, and:
  - the information giving rise to the person's knowledge/suspicion came to them in the course of their trade/profession/business or employment; and
  - the disclosure is not made as soon as is practical after the information came to them.
- In determining whether an offence of failing to report has been committed, courts are required to take into account whether industry guidance has been followed.
- Offence of failing to report is punishable by up to five years' imprisonment and/or an unlimited fine.
- Creates criminal offence of 'tipping-off' in relation to reports made regarding existence of terrorist property, and of prejudicing an investigation, punishable by up to five years' imprisonment and/or an unlimited fine.
- Gives authorities powers to impose orders on financial institutions to monitor client accounts (similar to the account monitoring order introduced under POCA – see above) and to provide information about clients and client activities.
- Authorizes seizure, freezing and forfeiture of terrorist property.

Terrorism Act 2006

- Does not contain provisions specific to terrorist financing but covers e.g. glorification, preparation, incitement and the publication of materials.

Money Laundering Regulations 2003 (as amended)

- Replaces previous money laundering regulations as issued in 1993 and 2001; introduced to implement Second EC Money Laundering Directive (EC Directive 2001/97).
- Specify arrangements that all firms undertaking 'relevant business' must implement in order to prevent money laundering including requirements for:
  - identification

- record-keeping
- reporting suspicious transactions
- appointment of nominated officer to receive internal reports
- staff awareness and training.

- Introduces requirements for registration of money service operators and high-value dealers (those dealing in goods involving €15 000 or more); includes powers of entry, inspection of premises and records, access to recorded information in respect of such businesses and imposes fines for breach.
- Makes the Financial Services Authority (FSA) the prosecuting authority for money laundering offences by financial services firms. Offence of failure to comply with Regulations punishable by up to two years' imprisonment and/or a fine.
- Individual officers may be held liable for breaches by a firm if any breach was done with their connivance or was due to their negligence.
- In determining whether a breach of the Regulations has occurred, it is irrelevant whether money laundering has in fact taken place: firms may be sanctioned for not having adequate AML/CTF measures in place.

Identification:

- ID requirements apply if:
  - a 'business relationship' is formed (that is, there is an ongoing relationship);
  - a one-off transaction takes place in which the client receives or pays €15 000 or more;
  - two or more linked transactions take place in which the client receives or pays in total €15 000 or more.
- ID requirements do not apply (subject to some exceptions) if:
  - client is another regulated business in UK;
  - client is another regulated business in a country which is covered by the Money Laundering Directives;
  - client is another regulated business outside the European Economic Area (EEA) but which has comparable AML laws to those implemented by the Money Laundering Directive.
- ID requirements do not apply if business relationship is with a person introduced by a regulated body *provided* that the regulated body has given written assurance that appropriate ID checks have been made and client has been identified.
- ID requirements do not apply if proceeds of one-off transaction are payable to the client but are instead reinvested directly on his behalf in a second transaction and the second transaction can only result in either further reinvestment for the client or payment directly to the client.
- ID requirements do not apply to certain long-term insurance schemes.

NB: exceptions to ID requirements do not apply in any situation where a person suspects or knows that the transaction involves money laundering and do not exempt firms from carrying out other due diligence checks.

Record-keeping:

- Records of ID obtained and of details of transactions to be kept for a minimum of five years from completion of either the transaction (if a one-off transaction) or the business relationship.

Bank of England Consolidated List

Background:

- UNSC passed UNSCR 1373 in 2001 calling on all member states to suppress financing of terrorist acts.
- UN published names of individuals/organizations subject to UN financial sanctions in relation to Osama bin Laden, al-Qaeda and the Taliban.
- Required all member states to freeze funds and economic resources of any person on list of published names and to report suspected name matches to relevant authorities.
- EU directly implemented UNSCR 1373 through EC 2580/2001 (as amended), imposing an obligation on EU member states to freeze assets of those listed and a prohibition on making economic resources available to those listed, whether directly or indirectly.

Content:

- Bank of England Consolidated List includes all individuals/organizations subject to financial sanctions in UK and targets identified by UN/EU.
- Sanctions usually include a prohibition on making funds available to the target/agent and implementing an asset freeze.
- Bank of England Consolidated List also includes names of individuals/organizations identified by UN as being connected with the political leadership of specified countries and to whom there is a prohibition on making funds available.
- Criminal offence to make payments/allow payments to be made to and/or provide financial services to any listed target or their agent. This includes dealing with targets directly or indirectly through intermediaries.
- Duty to report to Bank or England with details of any funds frozen or where a person knows/suspects that a client or a person with whom the firm has had dealings is a listed person or is acting on behalf of a listed person.
- Bank of England acts on behalf of UK Treasury by issuing sanctions notices whenever new name added to List or List details are amended.
- Consolidated List found at www.bankofengland.co.uk/publications/financialsanctions/index.htm.

NB: in addition to the Consolidated List, the UK Treasury may direct that financial services firms may not deal with individuals or organizations based in countries to which the FATF has decided to apply countermeasures.

Reporting requirements under UK law

To whom?

Serious Organized Crime Agency (SOCA):

- Took over responsibility in April 2006 from the National Crime Intelligence Service (NCIS) as the UK's FIU.
- SOCA receives and analyses reports about suspicious financial activity (suspicious activity reports (SARs)).

When?

- When a person knows/suspects that money laundering is taking place. (An objective, not subsective, test).

How?

- Employees report to the MLRO within their financial institution, who then has an obligation to consider the report and, if appropriate, make an external disclosure to SOCA.
- Reporting is by filing an SAR by post, by fax or email with SOCA:
  - Pro forma SARs are available from the SOCA website www.soca.gov.uk
  - SOCA operates an online reporting service, which users are required to register for.
  - Reports filed by fax should be sent to:

    020 7238 8286
  - Reports filed by post should be sent to:

    UK FIU
PO Box 8000
London SE11 5EN

What to report?

- Details of person/organization filing the report.
- Particulars of person/organization being reported, including:
  - name
  - address
  - date of birth
  - ID information

- if a company, its registration number/country of registration and type of business.

- Details of suspicious transaction.
- Reason why transaction is suspicious.
- Detailed guidance on completion of the SAR form is available from the SOCA website.

NB: once a report has been made, consent must be sought from SOCA to continue with the transaction/activity concerned.

Confidentiality issues:

SARs kept confidential:

- Subject of SAR not notified that SAR has been filed.
- Filing a SAR following appropriate procedures does not breach client confidentiality, as requirement to file SAR is overriding issue.
- Clients should not be informed by organization that SAR has been filed: tipping-off or revealing information that might prejudice an investigation is a criminal offence, punishable by up to five years' imprisonment and/or an unlimited fine.

Consequences of failure to report:

- POCA, TA and ML Regulations create a statutory duty to report.
- Criminal offence if failure to report, punishable by maximum of five years' imprisonment and/or an unlimited fine.

United States

Principal legislation:

- 1970 Bank Secrecy Act
- 1977 International Emergency Economic Powers Act
- 1986 Money Laundering Control Act
- 1988 Money Laundering Prosecution Improvement Act
- 1992 Annunzio-Wylie Anti Money Laundering Act
- 1994 Money Laundering Suppression Act
- 1998 Money Laundering and Financial Crimes Strategy Act
- 2001 Uniting and Strengthening America by Providing Appropriate Tools to Restrict, Intercept and Obstruct Terrorism Act (USA PATRIOT Act)
- 2002 Suppression of the Financing of Terrorism Convention Implementation Act
- 2004 Intelligence Reform and Prevention of Terrorism Act

- 2005 USA PATRIOT Improvement and Reauthorization Act

US AML and CTF legislation is codified in the United States Code, primarily in Title 31 of the Code (Money and Finance), Subtitle IV (Money), Chapter 53 (Monetary Transactions), Sub-chapters II and III (Records and Reports on Monetary Instruments Transactions and Money Laundering and Related Financial Crimes, respectively). Details of the applicable fines and sentences are set out either in Title 31 or Title 18 of the Code.

1970 Bank Secrecy Act (BSA)

- Established requirements for record-keeping and reporting by private individuals, banks and other financial institutions, enabling law enforcement and regulatory agencies to pursue investigations of criminal, tax, and regulatory violations, and to prosecute money laundering and other financial crimes.
- Designed to help identify the source, volume, and movement of currency and other monetary instruments transported or transmitted into or out of the US or deposited in financial institutions.
- Required:
  - reporting of cash transactions over $10000 via currency transaction reports (CTRs);
  - reporting of transportation to/from the US of currency or other monetary instruments of amounts in excess of $10000 via Reports of International Transportation of Currency or Monetary Instruments (CMIRs).

1977 International Emergency Economic Powers Act

- Enables the US President to declare a state of national emergency to deal with any 'unusual and extraordinary threat', having its source outside the US, and which threatens the national security, foreign policy or economy of the US. The President's powers include the power to investigate, regulate or prohibit financial transactions with, and to block the assets of, organizations or individuals associated with such a threat.

1986 Money Laundering Control Act (MLCA)

- Introduced to strengthen existing AML legislation, particularly the reporting requirements.
- Criminalized the act of money laundering, and of transporting laundered funds across US borders. Offence punishable by a fine of the greater of $500000 or twice the value of the property involved and/or imprisonment of up to 20 years.
- Criminalized the knowing acceptance of tainted funds of a value greater than $10000 even where there is no intent to promote money laundering activities. Offence punishable by a fine in accordance with Title 18 of US Code (or up to double the value of the transaction) and/or imprisonment for up to ten years.

- Criminalized 'structuring' (the unbundling of financial transactions into amounts of less than $10 000 to evade CTR filings). Offence punishable by up to five years' imprisonment and/or a fine in accordance with Title 18 of US Code. Enhanced penalties apply for aggravated cases, where a pattern of structuring is established involving more than $100 000 over a 12-month period. Enhanced penalties are up to ten years' imprisonment and/or a fine of up to double the amount of illegal funds involved.

- Introduced civil and criminal forfeiture laws on money launderers and financial institutions against property involved in or produced from breaches of the AML provisions, anti-structuring provisions or of the CTR filing requirements.

- Provided for forfeiture of any property located in the US which represents the proceeds of illegal drug activities.

- Required banks to establish and maintain procedures reasonably designed to ensure and monitor compliance with the reporting and record-keeping requirements of the BSA.

1988 Money Laundering Prosecution Improvement Act

- Introduced requirements for verifying identity of customers and record-keeping requirements on financial institutions selling bank cheques, cashiers' cheques, travellers' cheques, or money orders in amounts of $3 000 or more.

- Introduced geographical targeting orders. Purpose is to target specific financial institutions or groups of financial institutions in a certain locality and require them to maintain additional records and submit additional reports if reasonable grounds exist for concluding that additional record-keeping and/or reporting requirements are necessary to carry out the purposes of money laundering laws and regulations and to prevent evasions of reporting/record-keeping requirements.

- Strict confidentiality provisions (introduced in 1992 by the Annunzio-Wylie Anti Money Laundering Act – see below) prevent financial institutions from disclosing the terms or existence of a targeting order.

1992 Annunzio-Wylie Anti-Money Laundering Act

- Introduced further amendments to the BSA: (i) a significant increase in penalties for breaches of AML laws; (ii) a broadening of the scope of the BSA; and (iii) regulatory responsibility under the BSA given to financial institutions.

So, the 1992 Act:

- Created 'death penalty' provisions for breaches of the MLCA money laundering provisions and for wilful violations of the BSA. Under the death penalty provisions, the Office of the Comptroller of the Currency (OCC) may, and in some cases is required to, institute termination proceedings.

- Made it possible for individual bank officials to be banned from the industry if they are convicted of money laundering.

- Increased civil liability for breaches of the BSA to incorporate a civil offence of 'negligence'. A financial institution may be fined up to $500 for negligent breaches of the BSA. If a pattern of negligent activity is established, the financial institution may be fined up to $50 000.

- Broadened the definition of 'financial transaction' and included additional domestic and foreign crimes within the scope of existing AML provisions.
- Expanded the breadth of the MLCA's anti-structuring provisions.
- Criminalized the operation of an illegal money transmitting business, establishing a maximum penalty of five years' imprisonment and/or a $250 000 fine.
- Required regulations to govern the verification and record-keeping of wire transfers.
- Broadened the accessibility of the BSA reports filed by financial institutions, allowing the Treasury to make information included in BSA reports available to state financial supervisory agencies.
- Required financial institutions to file SARs.
- Required financial institutions to develop internal AML programmes. At a minimum, these programmes must:
  - facilitate the development of internal policies, procedures, and controls;
  - designate a compliance officer;
  - institute an ongoing employee training programme; and
  - incorporate an independent audit function to test programmes.

(An extension of these internal programs are the know-your-customer (KYC) requirements.)

1994 Money Laundering Suppression Act

- Required banking agencies to develop AML examination procedures.
- Revised the CTR reporting process to grant specified exemptions from reporting to help eliminate superfluous reporting on transactions that were not likely vehicles for money laundering activities. The exemptions in the MLSA do not apply to the filing of SARs: suspicious transactions must be reported regardless of the entity involved.
- Amended the BSA to require all money transmitting businesses to register with the US Treasury. Failure to register is punishable by a civil fine of $5 000 for each failure, with every day that a business does not file being considered a separate failure.
- Increased the penalties for 'structuring' (see above).
- Authorized the Treasury Department to designate a single agency to receive reports about suspicious transactions (as a result the Financial Crimes Enforcement Network (FinCEN) was established – see below).

1998 Money Laundering and Financial Crimes Strategy Act

- Required banking agencies to develop AML training for examiners.
- Required Treasury and other agencies to develop a National Money Laundering Strategy.
- Created the concept of High Intensity Money Laundering and Related Financial Crime Areas (HIFCA).

2001 Uniting and Strengthening America by Providing Appropriate Tools to Restrict, Intercept and Obstruct Terrorism Act (USA PATRIOT Act)

- Title III of the USA PATRIOT Act, the International Money Laundering Abatement and Anti-Terrorist Financing Act of 2001, is the relevant part of the Act. It is an Act of Congress in its own right.
- Further legislation was required to deal with CTF because terrorist financing might be derived from *legal* activities/sources, whilst existing AML legislation focused on the proceeds of *illegal* activities.

The USA PATRIOT Act and its implementing regulations:

- Makes FinCEN a statutory bureau in the Treasury Department.
- Expands the AML programme requirements to all financial institutions.
- Introduces a 'long arm' provision giving the US jurisdiction over foreign money launderers and over foreign financial institutions which have bank accounts in the US.
- Enables government–institution information sharing and voluntary information sharing among financial institutions. Where such sharing of information takes place it will not breach client confidentiality rules.
- Facilitates bank records access and requires financial institutions in banking sector to respond to regulatory requests for information within 120 hours.
- Requires verification of customer identity programmes to be established.
- Requires enhanced due diligence programmes for correspondent accounts and private banking accounts.
- Prohibits US financial institutions from having correspondent accounts with foreign shell banks (that is, a bank that does not have a physical presence in any country).
- Provides the US Treasury with the authority to impose 'special measures' on foreign jurisdictions, foreign financial institutions, or transactions involving such jurisdictions or institutions or on accounts that are of 'primary money laundering concern.' The special measures include additional record-keeping, reporting and identification requirements, and restrictions on dealings with such jurisdictions or institutions in connection with correspondent and payable-through accounts. Special measures may remain in force for 120 days.

- Increases the maximum civil and criminal fines to $1 m, for failures to comply with (a) due diligence requirements in relation to correspondent and private banking accounts, (b) the prohibition on correspondent accounts with foreign shell banks, or (c) with special measures requirements. Sets a minimum civil and criminal fine for breaches of those provisions of double the amount of the illegal transaction.

- Establishes civil penalties for violations of geographic targeting orders and structuring transactions to evade certain record-keeping requirements.

- Lengthens the effective period of geographic targeting orders from 60 to 180 days.

- Requires federal banking agencies to consider a bank's AML record when reviewing bank mergers and acquisitions.

- Includes foreign corruption offences within the scope of money laundering offences.

- Requires any person who receives more than $10000 in coins or currency, in one transaction or two or more related transactions, in the course of that person's non-financial trade or business to report the transaction(s) to FinCEN.

- Creates an offence of bulk smuggling, for the knowing concealment and attempted transport or transfer of more than $10000 into or out of the US, with intent to evade currency reporting requirements.

- Criminalizes 'providing material support or resources to terrorist organizations' within the prohibition against money laundering.

2002 Suppression of the Financing of Terrorism Convention Implementation Act

- Criminalizes the collection or provision of funds to support terrorist activities, or the attempted concealment of such fund-raising activity, regardless of whether the crime was committed in the US or by a US citizen.

2004 Intelligence Reform and Prevention of Terrorism Act

- Authorizes and provides funding for the development of FinCEN's internet reporting system, BSA Direct E-filing (previously known as Patriot Act Communications System – PACS), as required by the USA PATRIOT Act 2001, providing quick and easy filing of SARs and access to SARs information by law enforcement agencies.

2005 USA PATRIOT Improvement and Reauthorization Act

Title IV of the USA PATRIOT Improvement and Reauthorization Act, the Combating Terrorism Financing Act 2005, is the relevant part of the Act. It provides for:

- illegal money transmissions to be added to the list of money laundering and RICO (Racketeer Influenced and Corrupt Organizations) predicate offences which may result in confiscation of property. Illegal money transmissions are transmissions of funds directly or indirectly overseas without a licence;

transmissions by licensed businesses which fail to comply with Treasury Department Regulations; transmissions by licensed businesses in the knowledge that the funds will be used for or were generated by criminal activities.

- confiscation of property, whether based in the US or overseas, of any individual or entity planning or committing an act of international terrorism against a foreign nation of international organization. There is no requirement to show that the property concerned was used or is intended to be used for terrorist purposes: only proof of ownership by the individual/entity concerned is required.

- Closure of a loophole in order to prevent money laundering through informal money transfer networks (*hawala* schemes). The prohibition against financial transaction involving the proceeds of crime has therefore been extended to include related or parallel transactions 'any one of which involves the proceeds of specified unlawful activity and all of which are part of a single plan or arrangement'.

Reporting requirements under US law

To whom?

The Financial Crimes Enforcement Network (FinCEN):

- FinCEN is a bureau of the US Treasury and is the delegated administrator of the BSA. SARs must be filed with FinCEN.

- Established in 1990 to support federal, state, local and international law enforcement by analysing the information required under the BSA.

- FinCEN is the Financial Intelligence Unit of the US.

- FinCEN issues regulations and interpretive guidance, provides outreach to regulated industries, supports the examination functions performed by federal banking agencies, and pursues civil enforcement actions when warranted.

- FinCEN's other responsibilities include providing investigative case support to law enforcement agencies, identifying and communicating financial crime trends and patterns, and fostering international cooperation with its counterparts worldwide.

When?

- If a financial institution 'knows, suspects, or has reason to suspect' that it: involves, or is an attempt to disguise, proceeds from illegal activity; is designed to evade the requirements of the BSA; or appears to have no business or apparent lawful purpose; or involves using the reporting organization to facilitate criminal activity.

- The SAR must generally be filed within 30 days of the initial detection of the facts that gave rise to the need to file a SAR (an additional 30 days is permitted where the suspect is not identifiable at the time of the initial detection).

- In addition to filing a SAR, financial institutions should telephone the appropriate law enforcement officials without delay if the breach requires immediate attention, because, for example it relates to terrorist financing or ongoing money laundering schemes. FinCEN has established a 24-hour hotline for immediate reporting. (Hotline Number 1-800-566-3974). Written SAR must still be filed.

How?

- The SAR must be filed with FinCEN.
- FinCEN has pro forma forms for different financial institutions, available from its website:
  - depository institutions
  - securities and futures firms
  - casinos and card clubs
  - money services businesses.
- No supporting documentation needs to be sent with the SAR, although the financial institution is required to keep such documents as well as a copy of the SAR on file for a period of five years.
- New requirements (2007 onwards) on electronic filing or through magnetic media. Check details at www.fincen.gov

What to report?

- The SAR should include information on:
  - the reporting financial institution
  - the suspicious activity and relevant parties
  - witnesses to the event
  - the person who prepared the SAR.

Confidentiality issues:

- Financial institutions are prohibited from notifying customers that they have filed a SAR.
- Financial institutions, their directors, officers, employees and agents filing SARs benefit from a protection against liability for breach of confidentiality.
- Whistleblower protection is available for employees that have notified the authorities about breaches of the BSA, entitling a dismissed employee, acting in good faith, to reinstatement and compensatory damages.

Consequences of reporting failures (civil penalties):

- Wilful violation of reporting requirements: minimum fine of $25 000; maximum fine of $100 000 or value of relevant transaction.
- Seizure and forfeiture of property concerned.

Consequences of reporting failures (criminal penalties):

- Wilful violation of reporting requirements: fine of up to $250 000 and/or up to five years' imprisonment.
- Wilful violation of reporting requirements as part of pattern of illegal activity involving more than $100 000 over a 12-month period: fine of up to $500 000 and/or up to ten years' imprisonment.
- Knowingly making a false, fictitious or fraudulent statement or representation in a report: fine of up to $10 000 and/or five years' imprisonment.

Hong Kong

Principal legislation:

- Drug Trafficking (Recovery of Proceeds) Ordinance 1989 (DTROP)
- Organized and Serious Crimes Ordinance 1995 (OSCO)
- Organized and Serious Crimes (Amendment) Ordinance 2000
- United Nations (Anti-Terrorism Measures) Ordinance 2002 (UNATMO)
- United Nations (Anti-Terrorism Measures) (Amendment) Ordinance 2004 (UNATMO)

Drug Trafficking (Recovery of Proceeds) Ordinance 1989 (DTROP)

- Creates criminal offence of money laundering: offence if deal with property, including money, knowing or having reasonable grounds to believe that the property was the proceeds of drug trafficking. Offence is punishable by up to 14 years' imprisonment and a fine of up to HK$5 000 000.
- Introduces requirement to report if a person knows or suspects that any property represents the proceeds of drug trafficking, was used in connection with drug trafficking or is intended to be used in connection with drug trafficking.
- Creates criminal offence of failing to report, punishable by up to 3 months' imprisonment and a fine of up to HK$50 000.
- Creates criminal offence of 'tipping-off', punishable by up to three years' imprisonment and a fine of up to HK$500 000.
- Allows tracing and freezing of assets derived from drug trafficking and confiscation of proceeds of drug trafficking.

Organized and Serious Crimes Ordinance 1995 (OSCO)

- Creates criminal offence of money laundering in relation to the proceeds of indictable offences: it is an offence if a person deals with property, including money, knowing or having reasonable grounds to believe that the property was the proceeds of serious crime. Offence is punishable by up to 14 years' imprisonment and a fine of up to HK$5 000 000.

- Introduces requirement to report if a person knows or suspects that any property represents the proceeds of serious crime, was used in connection with serious crime or is intended to be used in connection with serious crime.
- Creates criminal offence of failing to report, punishable by up to three months' imprisonment and a fine of up to HK$50 000.
- Creates criminal offence of 'tipping-off', punishable by up to three years' imprisonment and a fine of up to HK$500 000.
- Allows confiscation of proceeds of serious crime, and the issuing of restraint or charging orders on the property of a person accused of money laundering.
- Broad definition of 'organized crime' to include crimes listed in OSCO, as committed by a triad society or by two or more persons where the crime requires substantial organization and planning. Offences include murder, manslaughter, kidnapping, drug trafficking, rape, assault, theft, robbery, obtaining money by deception, false accounting, bribery, smuggling and firearms offences.

Organized and Serious Crimes (Amendment) Ordinance 2000

- Requires remittance agents and money changers to verify the name and identity of customers and to keep records of transactions where the transaction is of HK$8 000 or more.

United Nations (Anti-Terrorism Measures) Ordinance 2002, as amended (UNATMO)

- Implements UNSC Resolution 1373 (dated 28 September 2001, which calls on all member states to prevent the financing of terrorism, criminalize the wilful provision or collection of funds to carry out terrorist acts, and freeze terrorist assets) and FATF's Special Recommendations.
- Prohibits the collection or provision of funds or the making of funds or financial services available to terrorists or terrorist associates.
- Creates a statutory duty to report any knowledge/suspicion that property is terrorist property.
- Creates offence of failing to report, punishable by up to three months' imprisonment and a fine of up to HK$50 000.
- Gives power to freeze and forfeit assets of terrorists and terror groups.

Reporting requirements under Hong Kong law

To whom?

The law applies to 'all persons' and reports are to be made to 'an authorized officer'. In practice, for financial institutions this means the Joint Financial Intelligence Unit (JFIU):

- Set up in 1989 to receive reports made under DTROP about suspicious financial activity.

- Run jointly by HK Police Force and HK Customs and Excise Department.
- JFIU does not investigate suspicious transactions; instead, following appropriate analysis, JFIU passes on STRs to appropriate local and overseas law enforcement agencies, e.g:
  - Narcotics Bureau
  - Organized Crime and Triad Bureau of HK Police
  - Customs' Drug Investigation Bureau of HK Customs and Excise Department
  - Agencies of other countries.

When?

- When a person knows/suspects that any property:
  - represents the proceeds of drug trafficking or a serious crime;
  - was used in connection with drug trafficking or a serious crime;
  - is intended to be used in connection with drug trafficking or a serious crime.
- JFIU recommends the SAFE approach to assist financial institutions in deciding whether a suspicious transaction report (STR) is necessary:
  - *Screen* the account for suspicious indicators:
    - JFIU has issued guidance on what are suspicious indicators.
  - *Ask* the customer appropriate questions:
    - If a transaction bears one or more suspicious indicators staff should question the customer to identify:
      - the reason for the transaction;
      - the identity of the source of the money being transacted;
      - the identity of the ultimate beneficiary of the money being transacted;
      - whether the explanation is reasonable and legitimate; if not or if a customer refuses or is unwilling to answer, an STR should be filed.
  - *Find* out the customer's records, by reviewing information already held about the customer from previous transactions – the KYC principle.
  - *Evaluate* all the information.

How?

- Reporting must be to an authorized officer (that is, a HK police officer or member of the HK Customs and Excise Department, or the JFIU). Employees may report to the compliance officer within their financial institution.

- Reporting is by filing an STR, by post, fax, telephone or email with JFIU, or by 'STREAMS', JFIU's new electronic reporting system.
- Pro forma STRs, designed by the relevant regulatory bodies, are available from JFIU website:
  - HK Monetary Authority (for banks)
  - Office of the Commissioner of Insurance (for insurance companies)
  - Securities and Futures Commission of HK (for stockbrokers)
  - HK Police Force (for all other reports).

What to report?

- Personal particulars of person/organization concerned, including:
  - name
  - identity card number/passport number
  - date of birth
  - address
  - telephone number
  - bank account number.
- Details of suspicious activity.
- Reason why transaction is suspicious.
- Details of the explanation, if any, given by the person of organization concerned for the transaction.

Confidentiality issues:

STRs kept confidential:

- Not used as evidence.
- Fact that STR been filed not usually revealed in court proceedings.
- Subject of STR not notified that STR has been filed.
- Filing an STR does not breach client confidentiality, as requirement to file STR is overriding issue.
- *But*, clients should not be informed by organization that STR has been filed: it is a criminal offence, punishable by up to three years' imprisonment and a fine of up to HK$500000 to reveal to any person information that might prejudice an investigation.

Consequences of failure to report:

- S25(A)(1) DTROP and OSCO, and S12 UNATMO creates a statutory duty to report.

- Criminal offence if fail to report, punishable by maximum of three months' imprisonment and a fine of up to HK$50000.

Guidance:

Detailed guidance on compliance with the reporting requirements of DTROP, OSCO and UNATMO has been issued by the Securities and Futures Commission of HK, the Office of the Commissioner of Insurance and the HK Monetary Authority.

REFERENCES

United Nations	www.un.org
Financial Action Task Force	www.fatf-gafi.org
Asia Pacific Group on Money Laundering	www.apgml.org
Caribbean Financial Action Task Force	www.cfatf.org
Eastern and South African Anti Money Laundering Group	www.esaamlg.org
Council of Europe	www.coe.int
IMF	www.imf.org
European Union	www.europa.eu.int
Wolfsberg Group	www.wolfsberg-principles.com
Egmont Group	www.egmontgroup.org
Basel Committee	www.bis.org/bcbs

CHAPTER 5

What is 'Suspicious'?

BACKGROUND

Front end vs back end in money laundering and terrorist financing

As we have seen already, there are key differences between the laundering of the proceeds of organized crime and the movement of money used to fund terrorist activities and these are shown at Figures 5.1 and 5.2. Criminal gangs seek to process their ill-gotten gains simply in order to become richer. So, viewed graphically on a page, left to right, the crime occurs at the back end of the laundering chain (that is, it is the first event which occurs – Figure 5.1).

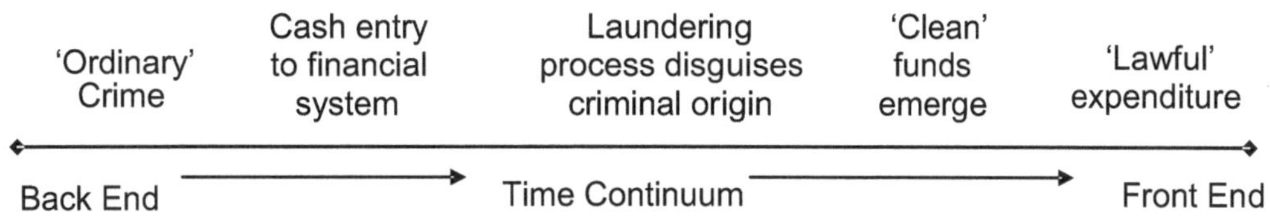

Figure 5.1 Laundering the proceeds of organized crime

In contrast, wealth is not the primary goal of active terrorist groups. Their actions are driven by an ideological, political or a religious motive, and the funds they raise, store, move and spend are a means to these ends. Consequently, the funds flowing into their coffers may well come from legitimate sources such as charitable donations or business profits and the crime will occur at the right hand, front end of the laundering chain (that is, it is the last event to occur – Figure 5.2).

Moreover, while the transactions involved in the laundering of criminal proceeds or in the initial collection and transfer of terrorist funds *may* attract

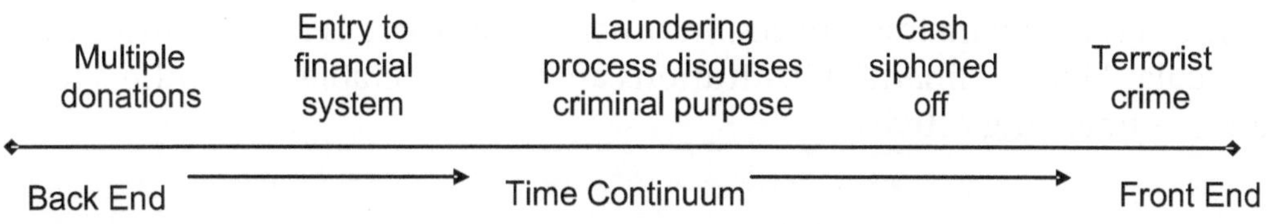

Figure 5.2 Movement of money to fund terrorist activities

attention because they are unusually large or are otherwise anomalous in some way, it becomes much harder to detect the movement of terrorist money in the system as it heads towards the front of the chain.

Reduced detectability

This reduced detectability in what we have called Type 2 terrorist financing is a particular problem. Those sums spent by active terrorist cells on the preparations for a conventional terrorist attack are typically so small as to be mere droplets in the ocean of daily financial transactions, and are often used to make entirely legitimate purchases – food, car hire, flights, accommodation. Looking for terrorist transactions immediately before the event, becomes an exercise with, one might think, little or no prospect of success. (1)

Nonetheless, financial institutions need to be aware of characteristics of individual transactions or customer arrangements which could, potentially, indicate some kind of link with terrorist financing, so that questions can be asked and, if deemed appropriate, reports filed and action taken. Moreover, just because the most high-profile attacks on Western targets – 9/11, Bali, Madrid and London – cost relatively little to finance, it certainly does not follow that *all* terrorist financing will necessarily follow a similar pattern. There is an enduring danger of 'fighting the last war' all the time, focusing on what has already been put into practice and ignoring the other possibilities open to terrorist activists in future financial dealings. The obvious example to pick would be the financing of a nuclear attack on a large city. We know that such an attack would not come cheaply for the organization which planned and executed it. Probably the cost in know-how and materials would come to many millions – a lot more, at least, than flight lessons, van rental and garden fertiliser. What must not happen is that while everyone is focused on name checking and the impossibility of detecting 'suspicious' $500 ATM withdrawals, some multi-million dollar nuclear-related financing scheme passes through the system undetected.

International vs local

There is an argument that large international banks and the domestic branches of foreign financial institutions may be more at risk of terrorist funding passing through their systems, because they have a wide international network and are oriented to the requirements of an international customer base. (2) That could suit those terrorist groups operating in the international arena or drawing financial support from around the world, but it is important to remember also that other terror organizations may have a much more local focus and therefore (to the extent that they use the formal banking system at all) relatively little need of international banking services. In other words, there is no guarantee that particular kinds of financial institutions are less vulnerable than others to terrorist financing activity.

Contribution of the Financial Action Task Force

The FATF has been producing annual reports on trends and new methods being used by criminals in the evolving science of AML since its inception, and these have been published since 1995. But it was only in 2000/01 that FATF experts turned their attention to the means by which *terrorists* in particular conceal or move funds, and the extent to which these may differ from those of other criminal gangs. Since then, the FATF has expanded its perspective and remit to incorporate terrorist funding into its annual exercise in identifying global trends and indicators in money laundering.

Generally, FATF experts have concluded that not only is there much overlap in the sources of funding used by the two types of group (which may include activities such as drug trafficking, extortion, robbery and smuggling), but also that the laundering (disguise) processes used by them can be very similar. For example:

> *The money laundering method of the regional liberation movement is identical to that of traditional criminal groups: first, the money is deposited into various banks of the region, where the issue of certificates of deposit takes place. Then, these certificates are deposited through intermediary companies in numbered accounts in banks at offshore tax havens, which may only be accessed by code. In the third phase, some of this money is transferred to several European banks from which cheques of payment orders are issued from differing current accounts. Finally, the money is transferred to accounts without arousing suspicion in the territory where the liberation movement is active. (3)*

Treatment of suspicion indicators in this chapter

Given this backdrop, until somebody invents a method of predicting accurately that small sums are about to be used for terrorist purposes, it is clear that the efforts of financial institutions to identify terrorist funds will stay concentrated to a large extent on identifying the numerous and varied ways in which customers' particular usage of the financial system may indicate that they are trying to:

- hide assets with illegal origins;
- accumulate assets for illegal purposes;
- disguise the true ownership of assets;
- disguise their financial associations with proscribed terrorist groups and their sympathisers;
- facilitate the use of assets by terrorists, for terrorist acts.

We therefore summarize in the remainder of this chapter the key groupings of these usage types, together with some mini case studies, some of which are developed into more substantive training exercises in Part Two and the accompanying CD-ROM. Even though many of them will be familiar to MLROs in an AML context, we have tried to present the summaries in a way which emphasizes their relevance to CTF (as we have said, we believe that training on countering terrorist financing should take place in the context of a discussion about terrorist financing). The summaries and case studies are based primarily on FATF typology reports, but we have also drawn them from other relevant national (in the case of the United States) and international bodies. We have taken some licence with these. We have sought to make them more accessible by in some cases assigning real locations to them, converting them to the present tense and giving names to the parties. These alterations are arbitrary though, also we think, realistic. Not being privy to the information on which country or countries the typologies related to (this information is never revealed by the FATF in its typology reports), in particular our re-workings of these case studies should not be taken as guesses about which countries were actually involved, nor as allegations that those particular activities have actually occurred in the countries mentioned.

GENERAL BANKING EXAMPLES (4)

Customers providing insufficient information or information which is inconsistent with their conduct of business

Warning bells might ring, for example, in the case of a customer:

- presenting *unusual identification documents* that cannot readily be identified;
- having an *unexpected background* given their business activities;
- having *no employment record* but making frequent or large transactions;
- setting up a new business account, being *reluctant to provide the information required* about the location of the business or the names of its directors, the nature and purpose of the business, or the expected level of activity on the account.

Why? Because it need not be expected that all would-be terrorists, terrorist financiers or terrorist sympathisers would operate the kind of smooth entry into their relationship with an organization that would be affected by a slick money laundering operation. Such elementary errors could be made, either at the start of the relationship or could become apparent later on when perhaps an emergency required the use of the customer's relationship with the organization for a purpose not originally envisaged – for example, the death or incapacity of a usual, trusted *Hawala* dealer, leading to a calculated risk to undertake a larger-than-usual payment on a bank account.

Customers attempting to avoid reporting or record-keeping requirements

This might involve a customer:

- trying to persuade a bank employee *not to bother filing reports* or update records as required;

- *asking to be exempted* from reporting or record-keeping requirements;
- being *reluctant to provide information* needed in order to file a report;
- trying to *back out of a transaction* after learning that it involves a mandatory report; or making a series of *bank deposits below a specified threshold*, through an automated teller machine (ATM).

Again, one might ask, what terrorist financier would undertake such obviously suspicion-generating activities? But if money launderers depositing criminal cash will target the shift patterns of bank tellers known to be slack with, or ignorant of the institution's rules and policies, then it is equally possible that terrorist facilitators could do the same, or even target staff whom they believe may be sympathetic to their cause.

CASE STUDY (5)

Simple transactions may be suspect

Simple operations (retail foreign exchange operations and international transfers of funds) revealing links with other countries may give rise to suspicions, when other factors are present.

For example, a customer in the United States is the holder of a current account and a savings account with a bank; he has also purchased securities and a single premium life insurance contract from the same institution. He makes several transfers from his current account to recipients in various countries. A name similar to his appears on the consolidated list of persons and/or entities included in the UN Security Council Committee on Afghanistan (S/RES/1333(2000)) and Regulation 1354/2001 of the European Commission.

In addition the customer has been progressively withdrawing his funds. He has successively cleared out his savings account, sold the securities he had purchased (before their maturity date), surrendered his life insurance policy (again, before maturity) and finally transferred his remaining funds to the European country where he normally resides. The last operation he performs occurs two weeks before a major terrorist incident and the bank has no further contact with him.

Funds transfer activities

Look for:

- *money transfers* to or from high-risk regions or financial secrecy havens, where the purpose of the transfer is unclear;
- *a series of small deposits* in the form of electronic fund transfers or cheques and money orders, followed immediately by a wire transfer to another city or country, again, where the purpose is unclear;
- *large incoming wire transfers* on behalf of a foreign client, without obvious explanation;
- any explained, unusual or repetitive *wire activity*;
- payments and receipts apparently *unrelated to legitimate goods or services*.

The keys here are 'unexplained' and 'purpose unclear'; whenever there is some connection in the relationship with a country which has been assessed by the financial institution as being high-risk as regards terrorism or terrorist financing. The connection in question could be the nationality of the recipient/beneficiary, the location of one of the accounts and, in the case of a correspondence bank, knowledge, acquired through due diligence, that it has relationship connections with such countries.

Activity inconsistent with the customer's business

This could take the form of:

- a sudden *change in transaction patterns* in a business, that cannot be explained through normal activities or cycles;
- a large volume of cheques, money orders or wired funds being deposited into an account for a business account, where the *level of activity seems excessive* given the nature of the business;
- a retail business with very *different patterns of financial activity* from those of its local competitors;
- any unusual transfer of money between related accounts or accounts belonging to *the same or related individuals.*

These indicators might reveal themselves, for example, when a local business was being used by terrorists as a front company for receiving funds or donations before sending them on to another collection account. We looked in Chapter 3 at the money laundering activities of the LTTE (Tamil Tigers) and their use of front companies and other legitimate businesses to disguise criminal origin and purpose. The features described above could, for example, indicate that such a business had either volunteered or been forced to act as a conduit for terrorist funds.

Other suspicious customer activity

Additional features for staff to be aware of would include:

- frequent exchanges of *large currency for small currency* denominations;
- a series of currency deposits that are wrapped in rubber bands or currency straps but are presented in a *disorganized fashion* and do not balance when they are counted;
- a single customer buying a series of travellers' cheques or money orders worth *just below a specified threshold;*
- money orders deposited by mail and featuring *sequential numbers or unusual symbols* or stamps.

These may all be indicative of low-level, informal, organized, but fundamentally non-commercial (in the sense of legitimate commerce) cash collation practices – practices which are often associated with crime, but also, potentially with terrorism. For example, the use of numbering and/ or symbols on money orders and cash bundles is known to be a potential signal of organized protection racketeering or loan sharking: the numbers or symbols constitute a coding system by which the collection agent records who paid what. But as we saw in Chapter 3, terrorist groups also raise funds through these activities and through the extortion of 'donations' from unwilling agents, and so the methodology is equally as applicable.

Changes in bank-to-bank transactions

For example, a bank might notice:

- a rapid increase in the size and frequency of *cash deposits* from another bank, without a corresponding increase in non-cash deposits;
- a *high turnover of high denomination bills*, out of keeping with the bank's location;
- marked changes in the *patterns of currency* moving between correspondent banks;
- the bank being unable to trace the true account holder behind *correspondent account transactions*.

This latter point in particular is relevant to terrorist financing, where shell banks (pretending to be real institutions) might be used to disguise, for example, a financial connection with a proscribed organization or person.

Suspicious behaviour from bank employees

In the context of terrorist financing, this might involve, for example, a staff member being reluctant to comply with policy requirements in relation to a particular customer or customers suspected of terrorist involvement – for example resisting the filing of a suspicious transaction report or waiving KYC requirements. If such behaviour can be taken as being potentially indicative, in a money laundering context, of a member of staff being complicit in the activities of a money launderer, then it might also be taken as a potential warning sign that an employee was lending assistance to someone engaged in terrorist financing – whether for personal gain or from personal beliefs.

INSURANCE EXAMPLES

The insurance industry steps into the AML/CTF spotlight

Only relatively few cases of money laundering and terrorist financing via life or general insurance products have been uncovered. The FATF nonetheless sees the insurance sector as potentially vulnerable to the threat, for several reasons: (6)

- Insurance has not historically been associated with dirty money, so staff may not necessarily think in those terms.
- The industry is huge, with a wide and growing diversity of products which are easily available to anyone.

- Particularly in the case of investment-linked life policies, it is relatively commonplace for the policyholder and the beneficiary of the policy not to be the same person.

Brokers and intermediaries

The FATF, reviewing the vulnerabilities of the insurance sector in 2002–2003, pointed out that there is a particular risk attached to the large volume of insurance business carried out through brokers and intermediaries. They noted at that time that brokers had little or no training in AML, and that because they were focused on the sales process they often failed to follow up on potential suspicion indicators such as pre-signed forms or unusual premium payment methods. Brokers also had a lot of freedom in their operations, and in the drive to make a sale they might adopt unusual practices in the interests of flexibility – for example holding pre-signed payment instructions for policy withdrawals so that clients could carry out a withdrawal by phone.

Lower levels of awareness

In addition, some insurance companies themselves were observed to miss money laundering indicators, such as the use of consecutively numbered cheques, or premium payments by unrelated third parties. Not only were insurance companies short on knowledge about the client and the source of their funds but they often had little idea about the 'complex pyramid of sub-brokers employed by their agents'. (7)

In light of the FATF revised Forty Recommendations (which apply to the providers of life insurance and other investment-related insurance businesses), many jurisdictions have already put in place the obligation for insurers to carry out customer due diligence and to file suspicious transaction reports. The International Association of Insurance Supervisors (IAIS) has also produced new guidance notes setting out the main AML/CTF principles and procedures for insurance business (including non-investment linked), which covers KYC requirements and staff training programmes among other issues. (8)

AML and CTF in insurance – basic scams

How could money laundering and terrorist financing in insurance work? Typically, one or a series of single premium life policies may be purchased with cash – often through a broker or intermediary without direct answerability to the insurance company. Following the early surrender of the policy for cash (despite the fact that early surrender may attract a financial penalty which makes an economic nonsense of the move) the money may then be layered through a number of transactions over time, and eventually paid back out into the economy as clean funds. Alternatively, a policy may be used as collateral against the purchase of other investments. Another noted method is for a launderer to make overpayments of policy premiums and then ask for the reimbursement to be made to a third party. (9) All these, of course, are transaction types which have the effect if converting asset value into different forms, of creating multiple points of origin and destination for funds, and of switching ownership from one party to another.

Particularly at risk are life insurance products that have a cash surrender value (as opposed to term insurance contracts, which do not), according to the US's FIU, FinCEN. (10)

CASE STUDY

Medical insurance fraud used to fund terrorist groups

Mr Katin of Manchester, England, who secretly performs fund-raising duties for a terrorist group, buys an expensive new 5 Series BMW, using a loan to pay for the purchase. At the same time, he takes out medical insurance with the Happy Sure Insurance company, that will cover the loan payments in the unfortunate event that an accident or other disability make it impossible to continue repayments. A month or two later, Katin is 'injured' in an 'accident' with the vehicle and an injury severe enough to prevent repayment is reported; it is confirmed by Katin's doctor, who is working in collusion with him, and Katin makes a claim under the medical policy. The insurance company honours the claim and the loan is paid off. Katin subsequently sells the car for cash, and the proceeds are pocketed by the terrorist group for whom he works.

The Happy Sure Insurance Company loses $2 m in a series of connected scams. (11) This case is a classic instance where fraud methodologies and tactics are employed for terrorist purposes instead of self-enrichment.

However, other kinds of insurance policy may also be vulnerable to inflated or bogus claims, such as claims for arson; or they may be used in a similar way to life insurance. For example:

- a policy might be cancelled before expiry and funds returned in the shape of a cheque from the insurer;
- overpayments might be made and then a request made for the excess to be reimbursed, maybe to a third party.

As the International Association of Insurance Supervisors (IAIS) points out, the specific use of property and casualty coverage by terrorist groups could include, for instance, the use of workers' compensation payments paid to terrorists who are awaiting assignment. (12)

Warning signs

In looking at the potential use of the insurance industry for terrorist financing, it is important to remember that it is useful for terrorist organizations to have funds and assets available, and held in a wide variety of legitimate appearing formats, and that does not just mean money sitting in bank accounts. If an insurance product can be cashed in or transferred to a third party and then cashed in, at a time when the terrorist organization in question needs funds, then it will be of use to them.

A number of warning signs have been identified by the IAIS as worthy of further scrutiny. But it is important to remember that the presence of any of these indicators does not necessarily mean that anything untoward is going on, and also that the IAIS's list is not necessarily exhaustive; other money laundering and terrorist financing indicators (including those listed above) may also apply. Staff should look out for any special situations where the purpose of the policy or investment may not be the usual ones of financial protection or asset growth, but rather the maintenance of an easily redeemable asset according to circumstances which are questionable or which in some way or other do not make sense, for example:

- an application for a policy from a client based in another country, when a comparable policy could have been bought in the home country;
- an introduction from an agent or intermediary in an unregulated or lightly regulated jurisdiction, or one associated with criminal or terrorist activities;
- acceptance by the client of very unfavourable policy conditions that are not related to health or age;
- an insurance policy with a premium higher than the client can apparently afford;
- an insurance policy that does not seem appropriate for the client's insurance needs;

CASE STUDY

Terrorist financing through early redemption of policies

Individuals in France, Germany and Spain buy insurance policies from an intermediary in Italy; they provide ID cards as identification but this is not verified by the Italian insurer, as it relies on the intermediary to carry out customer due diligence. The intermediary makes the necessary payments to the Italian insurer and the policies are put in place. However, after only a couple of months, the insurer receives notification from the new clients, to the effect that circumstances have changed and it will be necessary to cash in their policies even though it means suffering a loss. The clients in France, Germany and Spain then receive clean money in the form of refunded cheques from the Italian insurer.

In other cases the policies are left to run for a couple of years, and then closed with a request that the refunds be paid to a third party. Because the refund cheques come from a reputable EU insurance company, the receiving bank has no cause to query them. The funds are then wired on to other accounts in other countries and used to fund training and indoctrination camps for potential suicide bombers. (13)

- early termination of a policy, especially at a loss, and/or where cash was paid in the first place, and/or where there is a request for the refund cheque to be sent to a third party;
- a change in the designated beneficiaries, especially in cases where this can be achieved without the consent of the insurer, or where the right to payment could be transferred just by signing an endorsement on the policy;
- the substitution of newly designated beneficiaries, with no apparent connection with the policyholder;
- an attempt to take out a large lump sum contract where the client's usual pattern is for smaller regular payments;

CASE STUDY

Cancellation and overseas payments arrangements dominate discussions

An attempt is made in the United States to purchase life insurance policies for a number of foreign nationals. The US underwriter is asked to provide life cover with an indemnity value equal to the premium paid. There are also discussions to the effect that if the policies should be cancelled, the returned premiums should be paid into a bank account in another country. (14)

- a client with no concerns about the performance of the policy but a lot of interest in the arrangements for early cancellation;
- a request to make a lump sum payment via wire transfer or using foreign currency;
- use of a home address outside the country where the insurance company is based, where it is discovered during the verification process that the home phone is not connected.

SPECIFIC BANKING EXAMPLES

Extraneous information from outside the relationship

Warning bells might ring as a result of the receipt of extraneous information, for example, from informal communication with the police intelligence

The FATF Report on pre-9/11 transaction sequence

Name on UN list reinforces bank suspicions

The FATF gives the example of an individual whose financial transactions, conducted through a bank in a neighbouring country, came under scrutiny in the months before 11 September. When a name very similar to that of the account holder appeared on the United Nations's list issued as a result of UNSCR 1333 prohibiting the financing of al-Qaeda, the bank in question immediately filed a STR to its FIU.

The FIU in question analysed the financial movements relating to the individual's accounts [a savings and a deposit account] using records requested from the bank. It appeared that both the accounts had been opened by the individual in 1990 and had been fed mostly by cash deposits. In March 2000 the individual made a sizeable transfer from his savings account to his checking account. These funds were used to pay for a single premium life insurance policy and to purchase certificates of deposit.

From the middle of April 2001, the individual made several large transfers from his savings account to his deposit account. These funds were transferred abroad to persons and companies located in neighbouring countries and in other regions.

In the course of the next couple of months he sold the certificates of deposit, and transferred the proceeds into the accounts of one company based in Asia and another based in his home country. He also cashed in his life insurance policy early, and transferred the cash to a bank in his home country. The last transaction occurred at the end of August 2001, less than two weeks before the 9/11 attacks. (15)

services or other sources. In the course of developing a lead from some other source, the intelligence services might ask a bank to take a closer look at the transaction patterns associated with a particular target group of consumers living in a specific area. Or suspicions might also be aroused as a result of paying attention to international current affairs. For example, a news announcement that insurgents may be operating from a new location not previously linked with terrorism might raise a question mark over certain transactions with that location. The value of staff being well briefed in such issues is discussed further in Chapter 6. (16)

Changes in relationship patterns and account activity

An emerging trend noted by some, is the 'purchase' by terrorists and terrorist sympathisers of an active bank account belonging to someone who is leaving the country and who has no further use for it. For the terrorist, this can provide a valuable legitimate screen for bank dealings, without the need to establish a personal bank record nor, indeed, to have any personal contact with the bank at all. It also has the obvious advantage that any investigative trail will stop at the door of the genuine account holder. (17)

There is no reason why this technique should be limited to personal customers. Corporate clients of banks and asset managers could be taken over by terrorist financiers or sympathisers and their newly acquired companies.

Staff should be trained to develop a heightened awareness for the following types of situations:

- *customers* who used to make personal contact but who no longer do so;
- *customers* whose accounts show sudden changes in activity patterns; for example, previous salary source eliminated and replaced with cash payments or, in the wholesale sphere, the replacement of reliable and long-established revenue sources with newer ones which have not been verified;
- *a change of address*, in conjunction with the above;
- *corporate clients* or investors changing their investment behaviour or channel of representation (for example 'please now deal with our investment representative Mr Tallin', who turns out to be an accountant at an offshore location).

  Accounts of investment vehicles may then be used by the new owners for terrorist financing purposes, such as paying in and drawing out cash to meet operational expenses, or converting financial donations, extorted payments and criminal proceeds into redeemable assets/investments, which can be sold and drawn down. These in turn are used either to meet a specific funding need in a particular country or as just another leg in a web of transactions designed to disguise ownership and the ultimate terrorist purposes to which they will be put;
- *customers who fail to provide information* requested by the financial institution, or who attempt to provide as little as possible, or who provide information that is either misleading or deliberately difficult for staff to verify;

- an account that receives periodic deposits, followed by periods of inactivity. The FATF points out that these accounts can be used in creating a *backdrop of apparent financial legitimacy*, behind which other fraudulent activities are being carried out;
- a dormant account containing almost nothing, which suddenly receives one or more deposits followed by *daily cash withdrawals* until the deposited sum runs out. Again, such accounts could be being used to fund operational expenses for terrorist operatives who wish to avoid opening and using bank accounts themselves.

CASE STUDY

Dormant accounts and a questionable business relationship

The manager of a chocolate factory, ChocCo, introduces his business bank manager to two other businessmen, both of whom want to open business accounts for new companies: TextCo is involved in textiles and PropCo is a non-trading real estate company. The two companies were established within a few days of each other but in different countries and with different managers. Bank accounts are duly set up for each, but both remain dormant for several years.

Eventually the manager of ChocCo announces the arrival of a credit transfer from PropCo to the account of TextCo, allegedly a down payment on a shipment of tablecloths, though no invoice is shown. When the money arrives in the TextCo account, the TextCo manager asks for it to be made available in cash at a bank branch near the border. There, together with the ChocCo manager, he withdraws the funds.

NB: the bank apparently reported this story to the FIU, who found that the two managers then took the money across the border, which is in an area of known terrorist activity. Further investigations revealed links between the managers of TextCo and PropCo and local terrorist groups. (18)

Unusual arrangements or high turnover

Staff should be aware of:

- an account for which several people, without any obvious business or family relation to each other, have *signature authority*; for example, a joint current account or a credit card being operated – or having the capability to be operated – by three separate, apparently unrelated individuals, yet which does not appear to be for business use. The benefits of such an arrangement to a terrorist cell, with each individual being able to use the account and access funds as required, are obvious;
- an account opened by an organization or business with *the same address as other legal entities*, and for which the same individual(s) has signature authority, yet where there is no obvious economic or legal reason for such an arrangement (such as there would be in the case, for example, of the directors of a group of related companies headquartered at the same location). Again, a useful arrangement if you want maximum flexibility in the collection, transfer and distribution of funds, such as would be the case with a terrorist funds handler;
- an account opened in the name of an organization involved in the activities of an association or foundation whose aims in turn are *related to those of a terrorist organization*, showing financial activity out of line with its expected level or geographic scope of payments – especially where such activity

involves higher risk locations. For example, a printing or publishing house in London involved with the production or sale of literature sympathetic to a terrorist group, remitting funds for no apparent commercial purpose to a company in Karachi, Pakistan.

CASE STUDY

High account turnover and false identity reveals terrorist funding through tax fraud

A person supposedly earning a salary of \$17000 a year in fact has a turnover in his account of more than \$350000. A subsequent investigation discovers that no such person in fact exists, and that the account has been set up using a false identity. It is then established that the account is linked to a foreign charity, and is being used in the fraudulent collection of funds for a terrorist organization via the charity.

This works on the following principle: in the country concerned, the government matches charitable donations to the tune of 42 per cent of funds received. Donations to the charity are paid into the account, and the charity claims government funds on that money. The original donations are then returned to the donors, while the charity holds on to the government contribution. In total more than \$1.14 m is fraudulently obtained in this way. (19)

Deposits, withdrawals and remittances

Automatic teller machines (ATMs) provide a convenient means of accessing relatively small amounts of cash without arousing any suspicion. Not only are they increasingly ubiquitous, but they are also valuable as a relatively anonymous means of accessing cash. Not only does the customer not have to confront a bank teller, but the ATM itself records only the time and amount withdrawn, and not the identity of the person who actually made the transaction. (20)

In general terms, suspicious transaction patterns on an account may be those that are atypical of the usual patterns for that account, or for comparable businesses in the locality. Unusual cash payments or deposit methodologies in particular should alert staff, as should apparent attempts to avoid reporting thresholds. Specifically, staff should be aware of:

- deposits for a business in *unusual combinations of monetary instruments* (for example a mix of business, payroll and social security cheques). This may be indicative of an account being used as a front company for the collection of terrorist funds, with the various donors or extortion victims (see Chapter 3 on terrorist financing methods) supplying funds in a variety of different ways;
- *large cash withdrawals* from a business account, when cash transactions are not normally associated with the account. For example, such withdrawals may be made according to a terrorist cell's operational needs, from a business whose owner is either sympathetic to their cause, or who is under threat of physical harm or death;
- *large cash deposits* made to an account, when the account holder's business transactions would normally be conducted via cheques or other forms of payment, and where the business explanation for the change in the receipt profile is unconvincing. This could be the case for example, where, a

CASE STUDY

Suspicious money transfers and a relief organization

A series of businesses and individuals in the United States make a mix of structured cash deposits and business, payroll and social benefit cheque deposits, with a total value of $9 m. The funds deposited are transferred within a day or two to a company located in Sri Lanka. The deposit and wire transfer activity involves 37 individuals, four businesses – one of which was the beneficiary of the funds transferred – and 44 accounts. Two of the other three businesses are ethnic-based money remittance companies based in the US; the third, at the same location as one of the money remittance businesses, is described as a 'relief organization'. (21)

business owner is cooperating with terrorists (whether voluntarily or under compulsion) in allowing a business account to be used as a collection and transmission point for their funds;

- a *mix of cash deposits and other monetary instruments* in a personal account, when such transactions appear to be out of keeping with the normal use of the account;
- a series of transactions carried out at the same branch of a bank, and on the same day, but with an apparent attempt to use *different bank tellers* or one particular teller – for example, who may have been threatened with violence not to report what is happening;
- the *structuring of deposits* through several branches of the same financial institution, or by groups of individuals who enter a single branch at the same time;
- a series of cash deposits or withdrawals for amounts just below the identification or *reporting threshold*;

CASE STUDY

Terrorists purchase bank cheques under the reporting thresholds

Individuals of the same ethnic origin use a single address. It is the address used by one of three grocery stores, two of which share a common location. Two individuals employed by one of the grocery stores, plus a third whose occupation is unknown (but who supplies the same address as the other two), each deposit funds just under the applicable reporting thresholds and immediately draw cheques payable to a fourth person. The cheques clear through two different banks in another country. In addition, two other people, both associated with the other grocery store located at the same address as the first, also each purchase a bank cheque worth just under the applicable reporting threshold; they do so at the same bank branch and at the same time, but from different tellers. One of those cheques is purchased on behalf of the second grocery store, and the other is on behalf of a third party; they are payable to two different individuals (one of whom has the same surname as one of the purchasers).

Finally, a third business uses the common address shared by the two grocery stores referred to above, in order to open a new business account, which immediately receives a $20 000 wire transfer from another grocery elsewhere in the country. Subsequent investigations reveal that altogether about $72 000 equivalent in cash is withdrawn from other accounts associated with this business.

Indicators that could be linked to the collection and movement of funds for terrorist financing purposes include:

- the use of a number of people to structure transactions just under the reporting threshold, (thereby sidestepping reporting requirements), and who then send funds on to a foreign beneficiary;
- a series of same-day transactions made at the same bank but using different cashiers;
- shared addresses, which are also business locations, by the individuals involved in these transactions;
- the use of cash-intensive businesses to cover up the sources of funds;
- the involvement of a group of nationals from countries of specific concern. (22)

- the presentation of uncounted funds at a bank – when they are counted and the value is found to be above the reporting threshold, the *transaction is reduced* to an amount just below that threshold (that is, the customer decides to deposit less);
- the deposit or withdrawal of multiple cheques or other monetary instruments for sums consistently just below the reporting or identification threshold – especially if they are *numbered in sequence*.

Characteristics of the customer or business activity

In broad terms, suspicion may be aroused by inconsistencies in the details supplied about an individual or business customer, or between the customer's background details and the way the account is used, particularly where there are links with countries of specific concern. Staff should be aware of situations where:

- unexplained inconsistencies are generated in the course of the identification or verification process. These might be to do with the applicant's previous or current country of residence, the country of issue of the passport, countries previously visited according to the passport, or documents provided to confirm the applicant's name, address or date of birth (for example, where the customer has declared residence in a country for two years, but the passport contains no visa/permit for that country);
- a shared address is given for individuals involved in cash transactions, especially when that address is also a business location, or when it does not appear appropriate for the person's stated occupation (for example 'Suite 3, Caledonian Business Park, High Street, Grangetown' for a customer whose stated occupation is student, unemployed and so on);
- the person's stated occupation is out of line with the level or type of activity on their account (for example, a student who receives or sends frequent wire transfers, or who withdraws the maximum daily cash allowance each day at various locations over a wide geographic area);
- funds are generated by a business owned by individuals of the same origin from countries of specific concern, or where there is the involvement of a number of such individuals, acting on behalf of similar business types and the funds are remitted overseas, for no commercial purpose, or where the stated purpose is open to question;

CASE STUDY

Unusual account activities and remittances to high-risk country spark concern

In the US, multiple cheque payments totalling around $420 000 are made from a business account to a securities brokerage. The business account is also used to make wire transfers totalling $2.1 m into and out of a number of business and personal accounts in Dubai. Additionally, a currency transaction report is filed on an $11 000 cash withdrawal from the account, made by a person with a foreign passport. Two individuals with signature authority on the account are also involved in other businesses, which between them make cash withdrawals totalling $43 000 (on which CTRs are also filed).

NB: a number of indicators in the above scenario could suggest the movement of terrorist funds. They include:

- the use of a business account to channel funds to a small number of overseas recipients;
- both individuals and businesses in a country of specific concern;
- an unusually high volume of wire transfer activity into and out of this business account;
- large currency withdrawals from an account where cash transactions are not usual;
- payments from a business account to a brokerage firm;
- funds generated by a business owned by nationals of countries of specific concern. (23)

CASE STUDY

Unlicensed money remitter sends funds to Afghanistan nationals for 'refugee relief'

A US export/import business generates $1.8 m in outgoing wire transfers through its business account during a five-month period. Cash, cheques and money orders are also deposited to its account, totalling around $1 m. Wire transfers are sent to beneficiaries, both individuals and businesses, in North America, Asia and the Persian Gulf. Around 60 per cent of the funds go to recipients in foreign countries, who are then responsible for disseminating the funds to the ultimate beneficiaries; a significant proportion go ultimately to Afghan nationals living in various countries.

Individuals conducting these transactions describe the export/import business as involved in 'refugee relief' or 'money transfer'. According to some CTRs filed, the person with sole signing authority on the suspect account also appears to be making deposits of $17.4 m and withdrawals of almost $60 000 payable to what appear to be 15 personal accounts at five different banks, over an extended period of time. He also travels on a US passport from the US to Europe and Asia several times over a three-year period.

Indicators suggesting potential linkage of the account activities outlined above to terrorist financing include:

- an import/export business acting as an unlicensed money transfer service;
- the use of individuals and businesses as intermediaries in the wire transfer process;
- wire transfer beneficiaries that include a large group of nationals of countries associated with terrorist activity or terrorist financing activity (Afghanistan);

- the fact that many of the beneficiaries are Afghan nationals living in other countries;
- the involvement in the transactions of a charity or relief organization;
- the use of both cash and monetary instruments;
- large amounts deposited in an apparently personal account held by the business owner. (24)

- a safe deposit box is opened on behalf of an individual or a business organization, when the nature of occupation or business is not known or does not appear to justify the need for one. This may appear to be a basic point, but the provision of secure, unquestioned safe deposit services would be an obvious benefit to a terrorist or accomplice. Staff should ask what the purpose of the box is, what kinds of valuables will be stored in it and if at all suspicious should report the matter to the MLRO;

- financial transactions are made on the account of a non-profit or charitable organization, for which there appears to be no logical economic purpose, or where there is no evident link between the stated activity or aims of the organization and the other parties in the transaction. These activities might include moving donated funds to a jurisdiction, such as an NCCT country, or to a lesser-known offshore institution, where they are less likely to be subject to scrutiny and from where they could be distributed to a correspondent bank in the country of terrorist activity (known as 'routing'). For example, a charity purporting to collect funds for poverty and famine relief in Sudan, remits funds to an investment company in the Turks and Caicos islands, from where they are remitted to a bank in Syria, withdrawn in cash and used to fund the terrorist insurgency in Iraq.

Locations associated with terrorist activity

Any unusual movement of cash to, through or from a location of concern should be cause for further scrutiny by bank staff. It is up to individual financial institutions to determine what are 'locations of concern' based on international findings and their own business profiles. Examples of potentially untoward activity which staff should be aware of include the following scenarios:

- foreign currency exchanges that are swiftly followed by wire transfers of the cash to high-risk locations;

- deposits that are rapidly followed by wire transfers of funds, particularly to or through such a location;

- a business account through which a high volume of wire transfer activity takes place, when there seems no obvious business-related reason for this – particularly when the funds are being sent to, through or from a location linked with terrorist activity or terrorist financing;

- funds collected through a number of accounts and sent on to a small number of foreign business and individual beneficiaries, especially if these are based in locations of concern;

- credit arrangements or commercial transactions made for a customer and involving the movement of money to or from a high-risk location, when there is no logical business reason for doing so;

CASE STUDY

Structured daily deposits and wire transfers to a location of concern

A bank notices that daily deposits totalling over $340 000 have been made to the account of a foreign currency exchange in the course of a 2.5-month period. During that same period the business initiated ten wire transfers totalling $2.7 m, which were sent to a bank in the United Arab Emirates.

The business owner, when questioned, indicates that he is in the business of buying and selling foreign currencies in Iran, the Persian Gulf states and other Middle Eastern countries, and that his business never generates more than the current US reporting requirement threshold of $10 000 a day; CTRs for a three-year period indicate cash deposits totalling $137 000 and withdrawals totalling less than $30 000.

The 'cash out' transactions are conducted by nationals of countries which have been associated with terrorist activity or terrorist financing. Another US bank also files an STR on the same business owner, on the basis that he has made an $80 000 cash deposit which was considered out of line for his trade. He also cashes two negotiable instruments at the same bank, one for $68 000 and the other for $16 000.

Pointers suggesting a potential linkage to terrorist financing include:

- daily deposits – possibly structured to avoid reporting thresholds – to a business account;
- the wire transfer of money from the account shortly after the deposits are made;
- transfer to a beneficiary account in a country with terrorist or terrorist financing links;
- a currency exchange business that buys and sells foreign currencies from various countries in the Middle East – an area of known terrorist activity;
- transactions on a business account conducted by nationals of countries with links to terrorist activity or terrorist financing, who have no obvious connection to the business;
- a volume of transactions that does not line up with the business owner's stated occupation. (25)

- the transmission of funds by international transfer to or from locations of specific concern;
- the opening of accounts of financial institutions from such locations.

It is important to note that individually, these types of indicators are unlikely to mean anything. It is when they occur repetitively, or in combinations with each other or with other events or information, that they may become suspicious.

Wire transfers

As noted in Chapter 2, wire transfers are well suited to the terrorist's purpose in several respects: notably in the speed with which money can be transferred, and the discrepancies between jurisdictions regarding the amount of information about the sender's identity that has to be gathered, retained and sent with the fund transfer. As we have seen, whilst there is no reliable model for determining likely terrorist funds by amount, (26) there is some evidence that they may be structured in order to avoid triggering mandatory reporting requirements. (27)

The FATF workshop on wire transfers previously mentioned highlighted the use of 'straw men' or front companies in transactions, in order to provide clean names that will not trigger the suspicion of the authorities or recognition on circulated lists. Another scam involves the channelling of funds through several different financial institutions, to give the impression in the recipient account that the money is arriving from several and apparently unrelated sources. (28)

In particular, staff should look out for the following:

- a series of transfers ordered in small amounts, apparently to avoid triggering reporting or identification requirements;
- a series of transfers of low value received from disparate financial institutions, apparently to avoid triggering reporting requirements;

CASE STUDY

Payments structured to avoid detection

Mr Tal and his uncle run a money remittance business Money Vex in the US, as agents of a larger money transfer business suspected of being linked to terrorist financing. Money Vex is investigated by the authorities on the back of an STR filed by a financial institution. This investigation shows that over a four-year period Money Vex has received more than $4 m in cash from people wanting to send money to other countries. When payments are received, the cash is deposited to a number of accounts at various branches of banks in the US. So as to avoid US reporting requirements, Mr Tal and his employees always deposit the cash in sums less than $10 000, sometimes making several such deposits in a single day. (29)

CASE STUDY

Suspicious wire remittance movements

Both a wire transfer company and a bank file STRs outlining the movement of about $7 m in money orders through the US account of a foreign business. The wire transfer company report various people, mainly in the north-eastern United States, buying money orders for the maximum face value of $500 to $1 000 and in sequential order, made payable to various individuals, negotiated through banks in Lebanon and later cleared through three US institutions. They are all endorsed by the foreign business. In some cases the funds have then been credited to accounts at other US or foreign banks.

The bank reports similar purchases of money orders in the same region of the US and negotiated at the foreign business. The various beneficiaries, all with Middle Eastern names, received sums ranging from $5 000 to $11 000. The foreign business is also identified as a secondary beneficiary. The money orders are cleared through a foreign bank's cash letter account at the US bank.

Indicators of possible terrorist financing activity include:

- the use of a number of accounts at several banks in order to channel funds to a small number of foreign recipients;

- the use of sequentially numbered money orders;
- the possible structuring of money order purchases at a series of locations so as to avoid CTR and other reporting requirements;
- the apparent intent to sidestep the wire transfer company's identification checks by purchasing money orders in small amounts;
- the movement of funds through (what was at the time) a FATF-designated NCCT;
- the involvement of a number of nationals of countries which have been associated with terrorism or with terrorist financing. (30)

- wire transfers either to or from an individual, without the expected information on the sender or the person on whose behalf the wire was sent;
- the use of a series of personal or business accounts, or the accounts of NPOs or charities, to collect and channel funds on to a small number of foreign beneficiaries;
- foreign exchange transactions are made on behalf of a customer by a third party, and the funds are then wired to a country of specific concern, or which has no obvious business links with the sender.

This is all very well, but it is also worth pointing out that FATF is still very aware of the difficulties of coming up with useful indicators that will assist banks and other financial institutions in their efforts to detect possible terrorist use of wire transfers. Says the FATF 2003-2004 typologies report:

> *In instances when information is available on an individual cross-border wire transaction, often the only factors that may help to link the transaction to terrorism are the name of the originator or beneficiary, and the originator or destination location. The size of the transaction does not seem to follow any specific patterns, although … they are generally low. (31)*

Charitable organizations

As we saw in Chapter 2, there are various ways in which charitable and NPOs may be exploited by terrorist groups, either to raise funds or to launder and move them internationally.

It is important to note that different types of NPO have different risk profiles, and that therefore there may be some variance in the kinds of unusual characteristics which each displays.

Registered vs non-registered

There is a significant difference between those NPOs that are officially registered as charities, which can then use their charitable status to appeal to a broader funding base, and those that keep a lower profile, in some cases remaining unregistered and often focusing exclusively on the needs of a particular ethnic community (and, hence, the funding available from that community). These latter organizations may more commonly be known as 'cultural associations' or 'foundations' rather than charities.

CASE STUDY

Illinois charities – domestic charities accused of financing al-Qaeda

The Global Relief Foundation (GRF) and the Benevolence International Foundation (BIF) were two Illinois-based NPOs, both designated by the US Government as supporters of terrorism in 2002.

GRF had 'humanitarian aid' operations in 25 countries, with a focus on war-torn regions including Bosnia, Chechnya, Kashmir and Afghanistan. The organization raised millions of dollars in support of its cause: $3.2 m was sent overseas in 1999 alone, and $3.2 m in 2000, according to its tax returns. Even before the events of 11 September 2001, US investigators suspected that GRF was sending a substantial percentage of the funds raised to Islamist extremist causes and jihadists with links to international groups such as al-Qaeda, and an investigation was already under way when al-Qaeda struck in the US.

BIF had offices in at least ten countries and raised more than $15 m between 1995 and 2000; it, too, ran 'humanitarian aid' operations but was similarly believed to be diverting funds in support of the international jihadist movement, and it also was under investigation before 9/11. Funds raised would be pooled from many small donors and then sent as aid to an overseas office of the charity or an affiliated organization, and no diversion of funds to terrorist groups would take place until the money was well out of the country. The end result was that the operation would look to any bank simply like a charity sending money to troubled parts of the world.

In the aftermath of 9/11, the US Government froze the assets of both charities, effectively closing them down, and the FBI opened criminal investigations on both. The leader of BIF was convicted on non-terrorism charges, and a major GRF fundraiser was detained and eventually deported from the US. But the groups' supporters claim they were unfairly targeted and that the organizations were shut down without good evidence that they did fund terrorist groups.

As the NCTAUS Monograph points out, these two investigations highlight a fundamental challenge for governments, which is that whilst there is a crucial difference between *seeing links* to terrorists and *proving funding* for terrorists, there is not necessarily a clearly defined threshold of information beyond which the authorities are well enough informed to take action. (32)

International vs local

It is also worth distinguishing between international and local operations. Internationally active operations may be more widely vulnerable to exploitation, but local charities based in countries with an internal terrorist problem are also open to misuse by these groups. Nor is the exploitation of charities exclusively limited to terrorist groups fighting an extremist religious cause. For example, regional independence movements or groups seeking to overthrow governments are terrorist groups if they target innocents as part of their strategy, and they too may make use of charities and NPOs to finance their activities.

Degree of donor complicity

The FATF NPO workshop made a further very important point that there may be 'differing degrees of complicity between an NPO and its donors'. Thus, although most of the real-life case studies considered by the experts at the workshop did identify complicit or corrupt management of the charity as the main link with the terrorist group in question, there were also reports of cases where NPOs were *unknowingly* infiltrated by terrorist supporters (so-called 'cuckoo' charities), who diverted funds from the organization into the terrorists' coffers. In other cases, money could be siphoned off from an innocent NPO nearer grassroots level, at the 'front end' of the chain through a corrupted branch office or unrelated organization receiving support from the charity.

As far as financial institutions are concerned, the accounts of charities and NPOs may be open to abuse in many of the ways outlined above. Their reports of suspicious or unusual transactions, and the subsequent analysis of the data by FIUs is acknowledged by the FATF as '[playing] an important role in bringing certain cases of suspected terrorist abuse of NPOs to the surface'. In some cases STRs filed by banks and other financial institutions have actually instigated an investigation, while in others they have thrown up new leads in an ongoing case. (33)

NPO suspicion factors

What, specifically, should staff in financial institutions look out for in their dealings with the accounts of charitable organizations? The FATF workshop identifies the following 'red flags': (34)

- incongruities between the financial background of an NPO's apparent source of funding (for example, a relatively poor immigrant community) and the value of funds being deposited into the organization's account or moved through it;
- a mismatch between the pattern and size of financial transactions on the one hand, and the stated purpose and activity of the organization on the other. For example, warning bells might ring if a local cultural association, after ten years of existence, opened an account for the proceeds of a local music festival but deposited a much larger amount than would be expected for such an event based on the normal numbers of people attending;
- a sudden increase in the frequency of financial transactions and the sums paid in or out of an NPO account, or a sudden slow up, whereby the NPO

CASE STUDY

NPO network used to transfer funds illegally

A network of at least 215 NPOs established by the members of an immigrant community was found to be making regular transfers of large sums of money to a few accounts in another country, both through bank accounts and via money transfer services. Over a three-year period more than $160 m was sent overseas. The banks' suspicions were aroused by the incongruity of the sums transferred in comparison with the stated purposes and activities of the foundations, and they filed STRs. Investigations then revealed that one of the beneficiaries of these transactions was actually a company listed on a UNSC designated terrorist list.

The FIU forwarded the case to the law enforcement agencies, which concluded that the NPOs were probably a cover for an alternative remittance scheme; investigations were still ongoing at the time of the report, but the FATF commented that 'there is at least the possibility that the funds were raised within this immigrant community with the deliberate intent to support terrorist acts.' (35)

holds sums in its account for a very long period, rather than the steady level of turnover that might be expected of such an organization;

- large and unexplained cash transactions by NPOs;
- a lack of contributions from donors located in the NPO's home country.

More generally, several other characteristics may be significant, which may be picked up by staff of financial institutions. In teaching staff of these characteristics, we would stress again the importance of emphasizing the importance of accumulation of evidence. As a psychological process, suspicion-formation tends to be cumulative; a repetition of same/similar events, or a combination of different events, together with other pieces of information tends to be what makes people suspicious, rather than a single event – although that, too, can of course sometimes happen.

The FATF red flags continue:

- the existence of foreign directors, particularly in combination with transfers of large sums from the account to the country of origin of these directors, and especially if that country is a high-risk jurisdiction;
- the existence of a large number of NPOs with unexplained links – for example, several NPOs sharing the same address, managers or personnel, or transferring money to each other;
- a number of NPOs related to the same community and using the services of the same 'gatekeeper', who may be a signatory on all their accounts;
- NPOs with little substance, so that in relation to their stated purpose and financial flows they appear to have few staff or none, and no suitable offices, fund-raising capabilities or even telephone number ('shell' or 'paper' NPOs);
- operations in jurisdictions associated with terrorist or terrorist financing activity, or transactions to or from those countries, could also be treated as a reason for further scrutiny by financial institutions, or for them to alert the supervisory authorities, depending on the degree of accumulation of other factors.

Future use of NPOs

Terrorist groups will presumably constantly assess and change their tactics in response to counter-terrorism developments. So as the authorities and financial institutions become increasingly aware of charities' financial support for terrorist activities, the terrorists will most likely adapt their use of charities and NPOs.

As Matthew Levitt pointed out in a paper presented at a terrorist financing workshop in 2004, this can make the job of those fighting terrorist financing all the more difficult:

> *A troubling Catch-22 of counterterrorism is that every success breeds new, more difficult targets. The disruption of a group's known, centralized mode of operations (operational, financial, logistical etc.), while cause for celebration, frequently leads to groups becoming less centralized, more*

CASE STUDY

NPO used to transfer money to suspected terrorists

The FIU in the United Kingdom receives an updated list of designated persons and entities from the UNSC. The FIU notices that one of the designated organizations – a tax-exempt NPO, Path of Pity, whose stated purpose is to provide humanitarian relief to projects around the world – operates under different variations of the same name in a number of countries, with several branch addresses located in the United Kingdom itself.

The FIU also receives an STR on the Path of Pity, listing it at one of the addresses included on the UN list. The STR focuses on bank accounts and on three individuals with a controlling interest in them, for the branch of Path of Pity based at the main UK address. One of the individuals, Mr Sal, has an address that matches one of the other addresses indicated on the UN list, and the other two individuals have addresses in two different countries. A search by the FIU reveals that Mr Sal is linked to these other country branches of the Path of Pity and also to four other international NPOs. Reports received by the FIU include details of multiple wire transfers sent from countries associated with terrorist or terrorist financing activity to the different branches of Path of Pity, and to Mr Sal personally. (36)

> *nihilistic, with more localized funding and support networks. In other words, successful disruptions often make future disruptions all that much more difficult. In the area of terrorist financing, particularly through charities, that is very much the case. (37)*

Another response by terrorist groups has been to make use of the bank accounts of their own members and their families to transfer money within the organization; in some cases these funds may be transferred via a charity. (38)

Such changes can have significant implications for financial institutions as they attempt to detect terrorist finance movements through their systems. For example, according to Matthew Levitt, one trend is the likelihood that NPOs will:

> *cut back on their direct support for terrorist operations or operations and focus instead on laundering and transferring funds. Without other indicators suggesting illegal activity, money laundering [via a charitable front] can be especially difficult to identify. [Indeed, he believes that] charitable front organizations are perhaps most useful to terrorist groups as a means of laundering legitimate earnings, donations and ill-gotten gains through cascading levels of charities and companies, including shell companies and paper charities. Shuffling funds among fronts makes tracing these financial trails immensely difficult, as charities and companies layer their transactions and obfuscate the terrorist intentions of their myriad transactions. (39)*

In other words, the increasing focus on the involvement of charities in terrorist movements may lead to a shift by those charities away from direct logistical support for the terrorists, in order to avoid the glare of public scrutiny. Instead, they may increase infrastructure support in various ways, including the laundering of terrorist funds through strings of charities. (40)

Banned charities may also make efforts to sidestep the sanctions imposed on them. Levitt reports that 'Many charities are incorporating under new names, either in response to being designated as banned terrorist entities or in an effort to evade attention.' He cites several examples, including that of the Al-Rashid Trust, which was designated by the UN1267 Sanctions Committee on 6 October 2001; the US Government discovered that by March 2002 all its activities were being conducted by the Al-Akhtar Trust. (41)

As unrest flares in new trouble spots around the world, terrorist-linked charities may expand into new territories in order to capitalize on opportunities to further their aims in an unstable environment. The war in Iraq has turned that country into 'the latest jihadist arena of preference', with radical Saudi and Iranian-sponsored charities reportedly involved in terrorist funding. Other reports suggest that these charities have been established there to recruit terrorists for organizations such as Hezbollah. (42) Whatever happens, one can be sure that new ways of using the financial system will always be developed and the challenge is both to counter such moves and to anticipate future developments.

SOURCES

1. Phil Williams (2005), 'Warning Indicators, Terrorist Finances, and Terrorist Adaptation,' *Strategic Insights IV*, January.
2. Office of the Comptroller of Currency (OCC) (2002), *Money Laundering: A Banker's Guide to Avoiding Problems* (Washington DC), December, p. 21.
3. FATF, *XII Report on Money Laundering Typologies 2000-2001*, p. 19.
4. Taken from OCC (2002).
5. FATF typology, quoted on the Joint Money Laundering Steering Group website www.bba.org.uk.
6. FATF, *XV Report on Money Laundering Typologies 2003-2004*, p. 15.
7. FATF, *XIV Report on Money Laundering Typologies 2002-2003*, p. 26.
8. International Association of Insurance Supervisors (IAIS) (2004), *Guidance Paper on Anti Money Laundering and Combating the Financing of Terrorism*, October.
9. FATF, *XV Report 2003-2004*, pp. 16–17.
10. FinCEN: Guidance Concerning Anti Money Laundering Program and Suspicious Activity Reporting Requirements for Insurance Companies (amendment to the US Bank Secrecy Act) www.fincen.gov.
11. IAIS (2004), *Guidance Paper on AML/CTF*, p. 34.
12. Ibid., p. 6.
13. Ibid., p. 31.
14. Ibid., p. 28.
15. FATF (2002), *Guidance for Financial Institutions in Detecting Terrorist Financing*, 24 April, p. 3
16. Most of the following pointers for possible terrorist financing are taken from FATF (2002) *Guidance for Financial Institutions*, Annex 1.
17. Philip Robinson, Director of Financial Crime of the UK's Financial Services Authority www.fsa.gov.uk.
18. FATF (2002), *Guidance for Financial Institutions*, p. 6.
19. Ibid.
20. www.fsa.gov.uk.
21. FATF, *XIII Report 2001-2002*, p. 5.
22. US Department of the Treasury (2002), *SAR Bulletin*, January, p. 2.
23. Ibid., p. 1.
24. Ibid., p. 3.
25. Ibid., p. 4.

26. FATF, *XV Report 2003-2004*, p. 6.
27. Ibid.
28. Ibid., p. 5.
29. Ibid., p. 6.
30. US Treasury (2002), p. 3.
31. As outlined in FATF, *XV Report 2003-2004*, p. 10.
32. National Commission on Terrorist Attacks Upon the US (2004), *Monograph on Terrorist Financing*, pp. 11, 53.
33. FATF, *XV Report 2003-2004*, p. 11.
34. Ibid.
35. Ibid., p. 9.
36. Ibid.
37. Matthew Levitt (2004), 'Charitable Organizations and Terrorist Financing: A War on Terror Status-Check,' p. 7 (paper presented at the workshop, 'The Dimensions of Terrorist Financing', University of Pittsburgh, 19 March, www.washingtoninstitute.org).
38. Ibid., p. 8.
39. Ibid., p. 9.
40. Ibid., p. 8.
41. Ibid., p. 9.
42. Ibid., p. 8.

CHAPTER 6

Best Practice

INTRODUCTION

Why we act

Why should financial institutions bother adhering to best practice guidelines when it comes to CTF efforts?

In part, of course, it is because they are obliged to by law and because of the very serious reputational and legal issues referred to in Chapter 1. Nobody wants to be the organization which gets this wrong. But is it not also true that they are 'playing their part'? The presence of CTF measures is believed to have a deterrent effect on potential terrorists, forcing them out of the formal financial system in search of other means of moving money around – less tightly regulated, but also posing other kinds of risks for them. If it becomes very difficult for terrorist groups to collect and administrate large asset bases, then the hope has to be that this will at least ensure that their campaigns remain fractured, unable to gather strength in any one time or place, and that the toll in innocent lives will be reduced.

Furthermore, financial institutions have a valuable reactive role to play after an incident has taken place in supporting intelligence and law enforcement agencies by supplying customers' financial details if they are requested. The financial records of suspects and details of their account activity, if properly maintained, can shed light on the money movements, people and places involved in the network behind the attack. So there is a real practical contribution to be made in this respect.

The thrust of the guidance which has been issued is therefore to enable financial institutions both to deter terrorists from making transactions in the first place, to do what they can to detect suspicious transactions if they do occur and to assist law enforcement with further investigations, either pre- or post-terrorist action. It is worth underlining to staff the fact that it is generally not the responsibility of the financial sector to establish whether or not funds actually do come from an illegal source or are bound for an illegal destination – that is the job of the country's financial intelligence unit or enforcement authority. Rather, the role of the financial institution is simply to identify questionable transactions which may indicate some kind of terrorist or other criminal activity and to pass the information on as necessary, together with the other important administrative duties (including name checking) referred to elsewhere. (1)

Relevance of AML and other controls

As already mentioned, comparatively little in CTF policy is unique to the business of catching terrorists. Most of it is based in the broader compliance principles designed to manage operational risk, reduce fraud and minimize money laundering, all of which also contribute to the reduction of terrorist financing opportunities.

These principles vary somewhat in their minutiae from country to country, but they generally centre upon customer identification, due diligence and know-your-customer (KYC) requirements, suspicion reporting, record-keeping and staff training, along with of course name screening and cooperation with law enforcement authorities. The idea is that financial institutions have a clear idea of each customer's identity, business and lifestyle, and the main sources of finance flowing through their accounts, and can then spot anomalous account activity against the template of their information and the risk profile for that customer. That activity, of course, may take place anywhere in the world in today's global banking environment; as the Basel Committee for Banking Supervision (BCBS) observes: 'Recent initiatives to reinforce actions against terrorism in particular have underlined the importance of banks' ability to monitor their customers wherever they conduct business.' (2)

Not only do KYC policies play a valuable role in the fight against money laundering and terrorist financing, but they bring various other benefits. A bank's KYC programme can help promote good business and risk management practices generally within the organization, and provide a sound platform on which to base product sales strategies, as well as to reduce mis-selling risk, reduce the likelihood of fraud and other financial crimes, and protect reputation by minimizing the risk of association with criminals (sometimes referred to as 'integrity due diligence' or IDD).

CTF – specific controls

Within this overall framework, there are several best practice features which play an emphasized role in the prevention and even detection of terrorist financing activity, though as we've emphasized, probably not in the prevention of a specific attack. A financial institution that carries out thorough customer identification and verification, maintains comprehensive records on each customer and their transactions, and can make those records swiftly available to the intelligence services on demand (typically, in fast-moving situations either immediately before or after a terrorist attack) can play an invaluable role in their investigations.

Likewise, name screening against selected lists of designated suspect terrorist names has also become a key feature in CTF procedures, and has so far proved to be effective in at least prohibiting direct and untrammelled access to the financial system by those on the lists. Additionally, staff training plays a significant role. AML training for bank employees is well established, but as we have noted in Chapter 1, often it makes only a passing reference to the phenomenon of terrorist funds within the financial system, so there is a place for training that focuses staff awareness specifically on terrorist financing and the role of financial institutions in the fight against it. We will look later at what exactly is entailed in both these elements of CTF best practice.

Risk-based approach

No discussion of general principles would be complete without reference to the risk-based approach, whose fundamental premise is that certain combinations of financial arrangements will be more likely to attract questionable business than others, and therefore need to be subject to more rigorous precautions and scrutiny. For example, consider a one-man independent financial adviser based in a community with little or no likely reasons – whether ethnic, religious or political – to become involved in terrorism, versus, say, an international bank with branches throughout the Middle East and Asia, with a much broader (and potentially higher risk) customer profile.

Strongly associated with this premise is the idea that individual financial institutions should concentrate their efforts on the types of customers, accounts, products and transactions which they have identified as being 'higher risk'. It is difficult for regulatory authorities to be prescriptive about what constitutes 'high risk', since this will vary from one institution to another; but in the words of one senior regulatory official with whom we spoke, 'Institutions need to ask themselves what the risk is of dealing with certain types of business, and what will be best for the organization.'

Sources of best practice

The World Bank and the IMF have produced a guide to best practice, grounded in the FATF Forty Recommendations and the BCBS's international standards and we have drawn widely from their consequential guidelines. (3) In addition, we have gathered guidance from other industry-specific bodies and relevant sources including IAIS (insurance), IOSCO (Securities), the Wolfsberg Group (international and private banking), the Joint Money Laundering Steering Group (UK consultative body) and the US Department of Treasury Anti-Terrorist Financing Guidelines (re charities). We would stress here again that our purpose is to summarize and provide material for training purposes, so that staff in many different countries can be made aware in the broadest sense of what constitutes global best practice. What we have not attempted to do is provide operational material for direct insertion into financial institutions' policies and procedures.

BANKING

Customer identification and due diligence (4)

The global KYC standard outlined here is based on the four-point plan drawn up by the BCBS and widely promoted as a benchmark for the banking sector, as well as a best practice reference point for other financial sectors. It comprises policies on:

- customer acceptance
- customer identification
- ongoing monitoring of higher-risk accounts
- risk management. (5)

How far should the KYC policy extend?

Whatever regime is introduced at the headquarters of an institution must be applied to its branches and to any majority-owned subsidiaries, both domestically and internationally, unless it clashes with local law in that jurisdiction. If there are differences in regulatory standards between home and host countries, then the more comprehensive/stronger of the two should be applied.

Who is a customer?

Banks need to establish at the outset whether the person with whom they are dealing is acting on their own behalf, or whether there is a beneficial owner of the account who may not be identified in their paperwork. If a bank suspects the customer is representing a third party, it must carry out due diligence on that third party as well.

Third parties may be organizations or legal entities as well as individuals; it can be particularly difficult to establish who is the beneficial owner when 'tiered ownership' is involved, with a whole pyramid of companies controlling one another and in some cases a parent company at the top. Again, appropriate due diligence is necessary in such a situation to find out the precise identity of the parent entity.

Customer acceptance procedures

It is useful for banks to be able to identify which potential new customers represent a high risk in terms of money laundering and the financing of terrorism, by developing high-risk profiles against which they can be measured. Standard risk indicators for money laundering will include factors such as:

- the customer's country of origin (for example from an NCCT or a country habitually associated with the production, transit or processing of illegal narcotics);
- the type and country of business activity (for example arms, casinos, diamonds, jewellery, money exchange);
- any linked accounts, and whether or not they have a high-profile position and are 'politically exposed';
- the kinds of products which the customer wishes to use, and whether they are of particular use to someone wishing to launder money (for example no notice restrictions on withdrawals).

As regards terrorist financing, it simply is not possible to produce a meaningful profile for an individual terrorist financier, but clearly issues surrounding the general profile of an account will be relevant, such as:

- known connections with a conflict area or country associated with terrorism;
- business interests in or with such countries/areas;
- frequent money transfers to and from such areas and travel to and from them (such as with associated charities and NPOs);
- complex ownership structures leading back to individuals or businesses with connections to such places.

Senior management approval

The risk-based approach generally means that the bank can afford to exercise reduced due diligence with low-risk customers; as the IMF/World Bank guidance puts it: 'The rigidity of the acceptance standards should be commensurate with the risk profile of a potential customer.' However, when new business deemed to be 'high risk' is up for consideration, the onus should be on the *senior* management to make the decision as to whether or not such business is appropriate for the bank to take on.

Customer identification

Bank staff should verify any new customer's identification to their satisfaction before an account is opened. Customers are not allowed to open accounts in fictitious names, and nor are numbered accounts permitted unless the usual customer ID procedures and supporting documentation are used as a matter of course.

Once they come to request identification documents, banks should ask for those that are hardest to forge; most suitable are official papers such as passports, driving licences, personal ID cards or tax identification documents. When an intermediary – for example a trustee, financial adviser or nominee – is opening an account or carrying out a transaction on behalf of an individual or a corporate customer, then unless legally sanctioned 'passporting' procedures apply (for example as in the EU, where business introduced by other EU-regulated entities may be assumed to have been correctly identified already), the financial institution needs to take steps to verify the identification of the beneficiary. This will include the following information:

- the name and legal form of their organization;
- its address;
- the names of the directors and the principal beneficiaries;
- the details of the agent acting on behalf of the organization and the organization's account number with the agent;
- the regulatory body to which the organization answers.

Detecting forgery

Particular care needs to be taken with the risk of forged identities, since this is a mechanism known to be used increasingly by terrorists, as well as criminal groups. For example:

- When dealing with a new customer face-to-face, it is important to check that the photo supplied is of the person actually opening the account, and that the date of birth given is realistic in the light of their appearance (an obvious point, but one easily missed in a frenetic retail environment).
- If bank statements from two financial institutions are presented as supporting evidence, check that the two show different transactions (one known method is to 'cut and paste' transactions to manufacture a second statement).
- Does the ethnicity of the name seem to match that of the customer?
- Is the content of each document consistent throughout – for example, do the dates match?
- Are the document margins straight?
- Are there any other signs that the document has been tampered with?

Originator information on funds transfers

Funds transfers of any description should be accompanied by accurate and meaningful originator information – including name, address and account number – and that information should remain with the payment all the way along the payment chain (we look in more detail at wire transfers later on).

Maintenance of KYC information

Knowing your customer is an ongoing exercise, which means that banks have to put some effort into keeping records up to date – for example if there are material changes in the way an account is run, or in the event of significant transactions being made on the account.

Low vs high risk accounts and transactions

As discussed above, the risk-based approach requires financial institutions to assess the AML/CTF risks attached to different types of customer profile. Similarly, financial institutions need to weigh up the potential for different kinds of product to be misused for criminal activities; for instance, a wire transfer service is a more obvious choice than a 90 days' notice deposit account in this respect.

For lower-risk categories of customer – for example public companies or government enterprises – financial institutions may be able to scale down or simplify the due diligence requirements, for example by requiring fewer details about the business relationship or expected transactions, though all customers should be required to prove and verify who they are. For higher-risk categories, banks should take additional precautions when they carry out customer due diligence. We look more closely at the various types of higher-risk customers, products and services later.

Record-keeping requirements (6)

Minimum periods

As already seen, when intelligence services or regulatory authorities are tracing the paper trail behind a money laundering or terrorist financing discovery, the availability of financial records for customers (whether current or historic) can be a significant help in the detection and prosecution of the individuals involved. Moreover, the very fact that records are kept as a matter of course is believed in some cases to deter would-be criminals from their original illicit plans. As part of any financial institution's obligation to be able to provide information to the regulatory authorities about past customers and their account activity, therefore, banks are required to keep customer identity records for at least five years after an account has been closed; and records on transactions for at least five years from the date of the transaction. The regulators of any country may choose to extend the minimum five-year holding period for institutions based there.

Type of information retained

The information retained by banks as a matter of course should include:

- a customer's name, address and account number;
- the date and nature of each transaction;
- the currency and amount involved; and
- any other information that is routinely recorded by the bank and could be relevant in piecing together a criminal paper trail.

INSURANCE

Due diligence and KYC

The insurance industry adheres to both the FATF Forty Recommendations and the guidelines issued by the International Association of Insurance Supervisors (IAIS). (7) The best practice procedures outlined in the IAIS document include the following recommendations on customer due diligence.

Customer identification

The insurance company should identify and verify the customer using reliable and independent sources; if the customer is acting on behalf of a third party then the company should carry out a similar exercise on that person, too. It should also establish who the ultimate beneficial owner is; and in cases where the customer is a legal person or legal entity, it should try to clarify the nature of the ownership and control structure. In addition, the insurance company should establish the nature of the business relationship between the various parties involved.

Ongoing due diligence

Once the insurance arrangements are up and running, the insurance company should maintain ongoing due diligence to ensure that the transactions being made are in line with what is known about the policyholder, the beneficial owner and their business and risk profile. Depending on the customer's risk profile (see below), this may involve establishing the source of funds used to fund the premiums. Due diligence should be increased if the flow of premiums or transaction patterns of the policyholder change substantially, unexpectedly or in an unexplained way.

Risk profiling

Like banks, insurance companies need to work out a risk profile for each policyholder before the business is accepted. This may be based on a wide range of factors, including:

- the kind of insurance product being bought;
- the background and geographical location of the customer and the beneficial owner;
- the nature and extent of their business;
- the source of funds;
- the method of premium payments;
- whether or not payments will be made to third parties.

Again, like banks, insurers need to be especially vigilant when it comes to higher-risk clients.

Importance of trigger events

As far as beneficial owners are concerned, the IAIS identifies 'trigger events' in the life of an insurance policy, including:

- claims notifications
- alterations to the terms of the policy
- changes of beneficiary
- policy surrender requests.

These will require further due diligence procedures to try to establish that they are not in fact indicators of money laundering or terrorist financing.

Record-keeping requirements

Minimum periods

As in the banking sector, standard record-keeping requirements for insurance companies involve the retention of customer information for a minimum five-year period after the end of a business relationship, which in this context generally means the maturation or expiry of the policy.

Type of information retained

Insurers are expected to keep the account files and business correspondence for each customer, including records of their risk profile (and that of the beneficial owner where this is not the customer), plus the data gathered as part of the customer due diligence process. Full details of all transactions, both domestic and international, should also be retained. These details should encompass the whole life of the policy, including:

- the location where the initial transaction was carried out;
- the client's financial assessment and needs analysis at that point;
- details of the method of payment;
- an illustration of benefits and copies of documentation used to verify the customer's identity;
- the post-sales records on the account for subsequent years;
- any details of claims settlements and maturity processing, including completed 'discharge documentation'.

Use of representatives for record-keeping

A representative for an insurance company may hold the required documentation for a client on behalf of an insurance company, but the integrity of the records is ultimately the responsibility of the insurer.

SECURITIES

Client identification

In line with the bodies overseeing other sectors of the financial services industry, the International Organization of Securities Commissions (IOSCO) has also produced a set of principles on client identification for the securities sector. (8) The principles follow the standards set such as the FATF Forty Recommendations, but are geared to the priorities and perspectives of securities firms and regulators.

Client due diligence

As far as anybody is aware, the securities sector has not so far been singled out as a particular target for terrorist funds. At the time of 9/11, numerous theories abounded that Osama bin Laden and al-Qaeda had shorted the world's stock markets ahead of the attacks (sold stocks which they did not possess at pre-attack prices, in order to purchase, prior to settlement, in a collapsed, post-attack market), but there is no actual evidence of that according to the National Commission, and the primary focus as far as customer due diligence is concerned has been to protect investors, ensure that markets are safe, fair and efficient and that they minimize systemic risk. Nonetheless, the application of customer due diligence in the securities industry should also help minimize the risk of criminals or terrorists misusing it for their own financial ends in the future. To that end, client identification and verification procedures (adjusted according to the risks presented by the client) are set out, along similar lines to those followed by banks and insurers.

Risk-based approach

More stringent measures to establish the client's identification could be applied in the case of higher-risk accounts, including, among others, those for politically exposed persons (PEPs) and those for nationals, residents or other securities firms from NCCTs.

Omnibus accounts

Omnibus accounts – established by financial institutions in their own name, in order to engage in securities transactions on behalf of their own clients – require special due diligence policies, specifically where the client institution is a foreign business. In these cases, the securities firm needs to gather enough information about the client institution to:

- understand its business;
- gauge its professional reputation;
- assess the adequacy of its due diligence processes; and
- take a view on the regulatory regime of its home jurisdiction.

The decision of whether or not to accept new omnibus account business should be taken by the senior management of the securities firm.

Beneficial ownership

When an account has an ultimate beneficial owner who is not the securities firm's client, the beneficiary's identity should also be established. This will be necessary for accounts set up for a variety of legal vehicles, including corporate structures, partnerships, companies that issue bearer shares, unregistered or unregulated investment vehicles, highly leveraged institutions, joint ventures, mandates and trusts. However, in the case of listed companies and regulated or registered investment companies (for example collective investment schemes and mutual funds) which are already obliged to make these disclosures to the regulatory authorities, securities firms do not have to repeat the process.

Third parties and introductions

Third parties, which feature widely in the business dealings of securities firms, may be used to introduce new clients and carry out due diligence on them, but the ultimate responsibility for that data remains with the securities firm to whom they have brought the new business. It is therefore incumbent on the firm to satisfy itself that the third party is properly regulated, that it has the requisite due diligence procedures in place, and that it will be able to supply promptly any data requested. Third parties based in high-risk, non-cooperative or lightly regulated jurisdictions should not be relied on to carry out due diligence on new customers.

Know your customer procedures

Know your customer is another key strand of the principles set out by IOSCO. Again, this involves securities firms gathering information on their clients' circumstances, financial background and business objectives, maintaining the client's risk and business profile, and monitoring transactions on an ongoing basis to ensure they are in line with those profiles and with the source of the client's funds.

Risk assessment

Clients may be considered 'higher-risk' in the light of a range of factors – for example, if they are non-face-to-face clients, or are PEPs, or are corporate vehicles, or if they live in a lightly regulated country or one associated with financial crime, money laundering and conflict involving terrorism and the financing of terrorism. The nature of a corporate client's business activities, the origin of its resources and its public reputation could also help to influence its risk profile. As with banks and insurance companies, securities firms are meant to apply enhanced due diligence with higher-risk clients.

Record-keeping

Security firms need to keep details of each customer's due diligence findings on record for at least five years after the business relationship has ended. They also need to put in place policies to determine what should happen if due diligence on a customer cannot be completed or if illegal activities are suspected.

SUSPICIOUS TRANSACTION REPORTING IN FINANCIAL INSTITUTIONS

Suspicious transaction report (STR) (9)

STRs are the mainstay of AML programmes, which place the onus on financial institutions to spot suspicious or anomalous activities among the daily flood of transactions, and despite the difficulty in detecting financing activity at the front end of the terrorist financing chain, they have their place in countering terrorist financing, too. As the FATF puts it:

If a financial institution suspects or has reasonable grounds to suspect that funds are the proceeds of a criminal activity, or are related to terrorist financing, it should ... report promptly its suspicions to the financial intelligence unit. (10)

However, a financial institution should under no circumstances alert the customers under scrutiny to the fact that their behaviour has been monitored and reported to the authorities.

Characteristics of suspicious activities

As we saw in Chapter 5, 'suspicious activities' can take numerous forms, but they do share certain broad-brush characteristics. Most obviously, as far as money laundering in particular is concerned, they tend to involve transactions out of step with the usual patterns seen in that account, so any complex or unusually large deals, or unusual transactions without any obvious commercial or lawful purposes, should be viewed as suspicious and reported to the relevant authorities. As far as terrorist financing is concerned, a variety of indicators may give cause for concern, ranging from problems with identification documents, through to, for example unusual signing arrangements, evidence of ulterior control by undisclosed parties, and wire transfer activity which shows signs of manipulation or structuring in order to evade reporting requirements or disguise ultimate sources of funds information.

Extent of reporting duties

How far does the reporting organization have to go in its reporting duties? An STR comprises simply the factual details of a transaction or series of events; there is generally no reason why the reporting bank, insurer or other financial institution should necessarily know anything about *what* it thinks may be wrong, only that it thinks that something *may* be wrong. Given that the United States's Office of the Comptroller of Currency (OCC) guide identifies more than 200 predicate crimes for money laundering, of which terrorist funding is just one, anything else would be an unrealistic expectation. (11) In any case, anything more than initial attempts to try to clarify details by asking leading questions of the customer could amount effectively to a warning that their account was under scrutiny. Financial institutions' obligations to report are therefore based on nothing more concrete than suspicions, and once they have filed an STR then any further investigation is generally left in the hands of the authorities; although best practice would dictate that reporting institutions cooperate with the authorities within the law in order, for example, to further their investigations and, hopefully, bring about successful prosecutions.

An important consideration as regards the whole principle of filing reports to the authorities on customer transactions is the concept of what are known in the United States as 'safe harbour' laws – laws which protect financial institutions and their staff from criminal or civil liability arising from the alleged breaking of confidentiality or secrecy laws, provided they report suspicious transactions *in good faith*; that is, without malice. (12)

Currency transaction report (CTR)

Given the enduring presence of cash in money laundering or terrorist financing operations, (which in many ways goes against the global trend towards the use of plastic and the electronic movement of money), there is arguably a case for reporting any cash transaction above a certain threshold, on the basis that if everybody does it, such mass data can then be used for the purpose of trend analysis. The FATF Forty Recommendations go no further than suggesting that countries should 'consider' implementing such a regulation. (13) Some jurisdictions have taken this step (including the US, Russia, and all the countries of Eastern Europe and the former Soviet Union), but others have not, notably the UK and some other Western European nations.

For example, the US requires that financial institutions record and report to the authorities any currency or bearer instrument transactions of US$10 000 or more as a matter of course, and Australia has a similar A$10 000 threshold. The UK regime is entirely suspicion based, and has no automatic reporting threshold, although KYC procedures are required for one-off transactions above a €15 000 limit. The new Third EU Money Laundering Directive will extend this to cover other non-financial businesses such as casinos and estate agents, as well as anyone selling goods for which more than €15 000 is paid in cash.

Reporting obligations for transactions involving cash do apply across the board where same-day multiple transactions – known as 'smurfing' – occur. This process is used by money launderers as a means of avoiding a designated reporting threshold by breaking up the movement of cash into many smaller transactions. If smurfing is suspected, financial institutions need to report the entire series of transactions to the authorities, even though individually they do not breach any reporting threshold which may exist. Additionally, a single transaction could also be suspected on the grounds that the customer was trying to evade the reporting requirements, if it was for slightly less than the relevant reporting threshold. Again, in such cases the bank should look more closely at the transaction and file a report if it is suspicious.

INTERNAL CONTROLS AND TRAINING (14)

Controls and independent audit

All organizations covered by a country's AML and CTF laws need to set up their own internal policies and procedures to protect themselves against the risk of being criminally exploited in either way. A critical aspect of these internal controls is an independent audit function (whether based within the firm or brought in), which is separate from the compliance office and is therefore able to test the adequacy of the overall compliance arrangements.

Staff training

Equally significant is the requirement for ongoing staff training. As we argue in Chapter 1, while regular training programmes on how to recognize potential money laundering activity and what action to take have become a well-established feature of fully compliant financial institutions, much less attention is paid to the specifics of terrorist financing within the formal financial system. In the words of one senior compliance figure in the UK banking industry: 'There's not sufficient focus on terrorist financing generally. Banks should be able to point to specific CTF action that staff should take and training which they have undergone.'

What should such training entail? In the context of terrorist financing, employees need, first, to be aware of the ways in which terrorist groups may misuse the system, and of the similarities and differences between terrorist financing and money laundering within it. They also need to be aware of the applicable AML/CTF laws and regulations. They should be familiar with the company procedures designed to assess risk and to detect suspicious activities, and be able to work through a variety of different scenarios (relevant to their business) which illustrate potential causes for suspicion in different areas (documentation, account opening, customer behaviour, transactions, geographies and so on) in the specific context of terrorist financing.

They should also be familiar with the importance of screening customer names against sanctions lists, the processes involved in the event that a name matches with a target on a list, and the potential for getting a so-called 'false positive' (see below). For a more detailed description of a potential programme, see Chapter 1.

NAME SCREENING

Prior to 11 September 2001, the sanctions lists produced by international or national authorities focused mainly on specific countries or regimes, with the aim of prohibiting funds transfers to the sanctioned country and freezing the assets of the government, business and residents; either that, or else they targeted known political figures (for example Slobodan Milosevic or Saddam Hussein). Since that date, the composition of the lists has changed, as thousands of names suspected of having terrorist links, both individuals and organizations, have been added to it. Accessing and making effective use of the lists is a challenging operational requirement for all financial institutions.

United Kingdom

There are many sanctions lists available. The United Nations produces a broad global list, applicable to all member states, while the EU consolidated list comprises names featuring in the annexes to various EC regulations. In addition, individual countries may have their own domestic sanctions regimes. In the UK, the Financial Sanctions Unit (FSU) of the Bank of England consolidates the financial sanctions targets listed by the UN, the EU and the UK and issues them as a single list. Where there is a legal basis for freezing the assets of a suspect within the UK, that target should appear on the Bank's consolidated list. (15)

United States

For the US financial sector, the sanctions authority is the Office of Foreign Assets Control (OFAC). The OFAC list should include names listed under UN sanctions regimes, but it will not necessarily contain EU (or UK) sanction targets. Use of the OFAC lists as well as the national and UN sanctions lists would also be necessary for foreign institutions dealing directly with the US, and is generally considered good practice by UK financial institutions.

Pre-lists

In addition to these formal sanctions lists, the authorities from time-to-time issue warning lists of names deemed to be a source of concern to those institutions where those people are believed to have accounts, even though there are no legally binding sanctions attached at this stage. The purpose of the warning lists is to enable financial institutions to move immediately to freeze the target assets if/when these names are subsequently added to the formal sanctions list.

Initial and subsequent screening

Financial institutions are required to run all new accounts of any sort against the current updated versions of the relevant lists, and similarly to screen all existing accounts on a regular basis. Wire transfers should also be screened as a matter of course (see below) to establish that no person or entity whose name appears on a list is the recipient of the funds. It is a key operational responsibility for the MLRO/compliance officer to decide which lists the organization must watch and how often. This latter point will be a matter of each firm's internal policy, and a reflection of its size and character. For instance, a small insurance firm might choose to scan its database monthly, whereas an international bank opening 10000–20000 new accounts each day would need to scan on a daily basis. The Bank of England comments only: 'If you fail to identify and block a target account, this may lead to a breach of the legislation.' (16)

Name match vs target match

Lists should contain any alternative name spellings and aliases used by the suspects in question, but of course it is not possible to conclude that just because someone has a name that features on a sanctions list, they are the wanted individual. In the UK, the FSU makes the distinction between a 'name match', 'where you have matched the name of an account holder with the name of a target included on the Bank's consolidated list', and a 'target match', 'where you are satisfied that the account held is that of the actual target of the financial sanctions', that is, the suspected bad guy. (17)

Action when information is inconclusive

Full details of any target matches should be reported to the authorities and the account frozen immediately. However, it has to be said that target matches are a relative rarity. It is more likely that a name on the database will match with an entry on a sanctions list but there will be no conclusive evidence that it is the same person or organization. In that case it is the financial institution's job initially to look more closely at the KYC information and customer profile on record, and assess it against the details available on the list. If it is not possible either to confirm or to clear the customer's name on the basis of available information, the financial institution may be able to seek guidance from the sanctions authorities but in the meantime is faced with the intractable problem of how to treat the customer's account. Given the consequences and penalties of making a mistake, many financial institutions will feel that they have no choice but to adopt the somewhat brutal policy of blocking an account until they have satisfied themselves that they do indeed only have a name match. They will prefer to deal with the customer's lawsuit rather than a regulatory enforcement action or a criminal prosecution.

It is in these circumstances that the importance of painstakingly and diligently collected KYC information becomes all too clear, not to mention software programs which can analyse such data against list information and, for example, produce 'target match' probability scores.

Effective compliance programmes

As well as conducting the screening process on all new accounts, on existing accounts as often as is necessary, and also on wire transactions and one-off non-customer transactions, financial institutions need to establish and maintain an effective programme to ensure compliance with the sanctions authority in question. This should include:

- the existence and observance of written procedures for checking transactions against the relevant lists;
- open communication lines between internal departments;
- regular staff training;
- an annual, in-depth audit of the compliance function.

Other considerations include arrangements for maintaining current sanctions lists and distributing them throughout every subsidiary or branch office, both domestically and overseas.

False positives

Beyond situations where the available facts are inconclusive, are those where financial institutions will actually determine – erroneously – that their customer is the person named on the list – the dreaded 'false positive' scenario.

In such circumstances it is essential that financial institutions should be capable of demonstrating that even if the outcome was wrong, they followed their full and correct procedure and carried out checks with any other parties involved (for example with a remitting bank). It is vital to keep clear records of the decision-making process leading up to any action taken.

BEST PRACTICE IN HIGH-RISK PRODUCTS AND SERVICES

As discussed earlier, one of the fundamental tenets of a risk-based approach is that financial institutions should make judgements about the risks of misuse attached to each relationship, and then should focus the greater part of their attention in areas where the greater risks lie. In this regard, specific recognition should be given to the following.

International correspondent banking accounts

Correspondent accounts may be maintained between banks, for use in making transactions for customers or between themselves. They are generally quite above board, but as we saw in Chapter 5, certain cross-border correspondent arrangements are at risk of misuse by money launderers and terrorist financiers (the assumption being that due diligence and KYC will be dealt with by the respondent bank in the country of origin). Such accounts maintained with banks based in lightly regulated countries are particularly vulnerable, as they may offer a route for people or organizations to access the global financial system while sidestepping the standard checks.

As the IMF/World Bank document points out (18), before entering into such a cross-border arrangement, any financial institution should make an assessment of the respondent bank in question, establishing:

- its location
- the nature of its business
- the purpose of the proposed account
- the bank's reputation
- the quality of its supervision
- the extent of its in-house AML/CTF policy and training provisions.

The importance of the above cannot be over-emphasized in the training which you provide to relevant staff. If payable-through accounts are to be used, then the financial institution needs to ensure that the respondent bank will verify the identity of its customers and carry out ongoing due diligence on them. More generally, the respective responsibilities of the banks should be established and documented beforehand. Correspondent banking is another area where senior management should take responsibility for approving the business relationship before it actually gets going.

Banks should not set up correspondent banking arrangements with organizations located in jurisdictions featuring on the FATF list of non-cooperative countries and territories (NCCTs), nor with so-called 'shell' banks (banks which are unconnected with any effectively regulated financial system and which are incorporated in a jurisdiction where they have no physical presence or actual staff operations).

Electronic banking (19)

There has been a rapid and dramatic expansion in non-face-to-face business as a result of the development of financial information services and product delivery via electronic means, including ATMs, telephone and Internet banking. Although there is no inherently greater risk involved in applications received by phone or Internet than in, say, applications by post, a combination of other factors typically aggravate the risks involved.

For example, it is possible to make an application instantaneously, at any time and from any location; it is easier to make multiple fictitious or anonymous applications without any additional risk and with less danger of detection. Physical documents are not typically required as part of the application process, therefore making it relatively easier to apply using a stolen identity. All these factors increase convenience for criminals or terrorist groups, and correspondingly, the risks to financial institutions. However, the FATF leaves it to individual jurisdictions to work out and put in place appropriate regulatory measures for their financial institutions.

The new guidelines on customer identification provided by the UK's Joint Money Laundering Steering Group (JMLSG) are an interesting example of the approach being adopted in some quarters. (20) The JMLSG takes the view that:

> *The extent of the identification required in respect of non-face-to-face customers will depend on the nature and characteristics of the product or service requested and the assessed money laundering risk presented by the customer. Even though the same identity proof can be offered by face-to-face and non-face-to-face customers, there is more difficulty in matching the customer to the proof in the case of non-face-to-face approaches. Guidance needs to recognize the differences between these two approaches. (21)*

These guidelines then go on to state that financial institutions need to carry out an additional check on non-face-to-face customers. This could take the form, for instance (again, depending on the perceived risk presented by the customer), of electronic checks as well as documentary evidence, or a written communication to the customer's verified home address, requiring a form to be completed and returned by post. (22)

Wire transfers

As discussed in Chapter 5, electronic transfers pose particular concerns for financial authorities and regulatory bodies. FATF's Special Recommendation VII sets out in detail the steps that financial institutions should take when sending money electronically: (23)

- Transfers to other countries should be sent with 'accurate and meaningful originator information' attached ('originator' meaning the name of the person or company sending the funds). This must contain the name of the originator and the number of the account, if there is one. If there is no account number then a unique reference number should be included. The address of the originator, or other identifying information such as their date and place of birth or a national identity number, should also be included.

- Countries have the option of introducing a minimum threshold for this requirement but it seems clear that FATF favours an arrangement where full and accurate information on the sender must be attached in order for the wire transfer to be accepted by a bank, regardless of amount.
- When a single sender bundles a number of transfers destined for various recipients in another country into a single file, and sends them all together, there is no need to include full originator information on each one provided that the batch file contains all the relevant sender identification details.
- Domestic transfers must also include all the required originator information, unless the originating bank is capable of providing this on demand, in which case all that needs to accompany the money is an account number or some other effective means by which to identify the originator. On demand means within three days of the originating bank receiving the request for information from the receiving bank or the authorities, as the case may be.
- The originator information must be kept with the wire transfer if it is processed by one or more intermediary institutions; if this cannot be done because of technical limitations, then the intermediary must keep a record of all the information received with the transfer, and do so for at least five years.
- The bank receiving the wire transfer should have 'effective risk-based procedures' in place, which will pick up any transfer without the requisite information about the sender. Wire transfers lacking that information may be treated as suspicious and scrutinized further or reported. The FATF suggests that the receiving bank should consider limiting or even terminating its business dealings with those financial institutions which do not comply with these basic requirements.

Private banking

Private banking relationships are set up not only by wealthy individuals and politically exposed persons (PEPs) but also by law firms, investment companies, investment advisers and trusts. Particularly with regard to money laundering, private banking is viewed as a particularly high-risk sector of the banking universe for various reasons – not least because of the typical levels of wealth, the complexity and sophistication of financial services available (in particular, so-called 'secrecy' products), and the number of advisers and intermediaries that may be involved in a client's financial affairs. Often, too, the very purpose of starting a private banking relationship is to hide wealth and put it out of reach (whether from the tax authorities, probing journalists or a vengeful spouse) – a process which is just as effective for criminal proceeds as it is for legitimate funds.

On the other hand, private bankers are likely to have more proactive and personal relationships with their client than would be the case in retail banking, and may therefore have additional insights into anomalous account activity. In this regard it is important to remember that the wealthy client issuing execution-only instructions for transfers of funds between various investments and offshore vehicles could just as easily be a terrorist sympathiser and financial donor, as a genuine client, or a criminal money launderer. Because private banking relationships can be so complex, it is important also that there are effective systems in place within each bank to monitor and report suspicious activity, and that they can do so based on a client's total activities. (24)

Standards for private banking have been largely driven in recent years by The Wolfsberg Group of international banks (see box), which has drawn up a set of best practice guidelines for global private banking. (25) These set out as the basic principle for client acceptance the requirements that banks will accept only those clients whose sources of wealth and funds can be reasonably established as being legitimate, and whose beneficial ownership is clear. It is the responsibility of the individual sponsoring private banker to make sure this is the case and, indeed, to be alert to suspicious activities on an ongoing basis. Importantly, say The Wolfsberg principles: 'Mere fulfilment of internal review processes does not relieve the private banker of this basic responsibility.' (26)

In addition, the principles address other key areas, as follows.

Wolfsberg Group

The Wolfsberg Group is an association of 12 global banks, which aims to develop financial services industry standards for KYC, AML and CTF policies.

The group first came together in 2000 (at the Château Wolfsberg in north-eastern Switzerland – hence the name) to draft AML guidelines for private banking in the wake of some very negative money laundering scandals which had affected the industry; *The Wolfsberg Anti-Money Laundering Principles for Private Banking* was subsequently published in October 2000 (and revised in May 2002). The group then published a *Statement on the Financing of Terrorism* in January 2002, and the *Wolfsberg Anti-Money Laundering Principles for Correspondent Banking* in November 2002. It has also produced a statement on *Monitoring, Screening and Searching* (September 2003).

Client identification and due diligence

Crucially, client identification requirements under Wolfsberg extend beyond the actual named client to the beneficial owners of account assets. The private banker is expected to understand the structure of companies and trusts sufficiently to establish who are the main players involved, and they must make a judgement as to whether to carry out further due diligence on the individuals and companies concerned. Due diligence must include:

- the client's reasons for opening the account;
- the client's expected levels of account activity;
- details of the business or other economic activity that has generated the client's wealth and an estimate of net worth ('Source of Wealth');
- details of the sources of funds to be paid into the account upon opening.

References or other corroboration of the details are also required, where that is possible, and it would normally be expected that a client would meet their banker face-to-face before opening the account.

Enhanced due diligence for higher-risk accounts

Extra caution is necessary, as would be expected, in cases where a client's money was sourced in high-risk or lightly regulated countries, or where the client is involved in an area of business known to be susceptible to money laundering activities, and where the client is known to send funds to countries associated with terrorist activity or where the client donates to causes in such countries. PEPs (who tend to favour the bespoke nature and privacy of private banking arrangements) also require additional due diligence (see below), and senior management must approve any new relationship with a PEP. Suspicious transactions (which may include large cash transactions, any account activity out of line with the customer profile, or 'pass-through' transactions) might be identified in a number of ways beyond the usual monitoring of the account. Suspicions might be triggered, for example, through third-party information from the media about a client, meetings with the client, or personal knowledge about factors such as the political situation in the client's country. The onus, according to Wolfsberg, is on the private banker to keep abreast of the 'bigger picture', as well as gaining and maintaining a thorough knowledge of the customer and their situation.

Specific CTF principals

The Wolfsberg Group supplemented its original principles, which focused on money laundering and other financial crimes in relation to private banks, with a further statement on best practice dealing with countering terrorist financing. This highlights the importance of name screening:

> *The proper identification of customers by financial institutions can improve the efficacy of searches against lists of known or suspected terrorists [applicable to that jurisdiction]. (27)*

To that end, it expands on existing identification, acceptance and due diligence best practice. Banks need to implement name-screening procedures and report any matches to the authorities; in addition they need to look at ways of speeding the retrieval of information about a customer if it is required.

Enhanced KYC policies should be in place for any customers involved in business sectors widely misused by terrorist groups, such as alternative remittance systems. Due diligence should be more extensive and rigorous on new business applications from such customers, and monitoring should be increased on both existing accounts and on those new accounts that meet the acceptance criteria. As a basic principle, banks should limit their business relationships with remittance businesses, exchange houses, bureaux de changes and money transfer agents to those which are subject to appropriate AML/CTF regulation.

The Wolfsberg statement recognizes that there is little chance that account monitoring will be able to identify individual transactions linked to specific terrorist attacks, but it emphasizes the importance of continuing to look for and report suspicious transactions on the grounds that such information could provide leads for intelligence services. In particular, it highlights the need to scrutinize more rigorously the account activities of any customer involved with business sectors known to be a conduit for terrorist funds, and the need for banks to try to spot patterns and trends in terrorist financing.

For film training on KYC in private banks, preview our DVD resource 'Too Good To Be True' at www.lessonslearned.co.uk/products.

Unusual/purposeless transactions (28)

As well as monitoring the various higher-risk categories of business outlined above, the World Bank/IMF guidelines emphasize the need for financial institutions to be alert, across the spectrum of their customer accounts, to any complex, unusually large transactions, and to unusual patterns of transactions without any obvious lawful purpose. They are instructed to look more closely at such transactions to establish as far as they can what is going on and why, and to keep a record of their findings. If they cannot obtain the information they want, or if their findings leave them still suspicious, they should consider turning the business away, and if necessary filing an STR.

BEST PRACTICE IN HIGH-RISK CUSTOMER GROUPS

Just as some kinds of financial services products are more likely than others to be exploited for illicit ends, so financial institutions are also expected to take a view on the likelihood that particular types of customer will pose a higher risk of involvement in criminal activity (including terrorist financing activity), and to adjust their due diligence, KYC and monitoring efforts accordingly.

Politically exposed persons (29)

Among the categories identified by the FATF, increased due diligence with regard to money laundering would be expected in the case of accounts for PEPs (senior people in prominent public positions in a foreign country, and their families or close associates). Bank staff would be expected to identify the PEP and their sources of wealth and funds; any new account in the PEP's name would have to be approved at senior management level, and more rigorous monitoring of the account would be required.

However, as the World Bank/IMF notes observe, 'Actually finding out whether a customer is a PEP is often the biggest challenge for a financial institution.' There is no official list of world PEPs to consult, for example, though 'rich lists' and other compilations are produced and updated commercially.

Business through intermediaries

Another potentially troublesome scenario involves clients introduced to financial institutions by intermediaries or other third parties, when the financial institution itself does not carry out the usual customer due diligence. In such instances, the IMF/World Bank guidance (30) recommends that banks should make sure that the agent who brought the new business is obliged by the relevant regulator in the agent's home country to perform customer due diligence, that they have in fact collected sufficient information about the customer in question, and that the information can be made available promptly if it is required.

Financial institutions need to be particularly careful when business is introduced to them by an agent based in another country. According to the IMF/World Bank commentary:

> *Several countries ... require that the introducer should be an individual or an institution that is subject to AML controls, is supervised by a regulatory body with responsibility for compliance with AML controls, and is located in a country that complies with FATF standards. (31)*

Customers from high-risk geographic locations

It is most important for financial institutions to be able to identify customers and transactions coming from high-risk parts of the world. They should exercise heightened caution dealing with countries branded by the FATF as non-cooperative in the fight against money laundering (NCCTs) and with countries in which there is terrorist-inspired conflict or where those who support such conflicts raise funds. Transactions with such countries are not prohibited, but they are considered to carry higher risks and should be scrutinized accordingly. Again, if a bank has any doubts that a transaction with an NCCT or country of concern is above board, it should think about declining the business and also consider filing an STR under its suspicion-reporting obligations. Additionally, the national security or regulatory authorities may have identified specific jurisdictions as being of particular concern (even though they are not on the NCCT list), as may the management of the financial institution itself if they have effective procedures in place for tracking the release of such information.

Banks and other financial institutions should also bear in mind that as the global marketplace becomes increasingly interconnected, it may become necessary to extend greater due diligence practices to other groups beyond their direct customers, particularly if there are higher-than-average risks attached to the relationship. These groups might include for example customer employees, correspondent banks as well as agents and suppliers working for their customers.

Charities and NPOs

As we have already seen in Chapter 5, charities and NPOs may be open to abuse by terrorist groups, often by diverting funds originally raised for humanitarian purposes. It is therefore crucial that financial institutions should carry out enhanced due diligence to ensure that they 'know their charity'. (32)

Senior management should approve any new relationship, and should bear in mind that there could be high risk attached to the business. A bank representative should visit the charity premises, meet the leaders and prepare a report on the visit, including such details as:

- the organization's legal type and the activities for which it is licensed, its sources of capital, the number of staff employed, number of years established at the present and previous addresses, the nature of its present activities and their geographical location;
- personal details for the directors/owners, and information about their powers;
- any involvement of a PEP;
- typical size and sources of donations;
- whether the charity is licensed to receive donations locally or overseas.

Financial institutions with charitable or NPO customers also need to monitor their accounts closely, and to be aware of potential red flags, such as the following:

- corporate layering or 'routing' – transfers between the charity's bank account and those of its directors or staff for no clear reason;
- wire transfers by charities or NPOs to beneficiaries based in countries known to be bank or tax havens, or countries of concern for terrorism purposes;
- lack of apparent fundraising activity (in other words, a lack of small cheques or typical donations) that would normally be connected with charitable bank deposits;
- transactions with no logical economic purpose (for example no link between the activity of the charitable organization and other parties involved in the transaction).

Voluntary best practice guidance for charities issued by the US Department of the Treasury is also worth mentioning. This guidance includes a section on financial accountability and practices (33) which may impact on charities' dealings with financial institutions holding their accounts, at least in so far as it shapes the typical NPO account activities and profile that a bank with charitable accounts might expect to see. These guidelines state that:

- the charity should have an annual budget, overseen by the board;
- there should be one individual appointed as the finance officer, with responsibility for day-to-day control over the charity's assets;
- charities with annual gross income over a $250000 limit should bring in an independent accounting firm to audit the accounts and produce a financial statement each year;
- full records of all money received and spent (including salaries and expenses both domestic and international) should be kept by the charity, with details of every charitable disbursement including the name of the recipient, the sum given and the date;

- as soon as money received has been recorded, it should be deposited in the charity's bank account;
- cash in particular should be paid in promptly;
- if possible, money to be disbursed should be sent by cheque or via a wire transfer rather than in currency;
- when the money is going to areas without normal financial services and there is no option but to send currency, funds should be provided in smaller increments for short-term needs, rather than large lump sums for longer periods;
- the charity should also keep detailed records of such currency payments.

SOURCES

1. FATF (2002), *Guidance for Financial Institutions in Detecting Terrorist Financing*, 24 April, p. 3.
2. Basel Committee on Banking Supervision (BCBS) (2004), *Consolidated KYC Risk Management*, October.
3. Drawn from Paul Allan Schott (2003), *Reference Guide to Anti-Money Laundering and Combating the Financing of Terrorism*, 2nd Edition (World Bank/IMF), Chapter VI.
4. Ibid., VI p. 3.
5. BCBS (2004), *KYC Risk Management*.
6. Schott (2003), *Reference Guide*, VI p. 16.
7. This section is based on IAIS (2004), *Guidance Paper on Anti Money Laundering and Combating the Financing of Terrorism*, October.
8. This section is drawn from IOSCO (2004), *Principles on Client Identification and Beneficial Ownership for the Securities Industry*, May.
9. Schott (2003), *Reference Guide*, VI p. 18.
10. FATF (2003), *Forty Recommendations*, No 13.
11. Office of the Comptroller of the Currency (OCC) (2002), *Money Laundering: a Banker's Guide to Avoiding Problems*, December, p. 13.
12. Schott (2003), *Reference Guide*, VI p. 21.
13. FATF (2003), *Forty Recommendations*, No 19.
14. Schott (2003), *Reference Guide*, VI p. 27.
15. Bank of England website www.bankofengland.co.uk.
16. Ibid., Financial Sanctions FAQs.
17. Ibid.
18. Schott (2003), *Reference Guide*, VI p. 9.
19. Ibid., VI p. 10.
20. Joint Money Laundering Steering Group (2006), *Prevention of Money Laundering/Combating the Financing of Terrorism*, April.
21. Ibid.
22. Ibid.
23. FATF, *Revised Interpretative Note to SR VII: Wire Transfers*, p. 2.
24. OCC (2002), *Money Laundering*, p. 15.
25. Wolfsberg Group (2002), *Anti-Money Laundering Principles for Private Banking*, May.
26. Ibid.
27. Wolfsberg Group (2002), *Statement on the Suppression of the Financing of Terrorism*, January.
28. Schott (2003), *Reference Guide*, VI p. 11.
29. Ibid., VI p. 8.
30. Ibid., VI p. 11.
31. Ibid.
32. Taken from Hany Abou-El-Fotouh (2005), 'Know your charity to protect against fraud and terrorist financing', *Money Laundering Alert* www.moneylaundering.com, December.
33. US Department of the Treasury (2005), *Anti-Terrorist Financing Guidelines: Voluntary Best Practices for US-Based Charities* (updated November), p. 4, www.terroristfinancing.com.

PART TWO

Training Activities

In the following chapters, we take some of the key learning points from the previous six chapters and convert them into ready-to-use training exercises. The materials in each case contain detailed trainers' notes dealing with the following:

'Training purpose' outlines the objectives of the training and the specific areas covered by it. It also suggests the context in which the training may take place – for example at induction, refresher or specialist training.

'Relevant reading' relates the training activity to the particular chapters within the book which are mostly closely associated with it.

'Overview' outlines the type of training activity, order and the format.

'Materials' lists the materials which are required in order to run the training session including which slides and handouts will be required from the accompanying CD-ROM.

'Timings' breaks down the overall timing of the whole session and the recommended times spent for each individual part of the session.

'Step-by-step session plan' describes in detail the steps needed to be taken to run the training session and also suggested words which can be used by the trainer. Many of the exercises involve the conduct of demonstrations or activities by the trainees themselves, and so there are complete instructions for this also.

The activities cover a range of different training tools and techniques and include videos, audio-visual slide shows, presentations, case studies, question-and-answer sessions, quizzes and account analyses as well as more traditional 'show and tell' slide presentations. Further details of relevant associated training can be found at our website www.lessonslearned.co.uk.

Money Laundering vs Terrorist Financing

Training purpose

Where training in countering terrorist financing gets tagged on to existing AML training, staff may come to the conclusion that there is no difference. There are, however, some distinct differences.

Put your scepticism aside when you read this activity. It is completely cross-cultural and actually demonstrates in a very visual and memorable way the essential components of both money laundering and terrorist financing, and the key differences between them. This exercise can be used as an ice breaker and as a lead-in to more detailed training on either topic.

Relevant reading

The issues dealt with in this activity can be further illustrated using details from the specific terrorist financing case studies described in Chapter 3 of this book. We would suggest in particular the case history for the funding of the Liberation Tigers of Tamil Elam, which we have referenced in the activity's closing comments.

Overview

The activity takes the form of two very simple demonstrations. With the help of volunteers selected from the group, and using real cash and other props, you demonstrate how items are bought and sold and the criminal or terrorist money 'turned over' many times in order to disguise the connection between source and criminal (in the case of money laundering) and source and terror attack (in the case of terrorist financing).

The power of the demonstrations is in the very visual format used. Participants can actually see the money moving around, they can see the process in action, and this makes the learning experience particularly memorable. A video showing this exercise in action has been included in the accompanying CD-ROM.

Materials

You will need to print out copies of the 'AML and CTF Demonstration Materials' from the CD-ROM provided with this pack. The materials include a 'deposit receipt', a 'share certificate', a 'property deed' and a 'banker's draft'. You will also need the 'Terrorist Financing Process' slide from the CD-ROM, and suitable projection equipment.

In addition you will need nine volunteers from the trainee group to assist you, plus a range of other materials:

- some small denomination currency notes
- a toy sports car (for example, a Porsche or Ferrari)
- a toy firearm
- some apples, oranges or other fruit as available.

Timings

You will need about 15 minutes in total:

- five minutes to brief and prepare participants
- five minutes for the demonstration activity
- five minutes to de-brief and summarize.

STEP-BY-STEP SESSION PLAN

Ask for seven volunteers to help you demonstrate how money laundering works. Select your volunteers, and ask them to stand in a line facing the rest of the training group. From left to right along your line of volunteers, distribute the following materials:

- Volunteer 1 (V1) – currency notes
- Volunteer 2 (V2) – deposit receipt/cheque
- Volunteer 3 (V3) – bond certificate
- Volunteer 4 (V4) – deposit receipt/cheque
- Volunteer 5 (V5) – property deed
- Volunteer 6 (V6) – banker's draft
- Volunteer 7 (V7) – a toy sports car.

Ask your volunteers to hold up the materials you have given them so they can be clearly seen by the rest of the group. Introduce your demonstration as follows:

- Money laundering always starts with a crime that generates illegal cash for the criminal.
- The crime might be anything – illegal drug dealing, extortion, fraud, people trafficking, tax evasion, and so on.
- The crime in this demonstration is going to be a theft.

Point to something to distract V1 and, whilst V1 is looking away, 'steal' the currency notes they are holding. Explain what has just taken place:

- You have stolen V1's cash.
- This stolen cash is *dirty money* – money which has been obtained criminally.
- Before you can use this money you need to hide where you got it from – you need to *launder* it.

Move down your line of volunteers, carrying out the series of transactions described below:

- *'Can I deposit this money please?'* Exchange your stolen cash for V2's deposit receipt/cheque.
- *'Can I buy that Government Bond from you?'* Exchange your deposit/cheque receipt for V3's bond certificate.
- *'Would you like to buy this Bond?'* Exchange your bond certificate for V4's deposit receipt/cheque.
- *'Can I buy that lovely house from you?'* Exchange your deposit receipt/cheque for V5's property deed.
- *'Would you like to buy this house?'* Exchange your property deed for V6's banker's draft.
- *'I really like this sports car, can I buy it from you?'* Exchange your banker's draft for V7's toy car.

Turn to the group to summarize what has happened:

- The money you originally stole has been converted into many different forms.
- The money you have at the end no longer has a clear connection with the original crime.
- The money has been *laundered* and can be used to buy something you really want, such as a luxury car.

Highlight that there are three distinct phases to the process you have demonstrated:

- the moment at which criminally obtained money is first put into the system (the deposit placed with V2) – called 'placement';
- the movement of the money through a series of transactions with no real economic purpose (the various interim transactions such as the buying and selling of shares) – called 'layering';
- the eventual use of the money for a genuine economic purpose (the purchase of a sports car from V7) – called 'integration'.

Ask for two additional volunteers to help you to demonstrate the difference between money laundering and terrorist financing. Position your new volunteers (V8 and V9) to the right of V7. Once again, distribute materials to your volunteers as follows:

- V1 – currency notes/cash
- V2 – deposit receipt/cheque
- V3 – bond certificate
- V4 – deposit receipt/cheque
- V5 – property deed
- V6 – banker's draft
- V7 – currency notes/cash
- V8 – replica gun
- V9

Introduce your demonstration as follows:

- The people who give money to terrorists can be perfectly law-abiding citizens, who may not even know that the money given will be used for terrorism.
- Or they may sympathize with the terrorist's cause and be prepared to fund it from their legitimate business activities.
- The methods used by the terrorists to obtain money might therefore not be criminal at all, they might be legitimate.
- Selling fruit, for example, is a perfectly legal way to obtain money from people.

Pick up a selection of fruit in your hand and turn to V1 to start your demonstration:

- *'Would you like to buy this fruit from me?'* Exchange your fruit for V1's cash.
- *'Could I deposit this with your charity?'* Exchange your cash for V2's deposit receipt/cheque.
- *'Can I buy that Government Bond from you?'* Exchange the deposit receipt/ cheque for V3's bond certificate.
- *'Would you like to buy this Bond?'* Exchange the bond certificate for V4's deposit receipt/cheque.
- *'Can I buy that house, please?'* Exchange your cash for V5's property deed.
- *'Would you like to buy this house from me?'* Exchange the property deed for V6's banker's draft.
- *'Can I deposit this and withdraw cash?'* Exchange bankers draft for V7's currency notes/cash.
- *'Will you sell me that gun?'* Exchange your cash for V8's gun.
- *'My friend, we meet again. Take this, and good luck.'* Give your gun to V9.

Highlight how this process differs from the process demonstrated previously:

- The origins of the money are not always criminal and can, in fact, be quite legitimate (for example, the legitimate purchase of fruit from V1).

- Whereas with money laundering the crime is what *generates* the money, with terrorism it is the money which *enables* the crime – the other way around.
- The money laundering activity is intended to disguise the connection between the fund-raisers and their activities, and the terrorist acts made possible by their fund-raising.

Show the slide, 'Terrorist Financing Process'. Use the slide to reinforce the point that funds for terrorism *can* be generated by crime (for example, drug trafficking, extortion) as well as from legitimate sources (for example, donations obtained via lawful means, profits obtained from legitimate business activity).

If you want at this point to use a specific case as an example, then we suggest you use the Liberation Tigers of Tamil Elam (LTTE). Chapter 3 of this book identifies five main sources of fund-raising by LTTE, some legitimate and some criminal:

- voluntary donations paid to LTTE by Tamil diaspora around the world;
- extorted 'donations' paid by Tamil diaspora who are threatened with exposure to the immigration authorities in their country of residence, or with harm to relatives back home;
- diversion of funds from NGOs and charities involved with Tamil social services and development programmes in Sri Lanka;
- profits from legitimate commercial ventures such as fruit canning, petrol retail, travel agencies, jewellery retail and so on;
- proceeds from criminal activities such as drug smuggling, people trafficking and so on.

Point out that existing AML measures are designed to help detect the proceeds of crime and can, therefore, have a counter-terrorism impact where the terrorist funds in question have originated from crime.

Point out in contrast that where legally obtained terrorist funds are concerned, there is nothing in the transaction itself to indicate any illegal intent or purpose, other than a specific knowledge or suspicion that the named parties involved might have a connection with terrorism. Stress the importance, therefore, of checking and cross-referencing customer entities' names against lists of known terrorists and terrorist supporters.

Distribute copies of the slide as a handout, check for questions, and close the session.

Overview of Terrorist Financing Typologies

Training purpose

Training in typologies is a powerful way to raise staff awareness of the various ways in which terrorist groups might use the international financial system to collect funds and move them around, ultimately distributing them to the active cells who commit the terror attacks.

This activity uses the vehicle of four real-life case studies to get participants thinking about terrorist financing typologies, familiarizing them with some of the methods typically used by terror groups to collect and move funds around.

Relevant reading

The cases used in this training activity are discussed in detail in Chapter 3 of this book. The audio-visual materials used by participants in fact mirror much of the content of Chapter 3. You may find it useful to read through this chapter in detail and to make your own notes as part of your preparation for this activity.

Overview

As explained above the activity uses the vehicle of four case studies to examine the methods used by four well-known terrorist movements: al-Qaeda, Jemaah Islamiyah, the Liberation Tigers of Tamil Eelam (Tamil Tigers) and the Provisional IRA. The activities of the last group have moderated in recent years as a result of political recognition and negotiation to resolve its grievances. The first three groups are still active.

The case studies are provided as an audio-visual presentation. Participants select from an on-screen menu listing the four case studies. Selecting any of the menu options will trigger off a short audio-visual presentation of the relevant case study.

Participants discuss the case studies they have been allocated. Their views and ideas are then pulled together in a facilitated full-group discussion. If they want to re-play any case study, then they can do so.

You do not have to use all four case studies. You can work with just one case study if time is short, although we would suggest a minimum of two as a better approach.

Materials

You will need to set up your training room with several sound enabled PCs or laptops spaced around the available area. Participants will need to work in discussion groups at these computers (we suggest a maximum of four participants per group).

You will need to have loaded onto each computer a copy of the 'Terrorist Finances Dissected' presentation from the CD-ROM provided with this book.

You will also need the 'Terrorist Financing Case Study Questions' slide from the CD-ROM, plus suitable projection equipment for yourself and your own laptop.

You will also need copies of the 'Terrorist Financing Case Study Notes' handout from the CD-ROM, for participants to take notes as they work through the activity.

Timings

For the small group discussions, we suggest at least 20 minutes per case study. For the full-group session we suggest ten minutes to discuss and debrief on each case study used. In short, you will need to allow approximately 30 minutes for each case study you decide to use.

STEP-BY-STEP SESSION PLAN

Divide participants into groups of about four people, and allocate each group to a PC or laptop. The menu for the case study presentation should be showing on the screen.

When groups have settled, take a couple of minutes to introduce the activity. Explain that they are going to be looking at some real case studies of terrorist groups and their financial methods. Explain which of the four cases they will be looking at (as stated above, you will need to decide beforehand which cases to use). Explain that they can access the case studies by clicking on the relevant link showing on their screen.

Show the slide, 'Terrorist Financing Case Study Questions'. Use the slide to introduce the questions that they will need to discuss and answer as they watch each case study:

- What legal and illegal sources of funding have typically been used by terrorist groups?
- How is this money hidden and moved around by the terrorists?
- To what extent might typical AML measures help in the detection and reporting of suspected terrorist financing?
- What additional CTF measures might also be necessary?

Set a time limit for each case study (as explained above, we suggest a total of 20 minutes per case study for group discussions).

Distribute copies of the 'Terrorist Financing Case Study Notes' handout. Check that participants understand what is required, and then set them working on their discussion tasks.

Stop group discussions at the end of the allotted time and bring everyone back into the main group. Taking each case in turn, work through the questions and debrief groups on their views, drawing together conclusions and summarizing key points as appropriate. Check for any final questions before closing.

Use the notes below as a guide to the key points that you could perhaps aim to draw out in your summaries. You may also find it useful to refer to Chapter 3 of this book, which gives a much more complete account of the fund-raising and terrorist financing activities involved.

GUIDE NOTES

Sources of funds

Al-Qaeda

- donations from charities, NPOs, mosques and individual donors, made via web links, fund-raising, intermediaries/facilitators, as zakat paid to imams and so on;
- criminal activities including drug trafficking, trade in 'blood' diamonds, gold, tanzanite and other precious gems.

Jemaah Islamayah

- funds diverted from charitable causes, with or without the donors' knowledge;
- criminally derived funds from robbery, kidnapping and extortion.

Tamil Tigers

- voluntary payments from diaspora (both legal expatriates and illegal immigrants);
- funds extorted from diaspora under threat of exposure to the immigration authorities, or harm to their families;
- funds diverted from charities and NPOs;
- legitimate business activities carried out by front companies;
- criminal activities including drug smuggling, counterfeiting, gun-running, people trafficking and so on.

Provisional IRA

- Noraid (funds raised by US-based Irish Catholics);
- state sponsorship from Libya;
- EEC farm subsidy scam (where 'farmers' claim financial support for exporting produce, and then smuggle the exported produce back in to the Republic, for re-export);
- legitimate business ventures including pubs and cab companies;
- protection activities (where protection money is extorted from local businesses, under threat of violence);
- other criminal activities including kidnapping, robbery, theft, fraud and smuggling.

Movement of funds

Al-Qaeda

- use of global banking system – wire transfers, ATM and credit card withdrawals – to move funds across international boundaries;
- use of *hawala* banking system – largely unregulated, allows for anonymous, global movement of money;
- couriers – physical importation and exportation of cash and other easily cashed assets such as gem stones.

Jemaah Islamiyah

- use of shell and front companies to clean criminally derived money and as a vehicle (via commercial transactions) for moving money across borders;
- use of *hawala* banking system as above.

Tamil Tigers

- movement of money via a global network of legitimate businesses and aid organizations (this network providing access to a range of commercial money transmission methods);
- investments handled through intermediaries – often Tamil diaspora resident overseas.

Provisional IRA

- use of couriers and bank transfers to collect money from American donors;
- use of loans to local businesses as a way to clean criminally derived money and extract a profit at the same time, in the form of loan interest payments;
- use of front companies and the commercial vehicles these provide for the storage and movement of money.

Effectiveness of AML measures in combating terrorist financing

The key conclusion has to be that AML measures are geared to the detection of criminally derived money, and that they are therefore as likely to detect terrorists' ill-gotten gains as any other criminals' profits from crime.

You might want to highlight a few specifics, for example:

- AML regimes typically require that customers are adequately identified before any financial transactions are executed on their behalf; the absence of such a requirement at the United Arab Emirates Exchange Center made it easier for al-Qaeda agents to move funds to their operatives in the US without being detected.
- The preference of Islamist terror groups for the *hawala* banking system highlights the potential weakness of unregulated financial systems that do not require specific records to be kept of transactions.
- The use of corporate structures – both front and shell companies – to launder, process and move terrorist funds around highlights the importance of understanding the ownership structures behind companies and their assets, and being able to ascertain whether or not a company is likely to have a terrorist connection.

A key problem with identifying Type 1 terrorist financing (that is, the back-end funding of the terrorist group itself) is that the sources of funds are not necessarily criminal. Detection measures which are geared to detecting the proceeds of crime may not, therefore, be entirely effective.

There is a further problem regarding the detection of Type 2 financing (that is, where the funds are moved to active terrorist operatives, for use in planning and executing terrorist attacks). The difficulty lies in the fact that terrorists' purchases, accommodation and travel arrangements and so on do not necessarily look any different from anyone else's. The transactions are often small, unremarkable and give no real grounds for suspicion.

Traditional KYC and due diligence measures are not necessarily effective in these circumstances. Unless there is something actively suspicious or unusual about the transaction, or about the actual customer, it is unlikely to be picked up by routine AML activities.

Additional CTF measures

One obvious measure which has been widely introduced is the requirement to screen customers' names against terrorist lists (for example the OFAC and EU lists). This is, of course, only effective insofar as a particular individual or entity has a known involvement in terrorism.

Participants may feel that there is nothing which financial institutions can do to detect the undetectable (that is, where the terrorists are individuals or entities with no known terrorist connections, engaging in what appear to be unremarkable activities).

You may want to point out, however, that there are some ways in which financial institutions can realistically minimise the risk of involvement with terrorist financing, for example:

- a 'risk-based' approach to new business take-on, where individuals and entities from jurisdictions known to constitute a higher risk, and engaging in transactions that present an increased risk, are subjected to an elevated standard of scrutiny;
- staff training and education (for example, this activity) to develop understanding of terrorist financing and ability in recognizing some of its possible features – particularly those of Type 1 financing.
- a rigorous adherence to identification and KYC procedures and other preventive measures.

Point out that there is also room for the international community to work more closely and effectively together in ironing out loopholes. For example, you could close by referring to the FATF's Nine Special Recommendations for detecting, preventing and suppressing the financing of terrorism and terrorist acts. These respond to many of the features specifically identified in the case studies. The Nine Special Recommendations are that countries should:

- ratify and implement UN instruments relating to the prevention and suppression of terrorist financing;
- criminalize the financing of terrorism and associated money laundering;
- freeze and confiscate terrorist assets;
- report suspicious transactions relating to terrorism;
- cooperate on an international scale with regard to counter-terrorist intelligence, investigations and proceedings;
- ensure that all money transmission services (including *hawala*-type schemes) are licensed or registered and subject to regulation;
- make it mandatory to attach originator information to wire transfers and to maintain a detailed audit trail of the transfer from origination to destination;
- review laws and regulations relating to NPOs and other entities which may be open to abuse for terrorist financing purposes;
- put in place measures to detect the physical movement of cash and bearer negotiable instruments across international borders.

Terrorist Financing and the Law

Training purpose

Staff in financial institutions who handle (or manage those who handle) customer transactions need to have an understanding of the law in relation to terrorist financing, the obligations which it places upon them and the penalties for non-compliance.

This activity provides a stimulating and interactive alternative to the usual dry 'law talk' that can be typical for the delivery of this kind of information to staff.

Relevant reading

Chapter 4 of this book provides a general overview of internationally agreed treaties and legal standards. It also provides specific information about the relevant local laws in the UK, the US and Hong Kong. If your jurisdiction falls outside of the scope covered by this book then you will need to refer to or seek guidance on your local laws and what they require. Use the quiz structure in this activity as a basis from which to develop your own, customized, local law quiz.

Overview

The activity takes the form of a competitive team quiz, with the facilitator in the role of quizmaster. Participants work in their teams to discuss and answer a series of ten questions about the law, which are projected one at a time on to a screen by the facilitator. When all ten questions have been completed, teams swap answer sheets and mark each others' answers. The winning team is, of course, the team with the most correct answers. This exercise can be used as part of a wider programme, leading into more detailed presentations about legal requirements and how they affect the organization's policies.

Materials

You will need:

- a relevant 'Law Quiz' presentation (if you are UK or US based, then you can use the presentations on the CD-ROM provided with this book);
- paper and pens for participants to take notes;
- sufficient space for participants to be able to talk and work in teams of 4–6 people.

Timings

You will need approximately 1 hour in total:

- 30 minutes for teams to discuss and answer the questions (three minutes per question);
- 30 minutes to review and debrief on the correct answers in plenary.

STEP-BY-STEP SESSION PLAN

Ask participants to form into teams of 4–6 people and distribute paper and pens to each team. Show the first slide of your presentation.

Explain that you are going to give teams an opportunity to prove that they know all about the anti-terrorism and anti-terrorist financing provisions of their local law.

Explain that to prove their knowledge they will need to complete a short quiz. Show the second slide in your presentation and give a brief overview of how the quiz will work:

- There are ten questions.
- Teams must discuss and write their answers to the questions on a single sheet of paper.
- At the end of the quiz, each team must pass its answers to another team for marking.
- The winner is the team with the most correct answers out of ten.

Check that everyone understands what is required of them. When you are ready, use your mouse to click on the box marked '1' on Slide 2.

Question 1 should now be showing on your screen. Give participants time to read the question at the top of the screen. Give them two to three minutes to discuss and agree their answers, then click on the '2' at the bottom of your screen to move to question 2.

As before, give participants a couple of minutes to read through and agree their answers to question 2, then click on the '3' at the bottom of your screen to move to question 3.

Repeat this process for the remaining questions. When participants have finished answering question 10, simply click where it says 'return to top' on your screen. This will take you back to Slide 2.

Ask teams if they would like to have another, final look at any of the questions. Click on the numbered boxes to link back to any of the questions as requested. Clicking on the 'return to top' box at the bottom of each question slide will always return you to Slide 2.

When participants have had time to review their answers, ask teams to exchange answer papers with each other.

Work through to discuss and mark the answers to the questions one at a time. Click on the box marked '1' on Slide 2 to go to question 1. When participants have given you their answers to question 1, click on the Forward (→) button on your keyboard and this will take you to the answer screen for question 1.

Click on the Forward button again to move to question 2, and again to see the answer screen for question 2. Keep clicking on the Forward button to move through the questions and answers until you have reviewed the answers for all ten questions.

Use the explanatory notes at the foot of each answer slide to help you explain and discuss the answers with the various teams. Additional notes are also provided below.

COMMENTARY TO QUESTIONS – UK LAW

Question 1

The UN International Convention for the Suppression of the Financing of Terrorism was first adopted in December 1999. The resultant Treaty criminalizes the act of providing or collecting funds that are intended or known to be designated for terrorist purposes.

There are a number of other international resolutions, treaties and agreements designed to ensure effective cooperation between countries in the fight against terrorism and terrorist funding. In particular you might wish to mention the FATF's Nine Special Recommendations in relation to countering terrorist financing:

- ratification and implementation of UN instruments relating to the prevention and suppression of terrorist financing;
- criminalizing the financing of terrorism and associated money laundering;
- freezing and confiscating terrorist assets;
- reporting suspicious transactions relating to terrorism;
- international cooperation concerning counter-terrorist intelligence, investigations and proceedings;
- requirement to ensure that all money transmission services (including *hawala*-type schemes) are licensed or registered and subject to regulation;

- requirement to attach originator information to wire transfers and to maintain a detailed audit trail of the transfer from origination to destination;
- requirement to review laws and regulations relating to NPOs and other entities which may be open to abuse for terrorist financing purposes;
- requirement to put in place measures to detect the physical movement of cash and bearer negotiable instruments across international borders.

Question 2

The Terrorism Act 2000 cites the names of various international organizations and entities which have been proscribed and outlawed within the UK as terrorist organizations. The list is reviewed and updated from time-to-time. At the beginning of 2006 as many as 40 organizations were listed as 'proscribed organizations'.

Under new UK legislation outlawing the *financing and supporting* of terrorism, it is now a criminal offence not only to belong to a proscribed organization, but also to give any form of financial or other support to such an organization.

The OFAC list given as the first answer option for this question is a US-generated list of 'specially designated nationals' (SDNs), that is, people or entities for whom it is against the law to provide financial services. SDNs on this list include known terrorists and terrorist organizations; known narcotics traffickers; organizations known to support or finance terrorism and other crimes; certain government entities and officials; certain shipping vessels known to have a connection with terrorism or other crimes.

The FATF NCCT list given as the third answer option is the Financial Action Task Force's 'Non-Cooperative Countries and Territories' list. The countries listed here are those identified by the FATF as being non-cooperative with its 40 AML recommendations. In 2000 and 2001 a total of 23 countries were listedbut the list has been reducing as countries have complied.

Question 3

All three of the actions described could be interpreted under UK law to constitute terrorism offences.

Section 11 of the Terrorism Act 2000 specifically outlaws membership of a 'proscribed organization', that is, an organization that has been identified under UK law as a terrorist organization.

Section 12 of the Act outlaws any action that invites or provides support for a proscribed organization, for example, attending meetings, or assisting in the arrangement of such meetings.

Section 13 outlaws the wearing of clothing, insignia and so on to indicate the bearer's membership of or support for a proscribed organization.

Section 15 outlaws any action designed to raise funds or make funds or property available to a proscribed organization.

Section 18 outlaws any action intended to launder or assist the laundering of terrorist funds.

Question 4

Section 15 of the Terrorism Act 2000 makes it an offence for a person to provide money or other property when they know, or have reason to suspect, that it will or may be used for terrorist purposes.

Clearly, if a person *knows* that a particular organization is involved in terrorism and, knowing this, still chooses to give a donation to that organization, then under Section 15 of the Act they will have committed a criminal offence.

Question 5

The answer here is that, if you have *any* suspicions at all, then you must make a report to your institution's designated reporting officer. There is no defence for giving someone the benefit of the doubt, for choosing to ignore a suspicion, or deciding not to report it.

Section 19 of the Terrorism Act 2000 makes it quite clear that it is a criminal offence to fail to report a knowledge or suspicion of terrorist financing.

Question 6

Section 11 of the Terrorism Act 2000 specifies that a person guilty of membership of a proscribed organization shall be liable upon conviction on indictment, to imprisonment for a term not exceeding ten years, to a fine, or both.

The penalty identified under Section 12 for those guilty of supporting a proscribed organization other than by financial means.

Question 7

Section 22 of the Terrorism Act 2000 specifies that laundering of terrorist funds (or involvement in such activity) may lead to a penalty upon conviction on indictment of 14 years in prison, a fine, or both.

Question 8

The UNSC has implemented a number of mandatory sanctions aimed at stopping the financing of terrorist organizations. UNSCR 1267 was aimed at cutting off funding to the Taliban, and a further resolution UNSCR 1333 specifically targets al-Qaeda. UNSCR 1373 extends the sanctions regime through the deployment of the proscribed list of Specially Designated Names and suspected terrorists and terrorist organizations. UNSCR 1390 further strengthened the sanctions against remaining elements of the Taliban, al-Qaeda and other terror groups. These UN resolutions require cooperating countries (including the UK) to freeze assets belonging to or connected with any individuals or organizations named in UN sanctions lists. In the UK, these lists are given on the sanctions page of the Bank of England website (www.bankofengland.co.uk). UK financial institutions are immediately alerted and kept up to date with any changes in the lists.

Section 17 of the Terrorism Act 2000 further reinforces the obligation on banks and financial institutions to disrupt the availability of terrorist funds, by prohibiting any involvement in any arrangement which would make funds or other property available where there is a known or suspected intention to use such property for terrorist financing purposes. In other words, if you went ahead and processed a requested transfer even though you suspected that its intended destination had a connection with terrorism, then you would be breaking the law.

Question 9

Section 4 of the UK Anti-Terrorism, Crime and Security Act 2001 extends the freezing powers of the authorities to virtually any entity at all, including funds owned by the governments of other countries or territories, where it is believed that those funds might have an intended or potential terrorist purpose.

Question 10

Section 11 of the UK Anti-Terrorism, Crime and Security Act 2001 requires only that the authorities 'reasonably believe' the persons who are the subject of a freezing order to have a connection with terrorism. The case does not have to be proven, or any formal charges made, in order for the freezing order to take effect or be lawful.

COMMENTARY TO QUESTIONS – US LAW

Question 1

The UN International Convention for the Suppression of the Financing of Terrorism was first adopted in December 1999. The resultant Treaty criminalizes the act of providing or collecting funds that are intended or known to be designated for terrorist purposes.

There are a number of other international resolutions, treaties and agreements designed to ensure effective cooperation between countries in the fight against terrorism and terrorist funding. In particular you might wish to mention the FATF's Nine Special Recommendations in relation to countering terrorist financing:

- ratification and implementation of UN instruments relating to the prevention and suppression of terrorist financing;
- criminalizing the financing of terrorism and associated money laundering;

- freezing and confiscating terrorist assets;
- reporting suspicious transactions relating to terrorism;
- international cooperation re counter-terrorist intelligence, investigations and proceedings;
- requirement to ensure that all money transmission services (including *hawala*-type schemes) are licensed or registered and subject to regulation;
- requirement to attach originator information to wire transfers and to maintain a detailed audit trail of the transfer from origination to destination;
- requirement to review laws and regulations relating to NPOs and other entities which may be open to abuse for terrorist financing purposes;
- requirement to put in place measures to detect the physical movement of cash and bearer negotiable instruments across international borders.

Question 2

Section 326 (Verification of Identification) of the USA PATRIOT Act (2001) specifies that financial institutions are required *as a minimum* to comply with reasonable procedures for:

- verifying the identify of any person seeking to open an account to the extent reasonable and practicable;
- maintaining records of the information used to verify a person's identity, including name, address and other identifying information;
- consulting lists of known or suspected terrorists or terrorist organizations provided to the financial institution by any government agency to determine whether a person seeking to open an account appears on any such list.

The last point is in essence a requirement that all US persons and companies must comply with OFAC (Office of Foreign Assets Control) Regulations. OFAC Regulations define 'Specially Designated Nationals and Blocked Persons' as '... individuals and entities which are owned or controlled by, or acting for or on behalf of, Governments of target countries ... [that is, blacklisted countries] ... or are associated with international narcotics trafficking or terrorism.' The Regulations go on to specify that 'These individuals and entities are listed on the Treasury Department's Specially Designated Nationals and Blocked Persons list so that persons subject to the jurisdiction of the United States will know that they are prohibited from dealing with them and that they must block all property within their possession or control in which these individuals and entities have an interest.'

In short, as part of account opening procedures, all US-based financial institutions must check the given identity of the account opening entity against this list and, if a genuine match occurs, to block all property they may hold in association with that entity. This name-checking and blocking is seen as an essential countermeasure against terrorist financing and exists not only in the US, but in many other territories too.

Question 3

As stated above, OFAC Regulations require that prospective customers' names are checked against any officially produced list of Specially Designated Nationals or Blocked Persons. Entities named in such lists will include any known or suspected terrorists, or terrorist groups, or entities known or suspected to support or facilitate terrorism.

If a genuine match occurs between the prospective customer and an entity named on such a list, then the institution in question must *not*: a) carry out further business for the customer; b) forward funds or assets for that customer to other locations; c) return any deposits to the customer. In short, it must place an immediate freeze on any deposits or assets placed with them by that customer.

Section 2339B of Chapter 113B, Title 18 of the United States Code (Providing material support or resources to designated foreign terrorist organizations) states the following (2339B, (b)):

> *Financial institutions: Except as authorized by the Secretary, any financial institution that becomes aware that it has possession or, of control over, any funds in which a foreign terrorist organization, or its agent, has an interest, shall-*
>
> *(A) retain possession of, or maintain control over, such funds; and*
>
> *(B) report to the Secretary the existence of such funds in accordance with regulations issued by the Secretary.*

Question 4

Banking services and facilities are clearly the kind of material support that terrorists might seek to obtain with or without the knowledge of the parties that provide it. The provision of such material is criminalized under US law. Section 2339B of Chapter 113B, Title 18 of the United States Code (Providing material support or resources to designated foreign terrorist organizations) states the following (2339B, (a)):

> *Unlawful conduct: Whoever knowingly provides material support or resources to a foreign terrorist organization, or attempts or conspires to do so, shall be fined under this title or imprisoned for not more than 15 years, or both, and, if the death of any person results, shall be imprisoned for any term of years or for life. To violate this paragraph, a person must have knowledge that the organization is a designated terrorist organization (as defined in subsection (g)(6)), that the organization has engaged or engages in terrorist activity (as defined in section 212 (a)(3)(b) or the Immigration and Nationality Act), or that the organization has engaged or engages in terrorism (as defined in section 140(d)(2) of the Foreign Relations Authorization Act, Fiscal Years 1988 and 1989).*

Question 5

Under the 'Travel Rule' (codified at 31 CFR 103.33) a financial institution must, for each funds transfer or transmittal of $3 000 or more that it executes, include information that can enable the transaction to be traced back to it as the executor and, as far as possible, to any previous institution or entity from which it received the original order. The idea is to ensure that, at each stage as a payment travels to and through various institutions, it should remain clear who the order came from, and who it is going to.

Information that must be transmitted within the payment order includes:

- name of transmitter
- account number of transmitter (if transmittal is ordered from an account)
- address of transmitter
- amount of transmittal order
- execution date of transmittal order
- identity of the recipient's institution
- name and address or numerical identifier of the transmitter's financial institution
- as many of the following items as are received with the transmittal order:
  - name and address of recipient
  - account number of recipient
  - any other specific identifier of the beneficiary, e.g., CHIPS or D-U-N-S identifier).

Question 6

As for question 4, the provision of material support to terrorist entities is a criminal offence. Section 2339B of Chapter 113B, Title 18 of the United States Code (Providing material support or resources to designated foreign terrorist organizations) states the following (2339B, (a)):

> *Unlawful conduct: Whoever knowingly provides material support or resources to a foreign terrorist organization, or attempts or conspires to do so, shall be fined under this title or imprisoned not more than 15 years, or both, and, if the death of any person results, shall be imprisoned for any term of years or for life. To violate this paragraph, a person must have knowledge that the organization is a designated terrorist organization (as defined in subsection (g)(6)), that the organization has engaged or engages in terrorist activity (as defined in section 212 (a)(3)(b) or the Immigration and Nationality Act), or that the organization has engaged or engages in terrorism (as defined in section 140(d)(2) of the Foreign Relations Authorization Act, Fiscal Years 1988 and 1989).*

Question 7

As for questions 4 and 6 above, the concern here is with the criminalization of any activity that knowingly provides material support to terrorists, including the giving of donations to support terrorism. Anyone found guilty of such an act may be liable to the penalties described under question 6, above.

Question 8

The Bank Secrecy Act ordinarily places very severe duties and obligations on financial institutions with regard to the confidentiality of any entities whose information they may hold. However, Section 351 of the USA PATRIOT Act (a reinforcement of Section 5318(g)(3) of Title 31 of the United States Code) assures civil liability immunity for disclosures of customer information by financial institutions in relation to known or suspected criminality.

Section 351 of the PATRIOT Act reads as follows:

> *Any financial institution that makes a voluntary disclosure of any possible violation of law or regulation to a government agency or makes a disclosure pursuant to this subsection or any other authority, and any director, officer, employee, or agent of such institution who makes, or required another to make any such disclosure, shall not be liable to any person under any law or regulation of the United States, any constitution, law, or regulation of any State or political subdivision of any State, or under any contract or other legally enforceable agreement (including any arbitration agreement), for such disclosure or for any failure to provide notice of such disclosure to the person who is the subject of such disclosure or any other person identified in the disclosure.*

Question 9

The USA PATRIOT Act amends Section 5318 of Title 31 of the United States Code, with regard to the timescales within which financial institutions must respond to regulators' and law enforcement agencies' requests for compliance information and customer information.

Section 319 (b) of the Act include the following paragraph:

> *120-Hour Rule: Not later than 120 hours after receiving a request by an appropriate Federal banking agency for information related to anti-money laundering compliance by a covered financial institution or a customer of such institution, a covered financial institution shall provide to the appropriate Federal banking agency, or make available at a location specified by the representative of the appropriate Federal banking agency, information and account documentation for any account opened, maintained, administered or managed in the United States by the covered financial institution.*

Question 10

A key aspect of the USA PATRIOT Act is its facilitation of 'special measures' which may be imposed as determined by the relevant US Government bodies, in relation to products, jurisdictions, entities and so on that are perceived to constitute a higher potential risk of association with money laundering or terrorist financing. This question is an opportunity for participants to identify as far as possible those activities which are subject to such special measures (as listed on the answer slide for this question).

'Does It Look Suspicious?' Case Study Exercise

Training purpose

This activity uses a case study approach to introduce participants to the kinds of indicators that might signal a potential connection with terrorist financing. In some retail environments where straight-through processing removes human review and where risk assessment mechanisms mean that many accounts will not appear above the monitoring radar, some of these cases would not be spotted. Nevertheless, if the exercise raises awareness then it will have achieved something. Human awareness needs to compliment the reliance on systems.

In other words, the aim is to help participants to develop an understanding of what to look for, so they are better able to recognize possible terrorist financing.

Relevant reading

The issues dealt with in this activity are discussed more fully in Chapter 5 of this book. In your debrief session you may find it useful to draw on the case studies in the chapter as further illustrations of the methods used by terrorists to conceal the origins and/or movements of terrorist funds.

Overview

The activity revolves around five case studies, delivered to participants in an HTML format on a PC or laptop. The case studies look at five separate relationships held at branches of the fictitious Alnabank. Each case study takes the form of a series of three documents. The documents in each case vary:

- in Case 1, participants are presented with an account application and two account statements;

- in Case 2, participants work through a series of three letters from an intermediary;
- in Case 3, participants examine the ID of the account holder, and two account statements for her account;
- in Case 4, they view a fund-raising leaflet issued by a humanitarian charity and two account statements for the charity's Alnabank account;
- in Case 5, they see a joint account application, a letter from the account holder to the Bank, and an account statement;

Working in small groups, participants select each case study on-screen. They are given some background information about the account holding entity/individual in the case they are studying. They are also given a series of questions to answer about the case. They access and view the case documents on-screen, discussing and answering the questions and making notes as they go. The activity closes with a plenary discussion, during which participants share and discuss their case study findings with the facilitator and other groups.

This activity can be used as a detailed session on suspicion recognition within a wider CTF training programme.

Materials

You will need to set up your training room with several PCs or laptops set spaced around the available area. Participants will need to work in discussion groups at these computers (we suggest a maximum of 3–4 participants per group).

You will need to have loaded onto each computer a copy of the 'Does It Look Suspicious? CTF Case Studies' presentation from the CD-ROM provided with this book.

You may also want to provide paper and pens for participants to take notes as they work through the case studies.

If you do not have access to sufficient PCs to give everyone access to the case studies, you could alternatively print the case study materials out. You would need to print:

- copies of the three documents for each case;

- copies of the background information for each case (you will find this in the presentation itself);
- copies of the questions to be answered for each case (again, you will find these in the presentation).

Timings

For the small group discussions we suggest at least ten minutes per case study, plus a further five–ten minutes per case for plenary discussion and feedback. In short, you will need to allow between one hour and one hour 20 minutes for the activity.

STEP-BY-STEP SESSION PLAN

Divide participants into groups, and allocate each group to a PC or laptop. The start menu for the case studies should be showing on the screen.

Allow time for groups to settle, then take a couple of minutes to introduce the activity. Explain that you have five client relationships for them to look at. Explain that the accounts are all held at a branch of Alnabank. Explain that their task is to:

- find out what they can about each account holder;
- examine the evidence available;
- answer various questions;
- form a view as to which of the accounts is potentially being used as a vehicle for terrorist financing.

Refer participants to the start menu on their PC or laptop screen. Explain that:

- clicking on the start buttons will take them to the various case studies;
- clicking on the on-screen links will take them through the case study, returning them to the start menu when they have finished.

Explain how much time you are going to give them. If your time is limited then you may want to work through just one or two of the five available cases. Be clear with participants which of the cases you want them to work on.

Distribute paper and pens for them to take notes as they work through the cases. Check that everyone understands what is required, then set the exercise going.

At the end of the time allowed, draw participants together to discuss and review their findings. Work through the cases one at a time, eliciting and discussing answers to each question in turn.

Use the guide notes below to help you in your discussion and analysis of the various cases.

GUIDE NOTES

Case Study 1: Felicita Imports

What level of risk might apply to this account, and why?

This raises the important point of which jurisdictions constitute a higher risk, and whether a person's or entity's association with a higher-risk jurisdiction should automatically place them under suspicion.

The company is registered in Pakistan. It clearly has business dealings with third parties in both Pakistan and the UK. One of the signatories is Pakistani, another is Afghan, another is a British citizen but his name indicates that he is of Pakistani origin. Pakistan and Afghanistan are both known and recognized to have connections with terrorism and in Afghanistan's case, with the drugs trade. Pakistan and Afghanistan are, therefore, clearly higher-risk jurisdictions. But does this association mean that the people involved are automatically under suspicion? No it doesn't – ethnicity alone is a poor indicator of risk. However, they *do* need to take an appropriate risk-based approach, and to conduct appropriate and relevant due diligence to ensure as far as they can, that they *know* the people they are dealing with, and that their business is legitimate.

The company is also an import/export business, and this raises risk levels in a CTF context, since one of the known methods of terrorists is to use the international banking facilities of import/export companies as a kind of 'unlicensed money remitter service'. The terrorists (either by guile, or by enlisting the assistance of people within the company) wire money through the company's accounts to third parties overseas – third parties who are active field operatives and who use the wired funds to plan and carry out terrorist attacks in their countries of operation. Given the higher degree of risk associated with import/export companies, it may make sense to subject such businesses to additional scrutiny and fact finding before opening accounts with them.

What else might you want to know about the company and the people involved?

One obvious point would be to find out as much as you can about the named signatories for the account. Who are they? What is their connection with the company? How long have they been with the company? What is their wider history and standing? Are there any facts about their past that may have an impact on their perceived integrity and legitimacy?

Another obvious point is to find out more about the company's ownership. The application attributes 20 per cent of shares to Mr Abid Ali (about whom we would presumably seek detailed information, since he is the main contact for the account and one of the signatories. But who owns the other 80 per cent? The account application mentions a 'consortium – Karachi/Islamabad based'. So who is in this consortium? What is their background? What is their interest in or connection with the import/export business? Do they have any known or alleged criminal or terrorist connections? Can they be identified at all? The key is to know who you are dealing with – and, if in doubt, not to deal with them further.

Further information about the company's likely business through the account is also essential for ongoing monitoring purposes. What are average 'money in' and 'money out' totals likely to be every month? How are regular transactions made – wire, cheque, cash? What is the average size of these transactions? When and in what jurisdictions might they typically take place? The more you can find out about an account and how it will be used, the more information you have available against which to gauge which transactions are unusual, and which are not.

Which transactions on the account appear unusual or potentially suspicious to you, and why?

Regular receipts from UK and European retail outlets (for example, Alfa Catalogue or Exotica Emporium) and payments to Pakistan-based suppliers (for example, AK Clothing in Islamabad) are in keeping with the known business of the company as an importer to Europe of ethnic crafts and other products.

What perhaps does not make sense, however, are the receipts from an entity called Antigon International, based in Faisalabad. Why would this Pakistan-based company be paying money out, rather than receiving it from Felicita Imports? What services or products is Antigon buying from Felicita Imports, that it could not buy more cheaply from a local provider? Why would a Pakistan-based business want to buy Pakistan-made products via a bank account in the UK? Does this make sense? Or is Antigon simply using Felicita Imports as a vehicle for moving money overseas?

There are also various forward payments from the account to entities and individuals based in America. Who are these people? What products or services have they provided to Felicita Imports? Does it make any sense for them to be providing such products or services? Or is the Felicita Imports account being used to channel funds overseas for unexplained purposes?

What do you think is happening in this account?

As stated above, one of the known methods of terrorist organizations is to use import/export companies as a conduit for the international distribution of funds. Money is collected together as a series of apparently legitimate business transactions, and distributed out again on the same basis. There are several signs that this may be what is happening with the Felicita Imports account, possibly with the complicity of one or more of its signatories.

Case Study 2: Ravonick & Gorston

What general risks of dealing via an intermediary are evident here?

The intermediary claims to have identified the client and verified his identity. To what standard was this identification process carried out?

The intermediary has provided a completed and signed application form. How do you know that the proposed client is the person who signed it? How do you know that the intermediary has carried out appropriate due diligence to verify the details given?

The intermediary himself is unknown to the Bank. Who is he? What are his credentials? What background checks have been carried out on him and his firm? What is his association with the client?

In short, the main risk is the extent to which the Bank has to rely on the integrity, thoroughness and professionalism of a third party for information relating to the assessment of the client and his business. Is the intermediary's information reliable? Is the intermediary's information honest?

Is there anything unusual about Mr Gorston's client's request to establish a life insurance policy with Alnabank?

Specifically, the fact that Mr Gorston and his client are seeking in the UK a product, the equivalent of which they could have sourced and obtained more easily at home in Kenya, is unusual. Seeking to purchase products overseas rather than at home might be intended as a cover for the transfer overseas of funds that are ultimately intended for another purpose – for example, for transfer to active terrorist cells. This is a known *modus operandi* of terrorist groups.

The heightened interest in cancellation terms is also unusual. Most clients would be more likely to be interested in the performance of the policy and the money it will pay out, rather than how much they will lose if they cancel it. If they intend to cancel the policy and incur big penalties for doing so, why take the policy in the first place?

What problems arise from the requests in the second and third letters?

In Letter 2, the client has asked to change the beneficiaries of his policy. The beneficiaries will be third parties. So what is their connection with the client? What business do they have with him? Why has he chosen two people with different names and no apparent family connection as his beneficiaries?

In Letter 3, the client has suddenly decided to cancel his life policy and wishes to transfer the monies paid out to a third party other than his named beneficiaries. This is unusual and, without explanation, potentially suspicious. Even the intermediary does not appear at this stage to know the identity of the beneficiary. Who is this person? What is their connection with Mr Allen? Why do they get the payout instead of Mr Allen or his beneficiaries?

Overall are there sufficient grounds for suspicion?

As with all suspicious activity, an element of judgement needs to be applied to the case. Any one indicator of suspicion might be an anomaly that can be explained. But in this case the indicators mount up:

- the decision to purchase a policy in a different jurisdiction, where an equivalent policy might just as well have been purchased locally;
- the level of interest shown in the cancellation arrangements and any charges that might be incurred;
- the change in beneficiaries – and the fact that the beneficiaries appear to have no immediately obvious link with the policy holder;
- the sudden cancellation of the policy after just two years;
- the instruction to send any money paid out to an unknown third party in yet another overseas jurisdiction.

Gathered together as a whole, there would appear to be more than sufficient suggestion here that something is not quite right about this client's account. Maybe it's terrorist financing, maybe it isn't. The point is to ensure that the anomalies on this account are promptly reported and investigated, so that any link to terrorism is quickly discovered.

Case Study 3: María Jesùs Jimenez

What is your view of this person? Is she a potential terrorist?

Certain jurisdictions pose a higher risk of involvement with terrorism or other crimes. Colombia is one such territory – a known centre for drug production and drug trafficking, and experiencing its own terrorist problems with insurgent groups such as the Revolutionary Armed Forces of Colombia (FARC), or 'People's Army'.

The same question arises here as with Case Study 1: is the individual in question necessarily any more suspicious or dangerous, simply because she happens to be a national of and resident in a higher risk country? The answer is 'no'. But you do need to carry out appropriate due diligence, and for some higher-risk jurisdictions the standard of due diligence may also be correspondingly higher.

There is, in fact, nothing to suggest that María is anyone other than she claims to be. She claims to be a student, and she has a university ID card for the university of which she claims to be a member. She has a valid reason for being in London, and this could be easily checked out via her UCL registration papers, or via a call to the UCL administration.

Does Account Statement 1 fit María's known business with the Bank?

Again, there is nothing here to suggest that María is anything other than a university student who earns a bit of money to pay the bills and have an occasional evening out with friends.

Sizeable transfers from Cartagena in Colombia correspond with sizeable payments out to UCL. María appears to be using savings or parental donations from back home to pay for her study fees and university accommodation, and to give herself a financial cushion she tops these up with earnings from part-time work.

Regular payments in from Body Shop and the Kings Arms Hotel are commensurate with the sums likely to be earned by somebody in part-time retail or waitressing work.

There is nothing unusual about the regular cash withdrawals and card payments. María doesn't live extravagantly, having the occasional night out and the occasional shopping trip. Most of her cash probably goes on incidental expenses.

There is one larger payment out to Going Places, which ties in with the Christmas holidays and is almost certainly an air ticket to return home for Christmas with her family.

In short, María's life is about as ordinary as it gets. There is nothing unusual or particularly suspicious about anything in this account.

Is there anything in Account Statement 2 which gives you pause for thought?

From 31 July onwards, a different transaction pattern starts to emerge:

- Whereas previously María might have used cheques and cards as well as cash, from 31 July onwards the account appears to be used only for cash; why the change?
- Whereas María might typically have made cash withdrawals in person at the bank, all withdrawals are now made via ATM; why would María change her behaviour in this way?
- Whereas María's life previously revolved pretty much around London, the pattern of ATM withdrawals shows a rapid circuit through various large cities – Birmingham, Newport, Cardiff, Bristol, Bath and Oxford; why would María do this?
- Regular payments from Body Shop and the Kings Arms Hotel have ceased; has María stopped working?
- Payments have been received, but from two previously unknown third parties; who are they, what is their connection with María, and why would they each have given her £2000?

What do you think is happening with this account?

Immediately prior to this sudden change in behaviour, María has:

- made another purchase at Going Places – presumably another air ticket;
- received a lump sum of £500 (curious in itself, since she previously did not earn as much as £500 in any one month);
- withdrawn virtually all of the money in her account and sent it back to her account in Cartagena.

It is possible, therefore, that the person using María's account from 1 August onwards is in fact not María.

Terrorists are known to have done something akin to this in order to gain access to banking facilities without having to reveal their identity. The way it tends to work is as follows:

- The terrorists look for foreign nationals who, perhaps, are thinking about returning home.
- They offer to 'buy' their banking facilities from them and are prepared to pay a reasonable sum for this.
- Payment cards, passwords and so on are handed over to the terrorists once the money has changed hands.

The terrorist can, from hereon, withdraw cash via an ATM, give money to third parties to deposit on their behalf, issue telephone or Internet instructions for the transfer of money to other accounts, and so on. In short, they can have a fairly full banking history without ever having to set foot in a bank and run the risk of being identified.

Case Study 4: Orphans of War UK

What level of risk might apply to this account, and why?

The account holding entity is a charitable organization, delivering humanitarian aid to Afghanistan, a country known to carry a high risk of involvement with both terrorist and drug crimes.

Whilst many genuinely worthy charities and other organizations have been set up to collect and send humanitarian funds to countries in need, there are also some less worthy entities which have been set up under the guise of a charity, but which in reality are vehicles for terrorist financing. The people who donate money to these entities may not even know that their money goes to fund terrorism – they are duped into thinking that they are contributing to a humanitarian cause.

Terrorists can not only set up their own pseudo-charitable organizations, but they may also 'hijack' real, legitimate charities with the assistance of employees sympathetic to their cause; these employees use their insider access to obtain and divert the charity's funds to terrorist causes.

The use of charitable organizations (or entities that appear to be charitable) as a conduit for terrorist funds is a well-known and widely recognized terrorist financing ploy. Charitable organizations operating in countries such as Afghanistan, therefore, are almost certainly going to constitute a far higher risk than many other types of entity. Due diligence procedures need to be designed to take account of this.

What else might you want to know about this organization and its activities?

Relevant due diligence information might include the following:

- a physical address in the UK (the address given is a PO Box in Birmingham – the organization itself could be virtually anywhere);
- some information about the charity's activities in Afghanistan – the kinds of projects it funds, the geographical location of these activities, the names of any recipients of regular funds, the typical amounts involved, the frequency of such transactions and so on;
- some information about the charity's founders/owners – Who are they? What is their background? What is their interest in Afghanistan? Where are they based? What other business do they have?

Is there anything in Account Statement 1 to indicate a terrorist link?

The account shows payments in by cheque or the Internet. Cheques are deposited as a lump sum over the counter – about £2 000 to £7 500 per day. Cheques presumably correspond to postal donations. Internet donations are made online and show people of all nationalities making small personal donations of anywhere from £20 to £100 or more. There are also a couple of corporate donations made over the Internet. These are for much larger sums – several thousands of pounds each.

One immediate point: whilst there is nothing to stop corporate donations being made via the Internet, arguably it is rather unusual as most companies would (when donating money to charity) allocate any donations rather more formally and issue a cheque, rather than doing it over the Internet.

One less obvious point is that the Al-Haramain Humanitarian Foundation, the Al Rashid Trust and Petra Navigation & International Trading are all listed in the US's OFAC list. US institutions and institutions operating within the US are legally required to check *all* new account opening entities' identities against the OFAC list. Not *all* countries require the scrutiny of names against the US-inspired OFAC list, but there are a number of other lists available – for example, the lists issued under UN Resolutions 1267, 1333 and 1390, or the European Union's own list. Institutions are required to scrutinize the identities of financial services clients against appropriate lists (normally it will be more than one), in order to identify where transactions may have a terrorist link. If a link is identified, institutions must take the action prescribed by local law – usually making an immediate report to the authorities and freezing any assets deposited with them by the entity in question.

A member of staff with access to the relevant lists should be able to spot any obvious name matches that may occur between clients and the names on the lists. This is an important defence against terrorist financing, given that terrorists' transactions themselves are often so unremarkable.

What about Account Statement 2 – what fits, what doesn't fit and why?

Payments to the Al-Fazir Orphanage in Kabul and the Angels of Peace Orphanage in Ghazni appear to fit the profile for this charity and the humanitarian work it claims to be involved in.

Payments to individually named accounts in New York, Sydney, Munich and so on, do *not* appear to fit the profile at all. Who are these people? What is their interest in or connection with Orphans of War UK? How will monies sent to them ultimately be used to help orphans in Afghanistan?

Case Study 5: Pello and Bagrat

What strikes you as unusual about the way this account is set up?

One immediate point is the fact that the account is going to have a total of four signatories, none of whom appear to have any family or other relationship with each other, other than acquaintance. There *are* circumstances in which it may make sense for relatively unconnected people to share banking facilities, but it is not the norm. It would be far more usual for the four people in question to operate their own individual bank accounts. Multiple account holders without apparent reason is one of the typologies associated with terrorist financing.

It is also not clear why Pello and Bagrat would want to set up an account in Moscow, when in fact they both live in Germany and appear to have no obvious ties (family or otherwise) with the Russian capital. Pello and Bagrat claim that they intend to move to Moscow at some stage in the future ... so why set up a bank account there *now*?

What else might you want to know about the people involved?

The point has already been made in Cases 1 and 3 that certain jurisdictions have higher risk attached to them, because of the relatively high prevalence of organized crime or terrorism in those jurisdictions. Pello is Basque, and Bagrat is an ethnic Chechen who was raised over the border from Chechnya, in Georgia. All locations have been associated with conflict, crime, the arms trade and/or terrorist activity. Does this association mean that Pello and Bagrat are potential terrorists? Not really; as stated previously, nationality or ethnicity alone is a poor indicator of risk, but when it is combined with other factors it may be significant and trigger further investigation.

In the current case, for example, it might be important to explore the relationship between Pello, Bagrat and the other two proposed signatories to their account. How do they know each other? What is their association? Do they have shared financial interests? Do they have any legitimate reason for needing to have an account that is shared between the four of them? The two proposed new signatories both have Georgian names, so are they associates of Bagrat, from back home? Who will be operating the Moscow-based account, given that Bagrat and Pello do not currently reside in Russia?

Is there anything inherently suspicious about Pello and Bagrat?

There is nothing particularly suspicious about either of them, but their rather peculiar account arrangements and how they behave is definately unusual.

Do any of the transactions on the account appear potentially suspicious to you, and why?

The account statement highlights a number of potentially suspicious features. Large chunks of money are being transferred into the account, via Pello's and Bagrat's separate accounts in Munich. Someone (presumably not Pello or Bagrat but possibly one of the other two people proposed as signatories to the account) has been steadily withdrawing quite large sums of cash from the account, from various locations around Moscow. This transaction pattern is clearly not typical or normal. Who is withdrawing the money? About 204 607 roubles – over £4 000 – in just three weeks is not remarkable, but is still quite a lot of money by Russian standards. What are they using it for? What do they intend to do with it? This type of pattern – unrelated people sharing an account and using it to distribute money to various unidentified others – is known to have been used by terrorists as a means to get money to active operatives on the ground.

Cumulative Suspicions – A Behavioural Analysis

Training purpose

Staff know that they must report any suspicions that they might have of a client's possible involvement in terrorism or other crimes. But how do you recognize behaviour that is suspicious? How can you know that a client is acting suspiciously? Staff do not always feel comfortable that they know the answers to these questions. They do not feel certain that they would know what behavioural features to look out for.

This activity uses a step-by-step case study approach to demonstrate to participants how, bit by bit, the accumulation of information about a client's behaviour can lead to very definite suspicions about their activities. Quite often it is not just one feature of their behaviour but a combination of features which leads to suspicion about a client. The aim of this activity is to help participants to develop an understanding of the kinds of patterns that might well cause them to be suspicious and to report their suspicions.

Relevant reading

The issues dealt with in this activity are dealt with more fully in Chapter 5 of this book. In your debrief session you may find it useful to draw on the real-life example in the chapter as further illustrations of the methods used by terrorists to conceal where their funds come from, or where they are going to.

Overview

The activity revolves around two case studies. Each case study is presented as a series of five slides. Starting with the first slide, participants read through and comment on the information provided about a particular client. With each new slide in the series, participants acquire a little bit more knowledge of the client. Over the complete series of five slides, a picture will start to build up of client behaviour that is definitely suspicious. Participants comment on the 'red flags' or behavioural features that concern them, as they work through the series of slides. By the end of the sequence, they should be able to give a full account of the cumulative reasons giving rise to their suspicions about the client.

Materials

You will need:

- the 'Cumulative Suspicions – A Behavioural Analysis' presentation from the CD-ROM provided with this book
- appropriate projection equipment and screen
- paper copies of the 'Red Flag' slide (one for each discussion group)
- paper and pens for participants to take notes.

Timings

We suggest that you allow about ten minutes for each case. Participants will need time to read and digest the information in each slide, and then comment on it. Each case contains five slides, so you should allow at least three minutes per slide, plus a couple of minutes to wrap up and summarize at the end of each case. If you are short of time then you may want to select just one or two of the case studies, rather than working through all four of them.

STEP-BY-STEP SESSION PLAN

Arrange participants in groups of 4–6 people. Give a red flag to each group.

Explain that you are going to show them a case study in five parts. Explain how the case study will work:

- You will show a slide, giving some information about a particular customer and their account.
- You will give them time to read through the information provided, and to decide whether or not there is anything in the situation that might give them grounds to suspect terrorist financing, or to fear an increased risk of terrorist financing.
- If they believe that there are grounds for suspicion, then they must hold up their red flag.
- Groups that have held up a red flag will be asked to explain the nature of their suspicion, or the risk they have identified.

- Once the first slide has been discussed, you will show a second slide, and the process repeats itself.
- The case study has five parts in total, so you will show five slides in total.
- Check that participants understand what is required. Distribute pens and paper for note-taking, and make sure everyone can see the screen clearly. When they are ready, show the first slide.

Work through the five slides in the case study as described above. When you have shown each slide, allow time for groups to discuss and comment on what they have seen. Whenever a group holds up their red flag, ask them to explain why they are suspicious, or why they fear an increased risk of terrorist financing.

If groups fail to recognize obvious risks or causes of suspicion, then you will need to discuss these and draw them to the participants' attention.

Repeat the exercise for as many of the case studies as you feel are appropriate to the group being trained. Use the guide notes below to help you in your discussion and analysis of any risks and suspicions identified.

GUIDE NOTES

Case 1: A charitable cause

Slide 1

The main issue here is the fact that the account holding entity is a charity. NPOs and charitable organizations have proved to be particularly vulnerable to infiltration by terrorist groups who then acquire and divert the organization's funds to their own terrorist causes.

Bank staff need to be aware of the enhanced risk associated with NPOs and charities. Some of the risk arises from the fact that where there is active terrorism there is often also some form of parallel humanitarian crisis, and that humanitarian organizations and charities are therefore often active in the very same geographical area as the terrorists themselves; as such, they make very convenient vehicles for the movement of terrorist money from overseas sources, and terrorist groups appear to have exploited this. Some of the risk also arises from the fact that NPOs and charities and their money movements are not always that effectively regulated; in fact the FATF's Nine Special Recommendations for countering terrorist financing specifically advocate a review of the laws and regulations relating to NPOs in order to manage this risk better.

How likely is it, then, that the charity in the case study is being used as a vehicle for terrorist financing? There are a number of factors which would suggest a relatively low risk of terrorist involvement: the charity is well-established, well-known, with high-profile patrons. The account holding bank has also known the charity and managed its money for a long time.

Slide 2

There is much here to indicate that AiN is a well-run and very professional operation. It has a substantial website. And it has internal rules and procedures for handling risk, and any threat to employees or the charity itself. Its 'personal safety first' policy recognizes that staff may, sometimes, be coerced into certain actions in order to preserve their safety – but it also places an obligation on them to report any such incidents immediately, so the charity can take appropriate measures. Clearly the charity has taken steps to protect itself from possible extortion or other threats.

However, it is important to note that this particular charity does indeed operate in exactly the war-zones and politically unsettled regions that might typically expose it to a higher risk of threat or infiltration by terrorist groups. Bank staff managing the charity's accounts need, therefore, to be extra-vigilant and aware of this enhanced risk to the charity's finances.

Slide 3

The main concern here is the background and previous history of the new Director of In-Country Operations. This is a very high-level appointment. The appointee will have a lot of influence over the charity's funds and how they are used. He is going to be a signatory, which means he has direct access to the charity's accounts. Who is he? What's his history? What are his associations? Prior to joining AiN he was involved in post-Tsunami relief work in Tamil-occupied territories. Has he therefore been exposed to Tamil extremism? Has he in any way been coerced, threatened or influenced by extremism? Is the charity going to be put at risk, via its appointment of this man?

Slide 4

The main causes for concern here are: a) changes in the personnel responsible for decisions about in-country project funding, and b) corresponding changes in the funding behaviour of the charity. AiN has always worked exclusively in Africa; so why is it now apparently supporting projects in Sri Lanka? And what is the purpose of withdrawing £150000 in cash? What are the 'unspecified purposes' for which this money is to be used? Is it normal for the charity to withdraw sums of cash (for example, to buy supplies locally) and if so, is it normal for it to withdraw sums of this size?

Slide 5

There seems to be a clear discrepancy here, between the content of AiN's web promotion of its activities, and the increasing levels of activity in Sri Lanka. Sri Lanka is the operational arena for the Tamil Tigers terrorist group. The changes in AiN's funding behaviour coincide with the arrival of the new Director of In-Country Operations, who previously worked in Tamil-controlled areas. He and his immediate team effectively have complete control of funding decisions, and the allocation of funds to projects. The charity's website makes no mention of funding projects anywhere other than Africa. Could it be that the Director and his team are in fact under the control of (or perhaps active supporters of) The LTTE (Tamil Tigers), and that they are diverting AiN's funds to Sri Lanka for use in funding terrorism?

Case 2: Hiding in the shadows

Slide 1

There are two features here which do match known terrorist financing typologies. First, El Corial makes its money by providing start-up capital to new small businesses, and then taking a share of the profits from those businesses. Some terrorist groups are known to favour this kind of approach, which has two significant benefits for the terrorists: a) they make money on the deal, and b) the network of corporate vehicles created by this activity provides the perfect cover for the terrorists to move their money around. Second, El Corial's Head Offices and primary centre of operations is in the Philippines. The Philippines have terrorist problems of their own but, on a more global scale, they are known to be a fund-raising centre for certain terrorist groups, notably Jemaah Islamiyah which has a known propensity for hijacking and diverting funds paid to charities, and which (in a 2002 UN Security Council report) was believed to have appropriated as much as 50–60 per cent of charitable funds in the Philippines.

The fact that El Corial is a Philippines institution and that its field of business matches an activity sometimes used by terrorist groups does not necessarily mean that it is linked to terrorism; but it does mean that there is a higher risk of terrorist involvement, and an increased need for vigilance and monitoring.

There is a further red flag – the lack of detailed knowledge of the ownership structure of the business. We know that 50 per cent of El Corial is owned by a man called Paulo Inquino; so who are the 'business consortium from Malaysia' who own the other 50 per cent? Does the account holding institution know? Have they identified and conducted appropriate due diligence for the various members of this consortium? Lack of clarity with respect to the ownership of funds is not necessarily a sign of terrorist involvement, but it is certainly typical of any criminal group that wishes to move money around without being identified.

Slide 2

The knowledge that something like 50–60 per cent of charitable funds in the Philippines are diverted to JI might make one cautious and more alert to possible anomalies with Philippines-based transactions.

The new knowledge that El Corial appears to have a close link with a charitable organization and, furthermore, that it donates 40 per cent of its profits to this charity gives rise to some quite serious concerns about the ultimate destination of that money. Who are the Trabuco Foundation? What humanitarian or other charitable purpose do they serve? Are the owners of El

Corial really such philanthropists that they willingly give 40 per cent of their income to charity?

Slide 3

We know that El Corial makes its money from providing capital investment to start-up businesses, who then pay a share of their profits to El Corial. Given this knowledge about the company, it is not surprising that the accounts show regular payments from around 700 small companies.

But what about the sizeable cash deposits? Payment of dividends to the legal owners of a business would not normally be carried out in cash, so where does the money come from, if it does not come from El Corial's legitimate business?

Also, why is El Corial taking receipt of payments transferred from overseas private individuals? Who are these people, and what is their business with El Corial? Are they private investors paying into El Corial's venture fund, or is their money intended for another purpose?

Slide 4

We know that El Corial pays 40 per cent of its profits to the Trabuco Foundation, but what about other payments to Australia, Japan and Indonesia? Are the beneficiaries of these payments the members of the mysterious consortium that owns 50 per cent of the company? Are these dividend payments to consortium members, or do the payments have some other intended purpose? Clearly the relationship between El Corial and any beneficiaries needs further clarification.

Slide 5

It is starting to look increasingly likely that a connection exists between funds that have moved through El Corial's accounts and at least one terrorist group. One of the recently arrested terrorists is a founder member of the Trabuco Foundation, which receives substantial funds from El Corial. Is the Trabuco Foundation perhaps a charity front for terrorist fund-raising, or is it a legitimate charity that has been infiltrated by terrorists? It is possible that the owners of El Corial are unaware of any connection between the Trabuco Foundation and possible terrorism; but, if they are aware, then that would make them active financial sponsors of a terrorist group. And if they are aware and knowingly contributing to terrorism, then maybe some of their other unexplained financial business is also connected with terrorist fund-raising – for example, the collection of cash deposits and sums wired from overseas individuals.

Terrorist Typologies Explained

Training purpose

Data gathered by intelligence agencies over recent years has helped to build up a picture of certain patterns or habits in the way different terrorist groups set about organizing their funding. An increased understanding of these funding typologies can enable staff to be more aware and more alert to the ways in which terrorists might try to use their institution's services and systems as a conduit for their funds.

This activity, a variation on Learning Activity 2, uses the example of four terrorist groups and their known funding habits as a means of introducing some of the more prevalent characteristics of terrorist funding. It can be used as an introduction to this topic, or as a reminder of how terrorist groups tend to operate for those who already have some familiarity with the issues.

Relevant reading

The cases used in this activity are discussed in detail in Chapter 3. The slide presentation summarizes the key points raise in this chapter. You may therefore find it useful to read through Chapter 3 in detail and to make your own notes as part of your preparation for this activity.

Overview

This activity can be used either as a straight presentation, with a question and answer session at the end, or as a facilitated group discussion exercise with participants working in small groups to answer a series of questions, which are then reviewed in plenary.

Whether you choose a presentation format or discussion group format, the aim of the activity is to examine and provide answers to the following series of five questions:

- What motivates terrorism?
- How do terrorist groups get their funding?
- How do they move and distribute their money?
- What transaction features might typically indicate a possible connection with terrorist financing?
- What CTF measures help to protect against involvement with terrorist funds?

Materials

You will need the 'Terrorist Typologies Explained' presentation' from the CD-ROM provided with this book. You will also need suitable projection equipment. You may also find it useful to have a flipchart and pens available for use.

Timings

If you opt for the presentation format, you will need around 15 minutes or so to deliver your presentation, with a possible further 15 minutes for any questions at the end.

For the discussion group format you will need more time. We suggest that you allow at least five minutes' discussion time for each of the questions, plus a further 20–25 minutes to review and discuss groups' answers in plenary.

STEP-BY-STEP SESSION PLAN

Slide 1

Show Slide 1 and welcome participants to the session. Ask for a quick show of hands: Who can confidently describe the difference between money laundering and terrorist financing? Who can confidently explain the methods most commonly used by terrorist groups to obtain funds and finance their operations? Explain that the purpose of this session is to find some answers to these very important questions.

Slide 2

If you are following a presentation format, use this slide to explain how your presentation is structured and what it will cover.

If you are following a discussion group format, use this slide to get your group discussions started. Ask participants to arrange themselves in groups of 4–6 people, and refer them to the questions on the slide. Set them the task of discussion and agreeing answers to these questions for presentation back to the main group. Explain that they will have 20-minutes discussion time – around five minutes per question. Check that they understand what is required, then set them to get on with it. At the end of the allotted 25 minutes, draw them together into the main group to share and explain their answers.

Whichever format you are following, work through the remainder of the slides as discussed below.

Slide 3

Use Slide 3 to introduce the example of four specific terrorist groups covered in detail in the book and to remind people of the ideological, political and religious causes which drive them:

- *Al-Qaeda*: aim is to confront America and reduce outside influence (in particular Western influence) upon Islamic affairs.
- *Jemaah Islamiyah (JI)*: aim is to force the creation of a single Islamic state throughout Southeast Asia.
- *Liberation Tigers of Tamil Eelam (Tamil Tigers)*: aim is to achieve Tamil independence on the island of Sri Lanka.
- *Provisional IRA*: aim to reunite Ireland as a single Catholic republic.

Use the notes below to provide some background information about these four terrorist groups, as appropriate:

- *Al-Qaeda*: has its origins in the Afghan mujahideen struggle against Soviet occupying forces in the 1980s; operates worldwide via a network of independent and collaborative terrorist cells.
- *JI*: established in the early 1990s in Malaysia by two exiled radical clerics; has a regional agenda and a regional sphere of operations, but also has close links with and receives financial support from al-Qaeda.
- *Tamil Tigers*: formed in 1976, with the specific aim of achieving Tamil independence from Sri Lanka; were amongst the pioneers of suicide bombing; have a regional agenda, but their fund-raising network is global.
- *Provisional IRA*: emerged as a radical splinter group from the IRA in the wake of the Troubles in Northern Ireland in the late 1960s; has a regional agenda, but once again the fund-raising capability is global.

Explain that you will be using the example of these four terrorist groups as a vehicle for illustrating the financing typologies typically used by terrorists.

Slide 4

Show Slide 4 to remind participants of the second question: *How do terrorist groups get their funding?* If you have a flipchart handy you may find it useful to draw two columns headed 'legitimate sources' and 'illegal sources'. Elicit suggestions and ideas from participants, writing their ideas into the flipchart columns under the appropriate headings. The range of sources is potentially very extensive, so keep going with this exercise for a few minutes, or until you have exhausted all the ideas.

Slide 5

Use Slide 5 to summarize and reinforce the point just made using the flipchart – that terrorists' sources are not always criminal. This is a key difference between terrorist financing and money laundering; with money laundering the source of the funds is always crime, whereas although terrorists do use crime as a means to generate income, they also take donations and profits from other more legitimate activities.

You may want to make the point that, although terrorism has long been a specifically identified criminal offence in many countries, it is only relatively recently that the act of providing funds or financial assistance to terrorist cause has *also* been specifically criminalized. An obvious effect of this change is that in many countries anyone who knowingly makes a donation or gives financial assistance to a terrorist group or an organization that supports such a group would now be committing a criminal offence.

Slide 6

Use Slide 6 to summarize and explain the main sources of funding for groups like al-Qaeda, Jemaah Islamaiyah, the Tamil Tigers and the Provisional IRA. Use the notes below to help with your summary.

Donations from charities and NPOs: these are a substantial source for al-Qaeda, JI and the Tamil Tigers. So why are such organizations so vulnerable to exploitation by terrorists? One answer may be that they are not always as strongly regulated as other types of corporate entity, which means that it is relatively a lot easier for terrorists to infiltrate them and to divert their funds. Another reason might be that the humanitarian, relief and aid work carried out by these organizations is typically most needed in the very centres of conflict which are also often a focus for terrorist groups. For example, in the aftermath of the Iraq conflict any number of humanitarian agencies are now active in Iraq, whilst in the same arena, insurgent terrorist groups are also extremely active. The fact that they share the same geographical arena makes these organizations particularly useful to terrorist groups who might want to use them as a cover for importing funds from overseas.

Collection of zakat: Muslims are required by their faith to pay *zakat*, that is, a proportion of their annual income to charitable causes. Terrorist groups with a specifically Islamist profile are known to have been beneficiaries of *zakat* payments which are paid over to them – sometimes knowingly and sometimes not – by the dignitaries or imams collecting the *zakat*.

Use of legitimate business structures: terrorist groups are known to use legitimate company structures in a number of different ways:

- as a front for laundering criminal proceeds;
- as a vehicle for moving funds around, particular across borders;

- as a fund-raising tool; for example, the Tamil Tigers have used a system whereby they provide start-up capital to help Tamil expatriates set up in business and, in return, they take an equity share of the business and a percentage of the profits.

State sponsorship: international sanctions against countries whose governments are known to sponsor terrorism have led to a very significant reduction in state sponsorship. The Provisional IRA may have received up to $20m from Libya between 1968 and the mid 1980s, but Libya no longer sponsors such groups, is no longer an international pariah and has been rewarded with the renewal of diplomatic relations with countries such as the UK and USA.

EEC farm subsidies: at a time when the EEC (now the EU) was providing subsidies to help farmers to export their produce to other member states, the IRA discovered a very effective way of exploiting the subsidies for fund-raising purposes. The scam involved:

- setting up as a farmer in the Republic of Ireland;
- exporting to Northern Ireland (effectively overseas) and thus receiving a subsidy from the EEC
- smuggling the exported produce back into the Republic and then re-exporting it and receiving a second subsidy.

Kidnapping and extortion: terrorist groups are clearly no strangers to violence and are not averse to using violent means to raise money. Money can be extorted from legally settled expatriates, by the threat of violence against their families back home. Money can similarly be extorted from illegal immigrants, by the threat of exposure to local immigration authorities. Several terrorist groups have been associated with kidnapping and ransom demands.

Voluntary donations from diaspora: terrorist groups with a specific regional agenda may find quite strong support amongst emigrants living overseas. The Provisional IRA, for example, received considerable funds during the 1970s and 1980s via Noraid, a US-based organization which raised funds for the IRA from among America's 9-million-strong Irish American community. The Tamil Tigers have also been able to secure strong support from Tamil communities in the UK, Australia and Canada.

Proceeds of crime: with the drying up of state sponsorship and the criminalization of donations and fund-raising for terrorism, terrorist groups may become increasingly dependent on the proceeds of crime for funds. The specific crimes they engage in are wide-ranging and to a certain extent determined by whatever is prevalent or convenient in their sphere of operation. For example, al-Qaeda has exploited the drug production industry of Afghanistan. The Tamil Tigers have used their own ocean-going freighter fleet for gun-running and people smuggling purposes, and so on.

You may want to refer to the FATF's Nine Special Recommendations for countering terrorist financing in relation to the funding sources above. For example, the Nine Special Recommendations include requirements for cooperative countries to:

- review and, where necessary, tighten-up laws and regulations regarding the governance of charities, and NPOs;
- criminalize the financing of terrorism, thus making it more difficult for terrorist groups to attract financial support from willing supporters and donors.

You can find a detailed explanation of the FATF's Nine Special Recommendations in Chapter 3 of this book.

Slide 7

Use Slide 7 to remind participants of the third question: *How do terrorists move and distribute their money?* Work round the various groups, eliciting ideas and examples. In particular, look for any specific case examples that they have read about in the media, or heard about via industry sources.

Slide 8

Use Slide 8 to wrap up the previous discussion about movement of funds, and to summarize the salient points.

Point out that terrorists can and do make use of the global banking system:

- Under the guise of shell and front companies, they are able to gain access to a range of money-transmission services.
- By infiltrating NGOs and charities and under cover of these organizations' own movement of funds to and from conflict areas, they are able to transfer terrorist funds to and from their operational arena.
- International wires under any guise (for example, a false name, a front-company name) are a quick and easy way to move money across international borders.
- The 9/11 terrorists simply set up bank accounts quite legitimately in the US, and then used ATM cards and credit cards from overseas accounts to draw cash funds into the US.

Point out that a very important aim of countering terrorist financing is to make it so difficult for terrorists to use the formal banking system that they are forced to rely on slower, less effective and less reliable methods such as the physical cross-border movement of cash and tradeable items such as gems. Terrorists do, to a certain extent, make use of couriers for this purpose. For example, in the early days of Noraid many of the funds given to the Provisional IRA were physically brought into Northern Ireland by Irish Americans on a visit to the 'old country' for their holidays. JI is also known to have been supplied by al-Qaeda with cash sums brought into Bali/ Indonesia by couriers from Malaysia and elsewhere, in the run-up to the Bali bombings. Al-Qaeda also used couriers as a means to get cash into the US and to the hijackers who carried out the 9/11 attacks.

There is also evidence that terrorist groups use the purchase of overseas securities and other investments as a means to move money abroad. The investments are made by intermediaries who purchase assets overseas. When cash is needed, the assets are simply sold and converted back to cash.

You also need to mention the *hawala* banking system, which is of specific relevance to Islamist terrorist groups. Almost entirely unregulated, the *hawala* system deals in cash and operates from countless stores, markets and bazaars with few, if any, intelligible records ever being kept of the transactions made.

Slide 9

Show Slide 9 to remind participants of the fourth question: *What transaction features might typically indicate a possible connection with terrorist financing?* Collect as many features as you can from participants, listing these up on the flipchart as you go.

Participants may contend that many of the features they are suggesting are in fact no different from the features that financial institutions might normally regard as potentially indicative of money laundering. Clearly this is true, so go ahead and agree with them, making sure also to point out that there are a number of additional features that are specifically associated with terrorist financing. You might even challenge participants to identify some of these features, for example:

- unusual transactions or a sudden change of behaviour on a charity or NPO account (the vulnerability of these accounts to exploitation by terrorist groups has already been discussed above);
- unusual funds transfers to and from regions specifically associated with terrorism (where there is terrorism, there is clearly a higher risk of terrorist financing, so any unusual transfers to and from such areas may well have a terrorist connection);
- dormant accounts which take receipt of deposits followed by daily cash withdrawals until the funds run out (such a pattern could be indicative of the distribution of funds to active terrorist operatives as they prepare for an attack);
- accounts where the signatory authority is shared between various parties with no obvious personal or business connection (such an arrangement might indicate a banking facility that is being shared by the various members of a particular terrorist cell in the field);
- personal accounts, often opened by foreign students or similar, which show a sudden change in financial behaviour (terrorist groups have been known to 'buy' bank accounts off foreign students or visitors who are returning home to their country of residence, and whose accounts the terrorists can then go on to use remotely, without ever having to be identified);
- wire transfers in small 'packets' at just below reporting thresholds, to or from small banks in offshore or lightly regulated locations.

Slides 10, 11 and 12

Use these slides to summarize the kinds of transaction features that might typically invite scrutiny or suspicion of a possible connection with terrorist financing.

General features are those features which are just generally indicative of a possible connection with terrorist financing or other criminal activity, for example:

- any apparent connection between the name of a client and the name of a listed known or suspected terrorist or terrorist group;

- clients who try not to give ID information, or deliberately obfuscate or try to give the minimum information.;
- the structuring of transactions in order to avoid the threshold for mandatory reporting requirements, in jurisdictions where such reporting requirements exist.

'Type 1' features are those associated with Type 1 terrorist financing, that is, fundraising and fund management. You could add to this list virtually all or any of the suspicious features otherwise commonly associated with money laundering as crime is, after all, a major source of revenue for terrorists.

'Type 2' features are those associated with Type 2 terrorist financing, that is, the distribution of funds to operatives engaged in planning for and executing an attack. These behaviours tend to be more specific to terrorist operations than Type 1 features.

Slide 13

Use Slide 13 to remind participants of the fifth question: *What counter-terrorist financing measures help to protect against involvement with terrorist funds?* Elicit and collect suggestions from participants, before using Slides 15 and 16 to summarize.

Slides 14 and 15

The ten items listed here include:

- the requirement to check the names of new or not previously known clients against lists of known or suspected terrorists (the lists to be used vary from country to country);
- the FATF's Nine Special Recommendations, which are in effect the FATF's response to the terrorist financing features and typologies discussed in this activity, for example:
  - the need to make people less willing to support terrorist causes, by criminalizing the financing of terrorism;
  - the need to tighten up the way in which charities and NPOs are regulated, so terrorist groups are less able to infiltrate and use such organizations for terrorist financing purposes;
  - the need to make it mandatory for originator information to follow transfers through from start to finish, thus making it more difficult for terrorists to move money without being identified.

Make the point that the fight against terrorist financing is ongoing. The FATF's Nine Special Recommendations are a first step in the international effort to defeat terrorist financing, but remind participants that new measures may evolve.

Check for any final questions, then close.

CTF Best Practice – A Short Briefing

Training purpose

In the last few years or so there has been increasing international pressure to do more in the fight against terrorist financing. The FATF, for example, have enhanced their original Forty Recommendations to combat money laundering with a further Nine Special Recommendations relating specifically to terrorist financing. Following on from this many countries have started to review and strengthen their anti-terrorist laws and their regimes for countering terrorist finance.

This activity is intended as a short briefing session to bring participants up to speed with international trends and views on CTF best practice and the potential implications for compliance measures and procedures within their own institution.

Relevant reading

Chapter 4 of this book examines the development of international (and some national) legal and regulatory frameworks in relation to countering terrorist finance. You may find this chapter useful as background reading.

Chapter 6 examines best practice trends and developments, and you may want to refer to this chapter for additional material to include in your presentation.

Overview

The activity is a straightforward presentation of certain key data about countering terrorist financing. The aim is, quite simply, to provide participants with a basic briefing on CTF best practice.

We would suggest that the presentation is used as an introduction to any session in which participants are receiving information about their institution's specific CTF procedures. Use this presentation to set the context, and then your own information about the specific procedures in question.

Materials

You will need the 'CTF Best Practice for Financial Institutions' presentation from the CD-ROM provided with this book. You will also need suitable projection equipment.

Timings

The presentation itself should take no longer than ten to 15 minutes. We recommend that the overall presentation time (including any additional material about your institution's specific CTF procedures) should be kept to one hour at the most.

STEP-BY-STEP SESSION PLAN

The notes below are offered as a sample script for the presentation. We would suggest that you do not try to learn this script off by heart or to use it verbatim, but that you use it as a basis from which to develop your own presentation ideas and format.

Slide 1

The purpose of this presentation is to raise your awareness and understanding of current thinking about the measures which financial institutions around the world can and should take, in order to prevent their systems, products and services from being used by terrorists as vehicles for terrorist financing.

Slide 2

Like most preventive measures, CTF measures are not absolutely effective 100 per cent of the time. However when effectively applied such measures do make it actively harder for terrorists to move their money around.

The application of CTF measures makes financial institutions more alert to potential terrorist financing, and increased alertness helps to prevent terrorists from gaining access to the formal financial system.

If they cannot gain access, then they cannot open accounts or wire funds via the international banking network, and so they are forced to rely on slower, less convenient and less reliable ways of moving their money around.

And the harder it is for them to move their money around, the harder it is for them to keep their organizations intact. If you can break down the terrorists' financial network, then you can start to break down the terrorists' organizations themselves.

CTF therefore has a powerful central role to play in the overall fight against global terrorism.

Slide 3

In the context of CTF, financial institutions have three critical obligations. These are to:

- comply with relevant anti-terrorist laws and regulations;
- cooperate and share relevant information with intelligence and law enforcement agencies;
- keep reliable, effective records so that investigators are better able to follow the trail of the terrorists' money and identify the people and entities involved.

Via these three areas of activity, financial institutions can make a significant contribution to the detection, investigation and prosecution of terrorists, as well as the appropriation by the authorities of any funds whose ultimate destination is terrorism.

Slides 4 and 5

In the aftermath of 9/11, the FATF enhanced its original Forty Recommendations for combating money laundering with a further Nine Special Recommendations relating specifically to terrorist financing. The Nine Special Recommendations constitute a response to specific identified risks, that is, vulnerabilities which are known to have been exploited by terrorist groups for terrorist financing purposes, for example:

- weaknesses in the regulatory oversight of NGOs and charities and their finances;
- weaknesses in cross-border controls regulating the movement of cash and other bearer instruments;
- the omission of originator details from wire transfer instructions and so on.

The FATF's Nine Special Recommendations require that cooperative countries should:

- pass relevant laws to prevent terrorist financing;
- make it a criminal offence to provide financial support to terrorist groups;
- extend their regulatory regimes to cover all money transmission services, including *hawala*-type schemes;
- tighten up the regulations governing how NPOs are funded and organized;
- share relevant intelligence and information with other countries and cooperate with their anti-terrorist efforts;
- freeze and confiscate terrorist assets as soon as any connection with terrorism becomes apparent;

- make it a mandatory requirement to report suspicions of terrorist financing;
- make it a requirement to attach originator information to all wire transfers;
- extend the measures used to detect the physical movement of cash and bearer negotiable instruments across international borders.

In response to these recommendations, anti-terrorist laws have been toughened in many countries, and higher standards of scrutiny and prevention imposed.

In compliance with these tougher rules, financial institutions have had to tighten up too, and to introduce more stringent due diligence and monitoring requirements for certain categories of riskier business. The remaining slides in this presentation outline the best practice approaches to CTF which have emerged as a result.

Slide 6

- To be effective in controlling terrorist access to financial services without at the same time constraining others' access to financial services requires a risk-based approach.
- A risk-based approach to CTF works on the premise that, whilst all business requires an agreed minimum of due diligence effort, there are some types of business where there is an inherently increased risk of terrorist involvement and where there should, therefore, be an intensified level of scrutiny.
- It is difficult for regulatory authorities to be prescriptive about what constitutes 'high risk' as this will vary from one institution to another, depending on the type and nature of each institution's business.
- The key, whatever the business, is to be clear about the level of risk involved, and to ensure that the preventive measures used are commensurate with that risk.

Slide 7

Obvious examples of where the risks might be greater and the required due diligence and monitoring standards therefore commensurably higher include:

- jurisdictions where there is political or religious unrest, insurgency or conflict (terrorist groups are often active in such areas);
- jurisdictions whose regulatory regimes do not meet international standards (given that lack of regulation is attractive to terrorist groups and other criminals who do not wish their financial business to come under too much scrutiny);
- individuals or entities having a connection with or transacting business to or from higher-risk jurisdictions;
- charitable organizations and NPOs (organizations which are often operational in areas where there is conflict and terrorism, and which are vulnerable to hijacking by terrorist groups wishing to use them as a vehicle for the international movement of terrorist funds);

- electronic banking (higher risk than face-to-face banking, because of the increased opportunity that it affords for individuals to assume someone else's identity and avoid identification themselves);
- wire transfers (higher risk, if relevant information about the originator of the transfer is not carried with the transfer to its ultimate destination);
- cash transactions (higher risk because cash is on the whole untraceable and cannot be reliably linked to an originator or ultimate beneficiary).

Slide 8

The level of risk involved is determined at the point of contact with the client, that is, before any business relationship has been established.

- Having determined the level of applicable risk, the institution has to decide whether or not it can accept that level of risk and manage it effectively. In other words, it has to decide whether it will accept the client and, if so, what the terms of that acceptance will be.
- If the client business is accepted, then the next step is to identify and verify the identity of the client. Institutions often have a range of procedures for identification. The higher the risk involved, the more rigorous the procedure and level of detail required.
- And once the client relationship is established, the institution has to decide on a monitoring routine – what to monitor and how often. Once again, the degree of rigour involved is commensurate with the level of perceived risk.

Slide 9

So, what level of risk is acceptable, and what is unacceptable? How likely is it that, by taking on a particular client, the institution will find itself being exploited by terrorists, and used as a conduit for terrorist funds? Institutions will have their own views on this, but factors that may be taken into account in the risk assessment process include issues such as:

- the client's country of origin (is it a high-risk jurisdiction, that is, somewhere where terrorist groups are very active?);
- the kind of business the client wants to engage in, and the countries within which the client wishes to transact such business (for example, a charitable organization based in the US and focused on supporting social development projects within the US itself is perhaps less vulnerable and less likely to have any terrorist involvement than a charity based in the US but funding overseas projects in conflict zones such as Sudan, or Somalia, or Afghanistan);
- whether there are any linked accounts and, if so, the nature and purpose of these accounts and the identities of their beneficiaries;
- whether the client has any known connections or business interests with individuals or entities in known conflict zones and, if so, the frequency and nature of any transfers to and from these individuals or entities;
- whether the ownership of any assets relating to the client can be traced back and linked to individuals or entities in known conflict zones.

It is not feasible to produce an infallible 'profile' for the individuals or entities involved in terrorist financing. However, it is clear that combinations of factors may denote increased risk and must, therefore, be taken into account when assessing whether or not to accept client business, and how to treat it once it is taken on.

When the client business is deemed to be high risk the onus should be on the senior management of the institution to make the decision as to whether or not such business is appropriate and the level of risk involved acceptable.

Slide 10

Let's move on now to the identification process itself. In recent years many countries have enhanced their minimum identification requirements by compelling institutions to ensure that clients' given identities are checked against official lists of persons or entities known or suspected to have an involvement in terrorism.

The system is not foolproof and mismatches can occur; for example, there are an awful lot of people called Ahmed Khan, John Smith or Juan Gomez, and although the name may appear on a proscribed list it clearly does not mean that every person of that name is therefore a terrorist.

However, where a true match is identified institutions are usually prohibited by local law from transacting any further business. In many jurisdictions the institutions involved would also be required to freeze any assets already held, and to report the incident immediately to the authorities.

In addition to name checking, there is also increasing rigour in the procedures required for verifying the identity documents and identity information provided by clients. Recent surveys have suggested that as many as one in four households in developed countries such as the US and UK have experienced identity theft. Identity theft is the perfect answer for terrorist groups who can provide their operatives in the field with access to funds via someone else's 'stolen' account, or by opening an account using a stolen ID.

To protect against identity theft or ID fraud, good practice dictates that institutions should accept only those forms of ID that are the most difficult to forge (for example, a national passport or identity card). Good practice also dictates that institutions should have rigorous procedures and guidelines for ensuring that ID is properly checked to ensure that it is genuine.

In addition to basic identification and verification requirements, enhanced due diligence should be used for higher-risk individuals and entities. Institutions will have different views with regard to the additional details required for higher levels of risk, but the basic principle is always the same: to be as sure as you can of whom you are dealing with, and of the purpose and intentions of their dealings with you.

Client identification requirements are universally more stringent, and there is also an increased focus on ensuring that the identity is known of all beneficiaries and owners who are party to a transaction in circumstances where the financial institution is not dealing directly with the customer:

- Where a transaction is handled by an intermediary, institutions should decline to proceed with the transaction without verified evidence of the beneficiaries, or the ownership of assets and funds involved.
- Where funds are transferred electronically, it is now a legal requirement in many jurisdictions to attach and transmit the originator's details with the transfer, so that the original ownership of the funds and their ultimate beneficiary can be clearly linked to one another (this tightening of the law regarding the linking of originator information and wired funds was just one of the Nine Special Recommendations published by the FATF after 9/11).

Slide 11

Once the client business has been accepted and the client identified, the ongoing monitoring of that client's business needs to be commensurate with the level of risk involved.

Client names should periodically be re-checked against proscribed lists of known or suspected terrorists and terrorist supporters.

Account activity should be monitored for changed transaction patterns, or behaviour that is not in keeping with the known business of the client. Some transaction patterns may invite particular scrutiny in relation to suspected terrorist activity, for example:

- a dormant account that suddenly receives large deposits followed by daily cash withdrawals until the deposits run out (is this account being used as a repository for the distribution of funds to terrorist operatives on the ground?);
- a sudden closing down of the activity on an account (for example, cancelling of standing orders, transfer of remaining funds to a third party, even, believe it or nor, the drawing up of a will, have all been noted in the financial affairs of both surviving and non-surviving perpetrators of terror attacks);
- sudden changes in the financial behaviour shown on an account (has this account been 'bought' or 'stolen' from its original owner, to be used as a conduit for terrorist funds?).

For certain types of product there are also specific 'trigger events' which should initiate additional due diligence procedures. For example, the sudden cashing in of policies for no apparent reason and in particular where a penalty charge is incurred is unusual and gives rise to a number of questions around the client's intentions. Additional due diligence procedures would need to be applied in order to ascertain whether there are plausible answers to these questions.

Institutions also need to decide the frequency with which client accounts should be reviewed. Clearly the frequency of these reviews needs to increase as the level of perceived risk increases. For lower-risk accounts, a view might be taken that detailed reviews are only required once every few years or so. For higher-risk accounts the review cycle might be considerably shorter – for example, every two months.

Slide 12

Adherence to the best practice principles and standards talked about here helps to minimize your institution's risk of exploitation by terrorist groups.

But risk can never be completely eliminated, and institutions still need to be prepared for the worst.

In the event that an institution suspects a link with terrorist financing then it must report that suspicion immediately. It should also:

- freeze any related assets (or otherwise dispose of them as instructed by the authorities);
- make all records and other relevant information available to the authorities;
- refer all decisions and instructions relating to the suspect business to the authorities.

Cooperation with the authorities and a willingness to make information available is absolutely paramount. There are sometimes concerns with regard to this disclosure of information to the authorities and the potential conflict which arises, in relation to the institution's duty of confidentiality to its clients.

In answer to these concerns it is important to be aware of the existence in any jurisdiction of what are known in the US as 'safe harbour' laws, that is, laws which protect financial institutions and their staff from criminal or civil liability arising from the alleged breaking of confidentiality or secrecy laws, provided suspicions are reported in good faith and without malicious intent.

In short, the imperative to prevent the funding of terrorist acts will tend to outweigh personal confidentiality considerations where there is a genuine suspicion of potential involvement in terrorist financing.

Five Training Ideas Using Posters

Training purpose

Training courses and workshops are just one of several ways in which you work towards building a better awareness and understanding of countering terrorist financing and related issues. Between one training course and the next, messages can start to lose their impact. People need reminders to keep key messages alive and fresh in their minds.

Workplace posters are just one of several ways in which organizations can keep the spotlight on important issues such as countering terrorist financing. This activity provides a range of different ideas for how to use 'key message' posters for training, for interim awareness campaigns and to encourage discussion of CTF issues in a more general context.

Relevant reading

The most relevant chapters from this book are probably Chapters 5 and 6. Chapter 5 looks at the whole issue of suspicion, and the kinds of activity that might arouse suspicions of a terrorist financing connection. Chapter 6 deals with best practice and the measures typically used within financial institutions, to counter the risk of involvement in terrorist financing.

Overview

We have supplied five ready-prepared posters on the CD-ROM provided with this book. Each poster shows a question and some related best practice reminders about financial institutions' expectations of their staff.

We have also supplied five different suggested ways of using these posters. Choose and use the methods that will work best for you and your institution.

Materials

You will need the 'CTF Key Message Posters' from the CD-ROM provided with this book. You will need these in electronic form or hard copy, depending on the training option you are using. For hard copy, you may want to enlarge the originals to A3 size.

Timings

There are no specific timings for Training Options 1 and 2, although you may need to set aside 10–15 minutes of your own time to prepare materials for distribution.

For Training Option 3 you will need about 20 minutes: five minutes for participants to prepare their presentations; two minutes for each group to deliver its presentation; and a further five minutes to discuss and review the presentations in plenary.

For Training Option 4 you will also need about 20 minutes: five minutes for participants to prepare their questions; and 15 minutes to work through and answer questions in plenary.

Timings for Training Option 5 will be very much dictated by the amount of time available. This is a matter for personal judgement, so we have not suggested specific timings.

STEP-BY-STEP SESSION PLAN

Training Option 1

Print the posters out (preferably in colour and A3 size) and place them around the workplace. This is a simple, effective way to help sustain people's day-to-day awareness of AML issues.

The posters by themselves can make an important contribution to continuing awareness but would, of course, work best as part of a wider awareness strategy. For greater impact over a longer period, phase the posters in and out sequentially so that they remain fresh.

Use occasional email campaigns to remind staff about the posters, and the countering terrorist financing controls to which they refer.

Training Option 2

Choose from the posters those which are relevant to any training sessions you have run recently. Attach these posters to an email. Using the question in the posters as a headline, write a summary of the key learning points from your training. Send your finished email out to everyone who took part in the training session.

This is a quick and simple follow-up activity which you can use to push your messages home, even after the training itself has finished.

Training Option 3

Divide participants into five groups, giving one of the five posters to each group. Distribute flipchart paper and pens.

Brief groups that they have five minutes to prepare a short presentation. The theme for their presentation should be the issue raised in the poster that has been allocated to them. The structure of their presentation should be along the following lines:

- a relevant example or story to illustrate the importance of the issue in a CTF context;
- a summary of the potential risks that might arise in relation to the issue;
- a description of the measures to be taken, in order to protect against these risks.

Training Option 4

Divide participants into five groups. Distribute one of the posters and a sheet of paper to each group. Instruct participants that they have five minutes to write down as many testing questions as they can think of, about the topic shown in the poster. They can write any questions they like – but they must know the correct answers. Reinforce that they should not write the answers – only the questions – on the blank sheet of paper provided.

At the end of five minutes ask each group to pass their poster and their list of questions to the group on their left.

Ask each group in turn to read out and answer the first question which has been passed to them. Check and confirm the correct answer with the group who supplied the question. When each group has answered a question, return to the first group for their second question, and repeat the exercise. Keep going for 15 minutes or so, or until all the questions have been exhausted.

This exercise is an effective and slightly more interesting way to test, evaluate and reinforce key learning points at the end of a longer training event.

Points system for scoring

- 1 point for each valid, correct or relevant question posed by a team;
- 2 points for correctly answering a question posed to your team;
- 1 bonus point for fielding and correctly answering a question posed to another team, where that team has been unable to give a correct answer.

Training Option 5

Display your five posters on the wall, and distribute Post-it® notes around the group.

Explain that you want to give participants an opportunity for free-form discussion about issues relating to the five topics shown in the posters. Ask participants to think about current situations or client issues which are relevant to these five topics, and which they are not sure how to resolve. Ask them to write these down on their Post-it notes (one per Post-it) and, when they have finished, to stick their Post-its near, on or around the relevant poster.

Select any of the Post-it notes, read it out and throw the issue open for discussion and comment. Discuss until a conclusion or clear course of recommended action has been reached, then move on to another Post-it.

Continue in this way until all the Post-its have been discussed, or until your time is up.

Note to cynics: some of the more hardened warriors of the Compliance world may be a little sceptical about these last two activities. Our advice is to try them. You may be surprised at the knowledge benefits gained from such 'free-form' sharing of questions, experiences and uncertainties. Training does not have to be all e-learning, presentations, films and case studies.

Index

U